DRUMS BOOK 3

by Maria Martinez and Terry O'Mahoney

I0794312

Guitar Center

LESSONS

INSTRUCTION & WORKSHOPS

DIGITAL DOWNLOAD CODE
To access audio visit:
www.halleonard.com/mylibrary/gc

Enter Code
5966-1093-6313-2544

ISBN 978-1-5400-1320-0

Published in cooperation between GC LESSONS and

HAL•LEONARD®

7777 W. Bluemound Rd. P.O. Box 13819 Milwaukee, WI 53213

Visit Hal Leonard Online at
www.halleonard.com

Visit Guitar Center Lessons Online at
www.guitarcenter.com/Services/Lessons

PERCUSSIVE ARTS SOCIETY INERNATIONAL DRUM RUDIMENTS

All rudiments should be practiced: open (slow) to close (fast) to open (slow) and/or at an even moderate march tempo.

I. ROLL RUDIMENTS

A. Single Stroke Roll Rudiments

1. Single Stroke Roll*

R L R L R L R L

2. Single Stroke Four

R L R L R L R L
L R L R L R L R

3. Single Stroke Seven

R L R L R L R
L R L R L R L

B. Multiple Bounce Roll Rudiments

4. Multiple Bounce Roll

5. Triple Stroke Roll

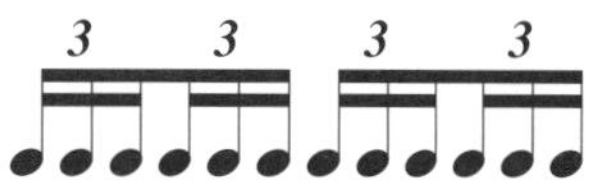

R R R L L L R R R L L L

C. Double Stroke Open Roll Rudiments

6. Double Stroke Open Roll*

R R L L R R L L

7. Five Stroke Roll*

R R L L

8. Six Stroke Roll

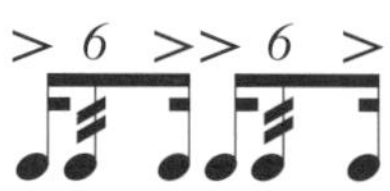

R L R L
L R L R

9. Seven Stroke Roll*

R L R L
L R L R

10. Nine Stroke Roll*

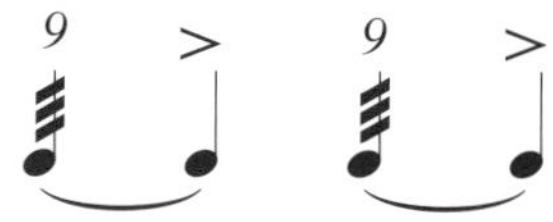

R R L L

11. Ten Stroke Roll*

R R L R R L

12. Eleven Stroke Roll*

R R L R R L

13. Thirteen Stroke Roll*

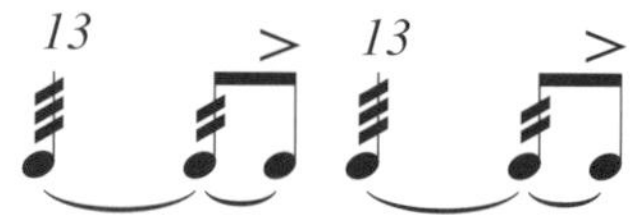

R R L L

14. Fifteen Stroke Roll*

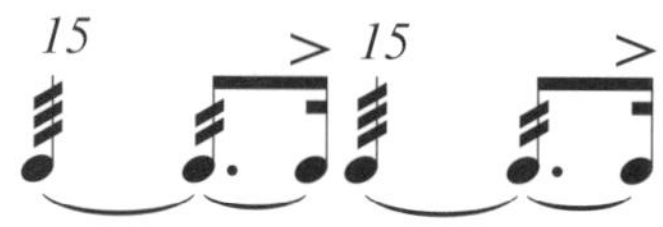

R L R L
L R L R

15. Seventeen Stroke Roll

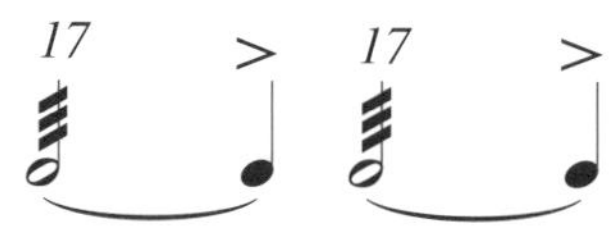

R R L L

II. DIDDLE RUDIMENTS

16. Single Paradiddle*

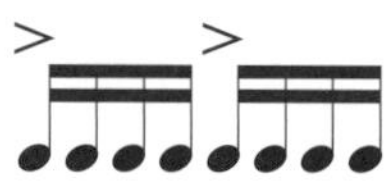

R L R R L R L L

17. Double Paradiddle*

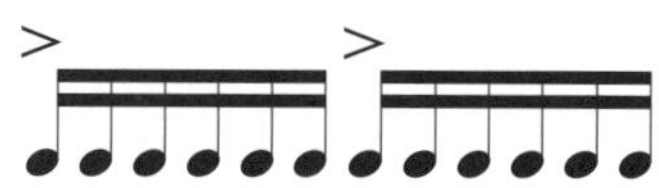

R L R L R R L R L R L L

18. Triple Paradiddle

R L R L R L R R L R L R L R L L

18. Single Paradiddle-Diddle

R L R R L L R L R R L L
L R L L R R L R L L R R

www.pas.org

*These rudiments are also included in the original Standard 26 American Drum Rudiments.

III. FLAM RUDIMENTS

20. Flam*

21. Flam Accent*

22. Flam Tap*

23. Flamacue*

24. Flam Paradiddle*

25. Single Flammed Mill

26. Flam Paradiddle-Diddle*

27. Pataflafla

28. Swiss Army Triplet

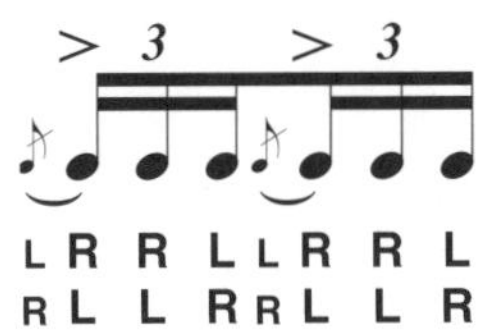

29. Inverted Flam Tap

30. Flam Drag

IV. DRAG RUDIMENTS

31. Drag*

32. Single Drag Tap*

33. Double Drag Tap*

34. Lesson 25*

35. Single Dragadiddle

36. Drag Paradiddle #1*

37. Drag Paradiddle #2*

38. Single Ratamacue*

39. Double Ratamacue*

40. Triple Ratamacue*

CHAPTER 1
SHUFFLE GROOVES

A *shuffle* is a triplet-based drumset groove that started in the 1930s and '40s during the swing era. There are many different types of shuffles that have developed over the years in a variety of musical styles—jazz, blues, country, and rock—and the shuffle can be found in most popular musical styles of the 20th century.

Early shuffles were played with two brushes on the snare drum. The right hand played the shuffle rhythm, and the left hand played the backbeat (beats 2 and 4):

1.

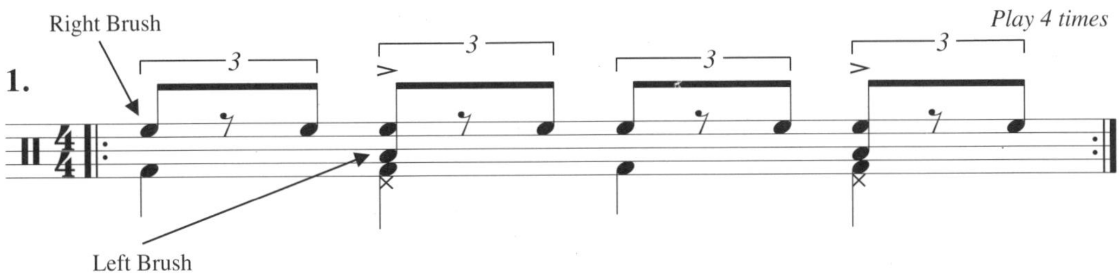

A jazz shuffle, which developed later, can use either the jazz ride cymbal pattern or a triplet ride cymbal pattern that omits the second partial of each triplet. The hands work together to gently stress beats 2 and 4, rather than heavily accent the beat, as is the case in later rock shuffle styles. In this style, the bass drum is "feathered," which means it's played very lightly on all four beats. The bass drum should be felt rather than actually heard and should be soft enough not to obscure the bass player's notes. This can be achieved by playing with the right heel completely resting on the bass drum pedal board (known as *heel down* technique) and playing the bass drum beater from a height of only 2–3 inches from the head.

2.

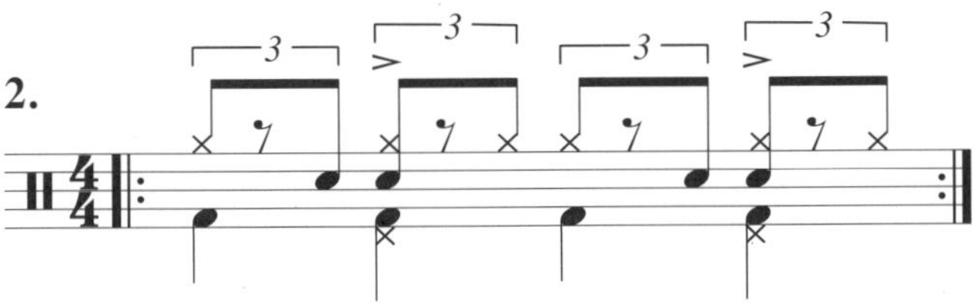

3.

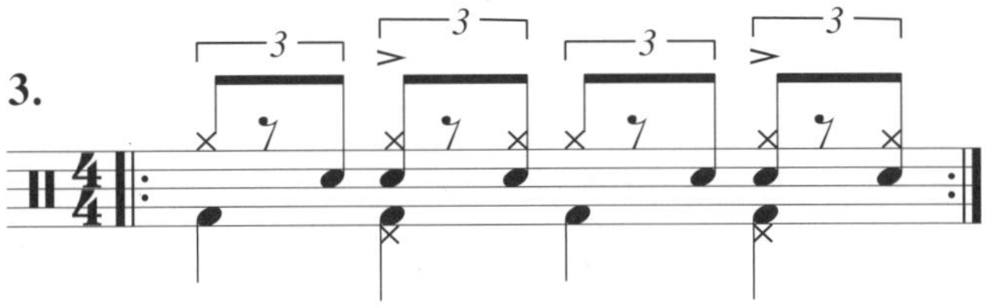

4.

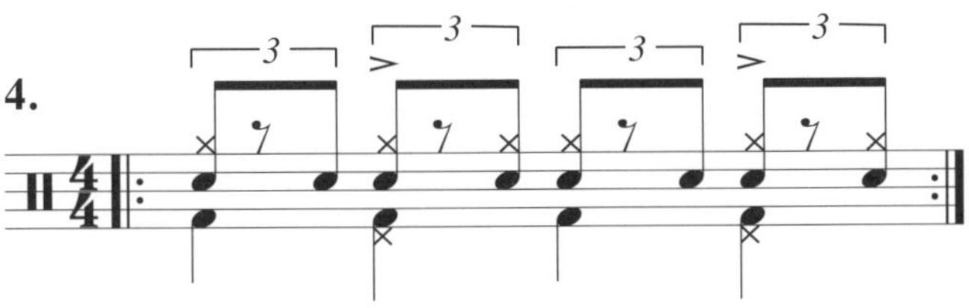

5.

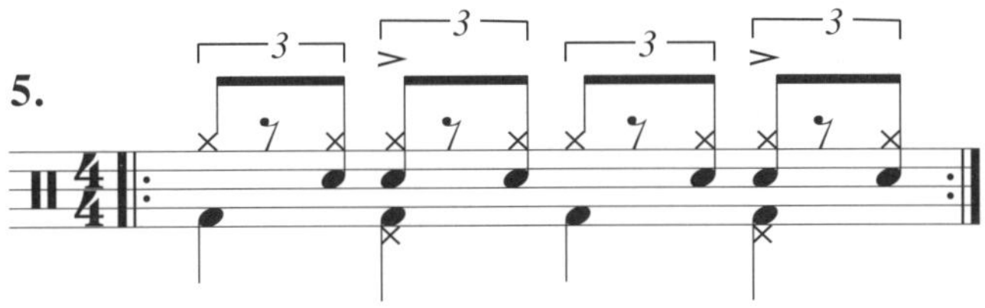

6.

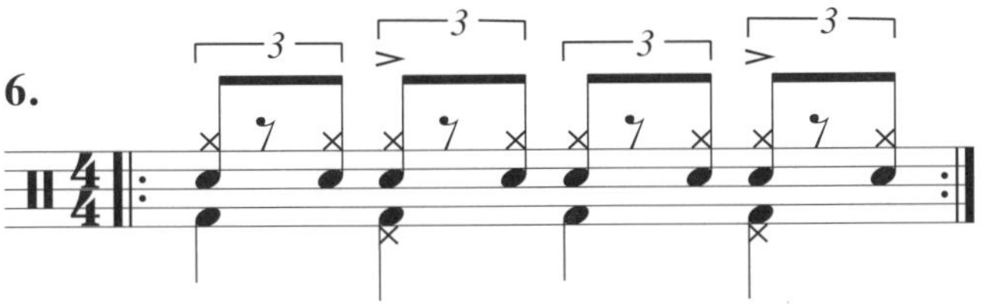

Jazz shuffles can also include some syncopated bass drum rhythms. Be sure to continue the accents in the snare drum while simultaneously adding the accents in the bass drum part.

7.

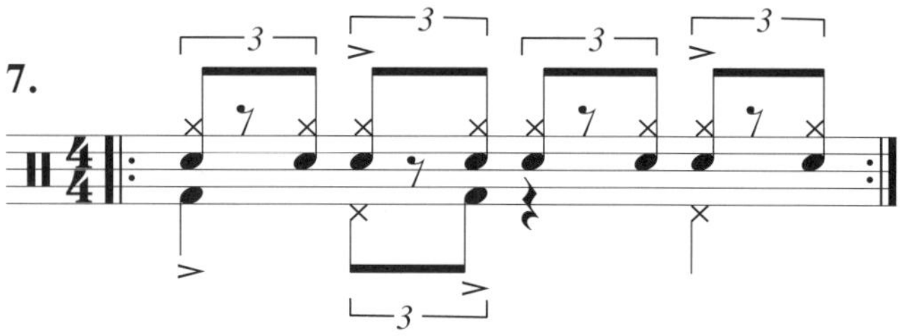

8.

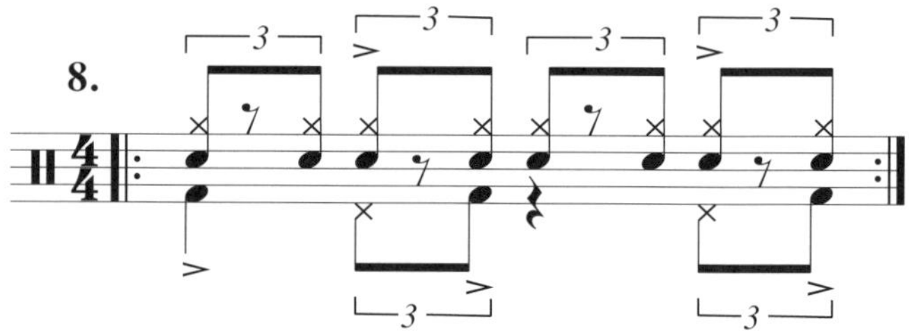

9.

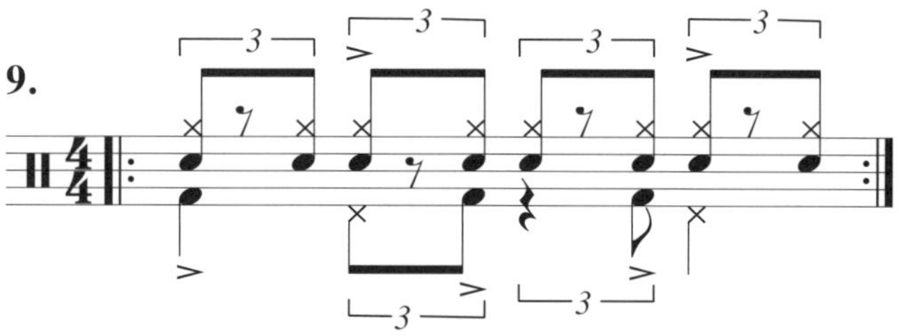

Blues shuffles developed in the 1940s and tend to be a bit heavier and louder than jazz shuffles, with more emphasis on the snare drum and bass drum. Notice that some of these examples are not written any differently than some of the previous jazz shuffles, but the balance between the snare, bass, and ride cymbal is different (the snare and bass are louder). Blues shuffles are often played on a closed or half-open hi-hat.

10.

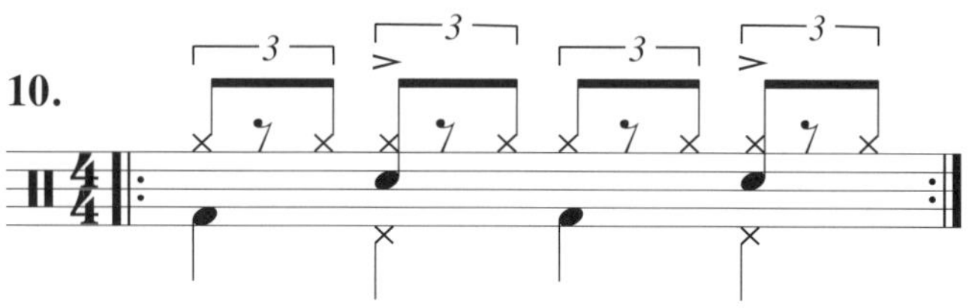

11.

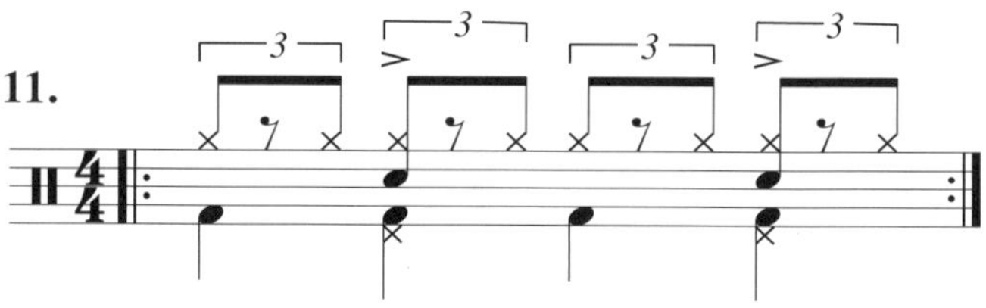

12.

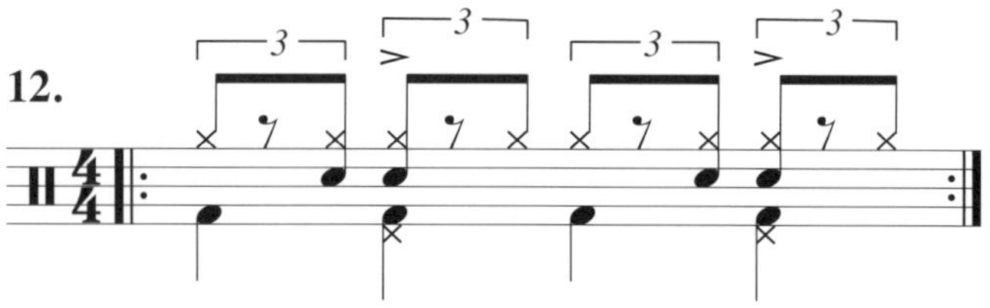

13.

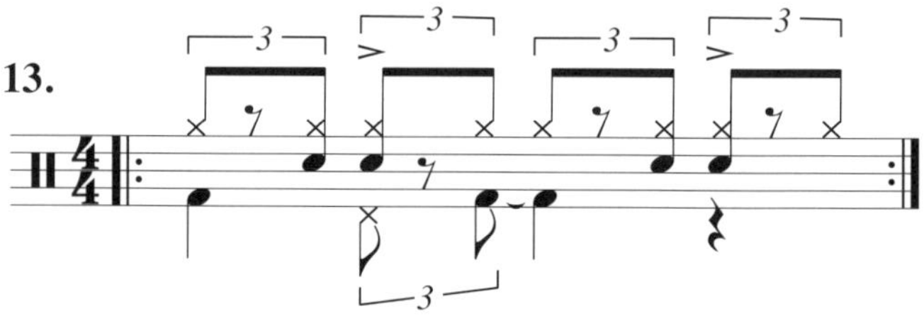

14.

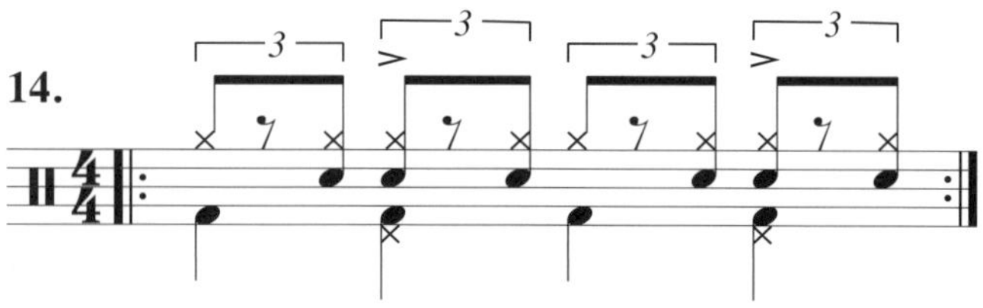

If a shuffle is too fast to play with all of the triplets in the ride part, you can substitute this groove, which uses a half-open quarter-note hi-hat part. To create the proper sound for these grooves, release the pressure on the hi-hat footboard slightly (but don't remove your foot completely from the pedal) to allow the two hi-hat cymbals to rub together and create a "sizzle" sound as you strike them. The "slushiness" of the hi-hat, combined with the triplets in the snare drum, creates an overall shuffle feel. The three examples are performed in three different tempos (slower to very fast); master all three and you will have a groove that you can use in almost any musical situation requiring a blues shuffle.

15.

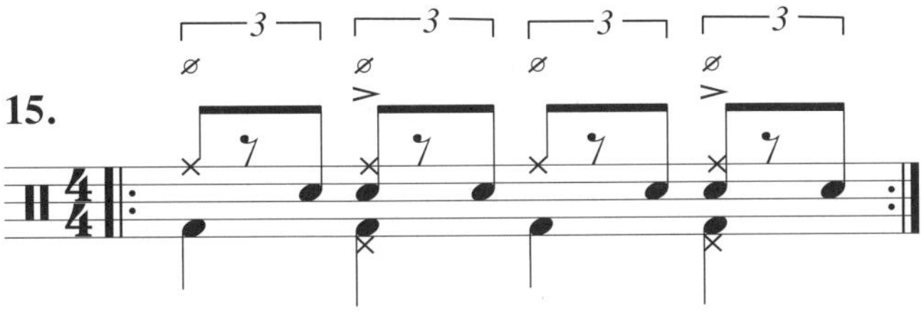

16.

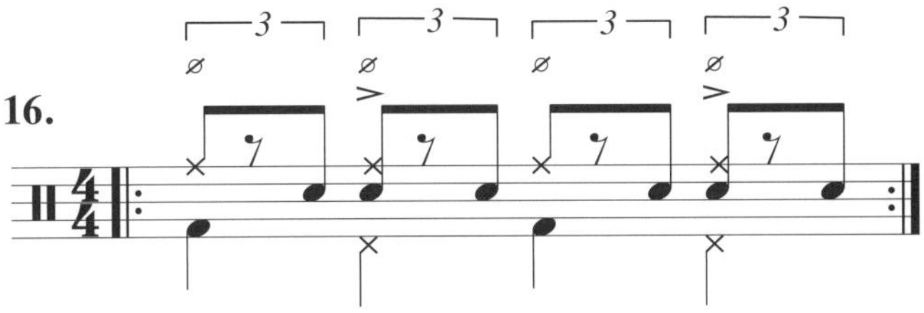

17.

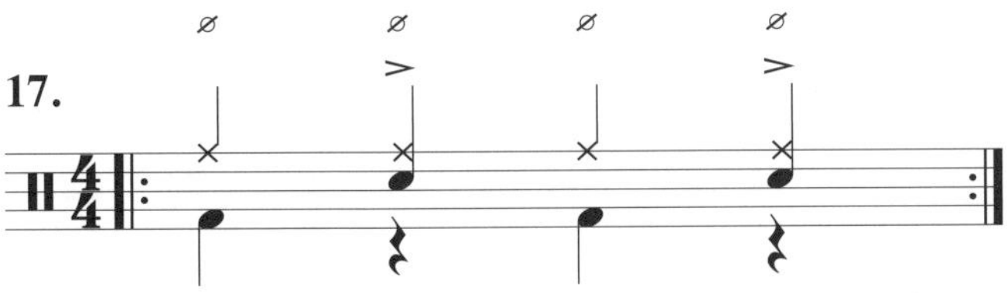

Rock shuffles are normally the heaviest and loudest shuffles and focus more on the "melody" created between the bass drum and snare drum. Often the left hand plays only the backbeat on beats 2 and 4, and the ride cymbal (or closed hi-hat) plays the triplets that give the groove its shuffle identity.

18.

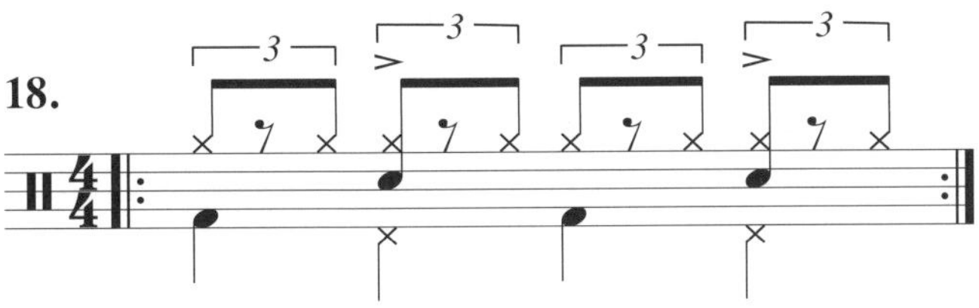

19.

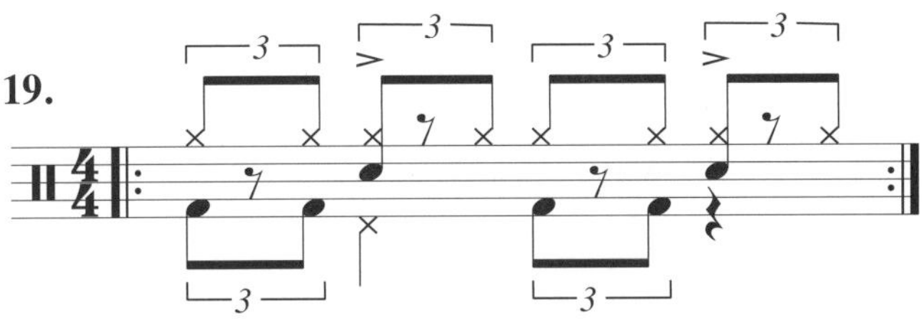

20.

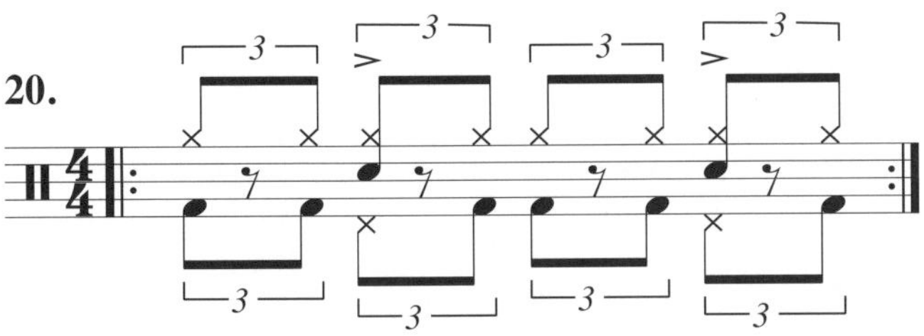

21.

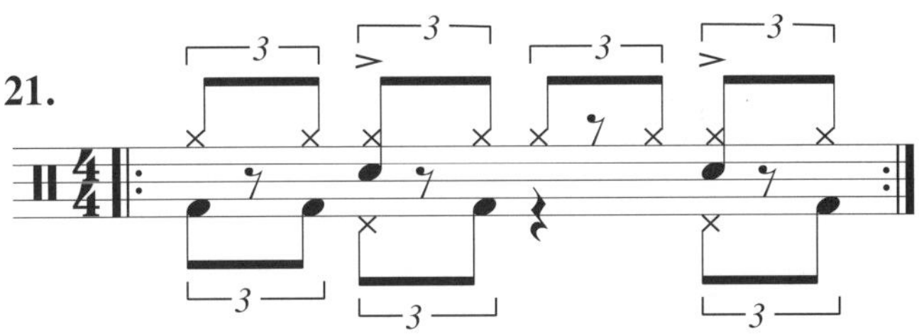

22.

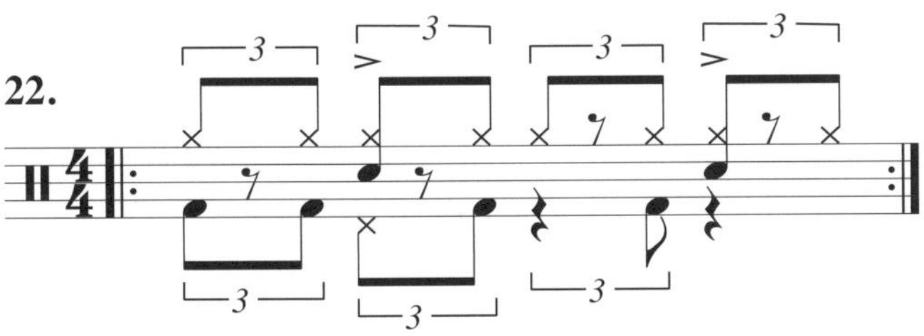

23.

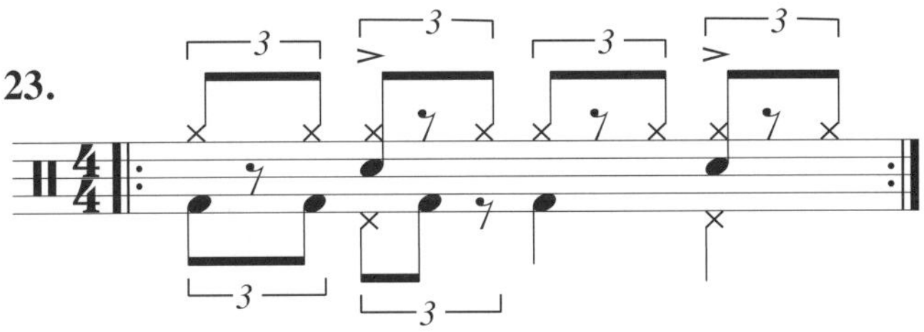

24.

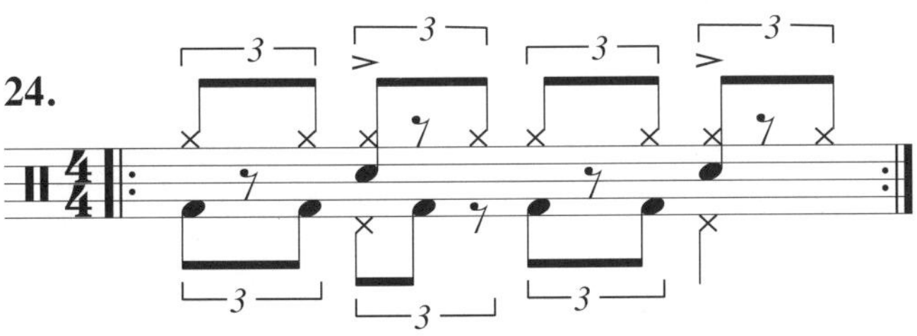

25.

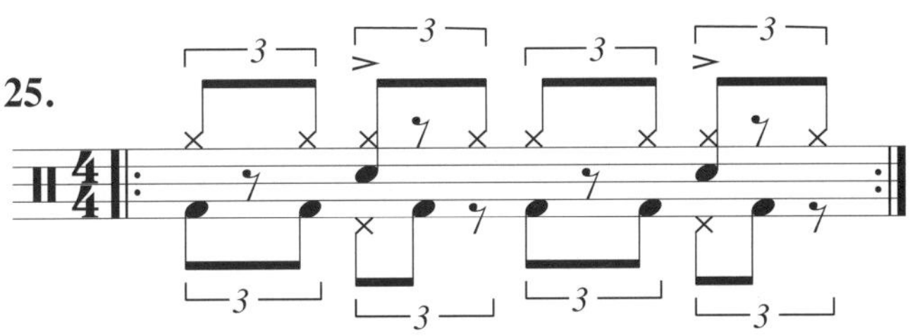

ODD-TIME ROCK

"Odd time" or "odd meter" are terms used to describe time signatures that are not divisible by the number 2. (*Meter* is another term for time signature.) The most common meter in rock and pop music is 4/4 (with the exception of a waltz, which is always in 3/4 time). Some styles, such as progressive rock, use odd meters to make their music distinctive.

Three-four (3/4) time is the best odd meter to study first. Practice these basic 3/4 rock exercises first.

1.

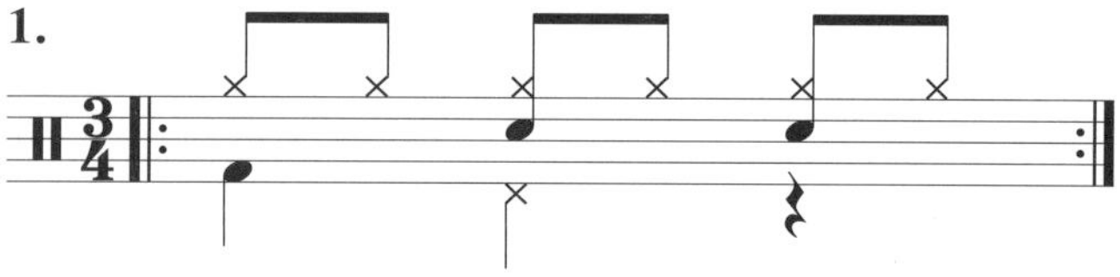

2.

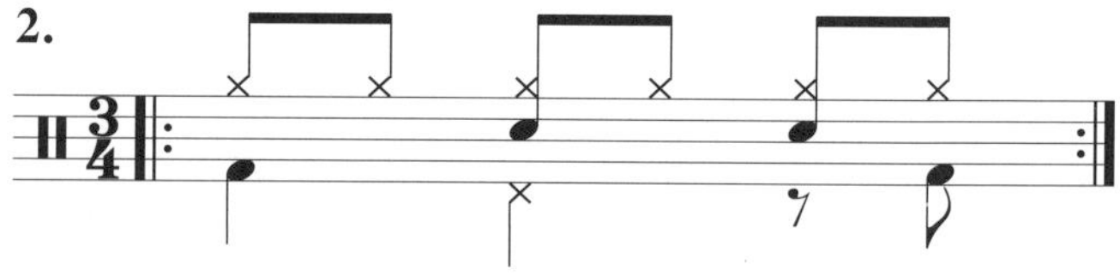

3.

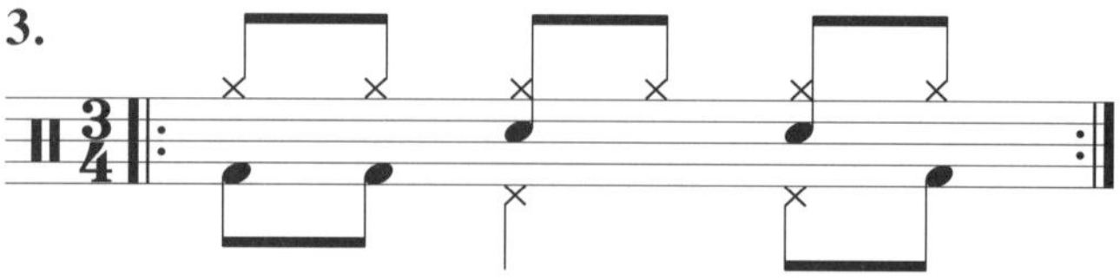

4.

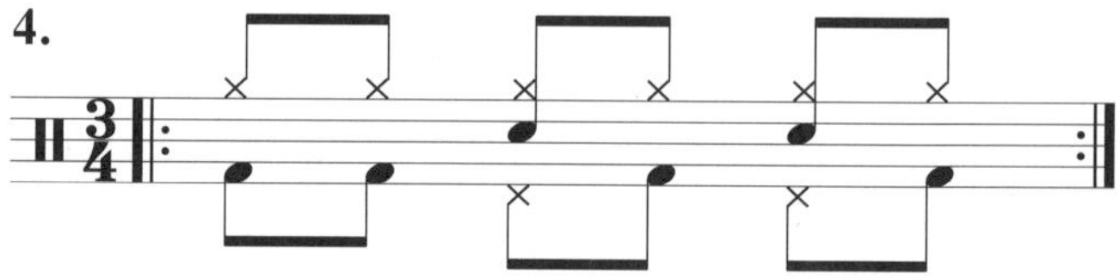

5.

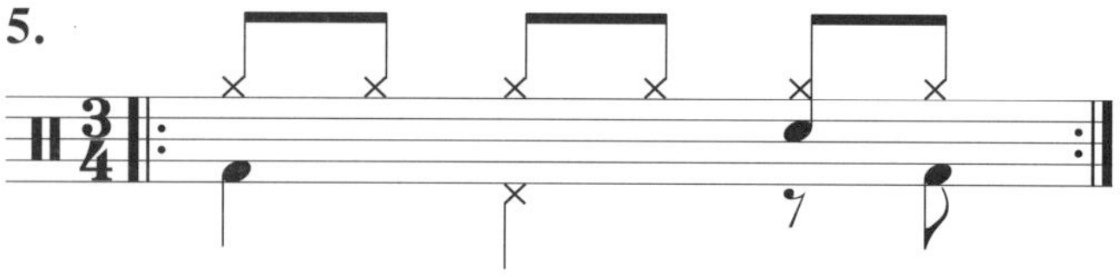

6.

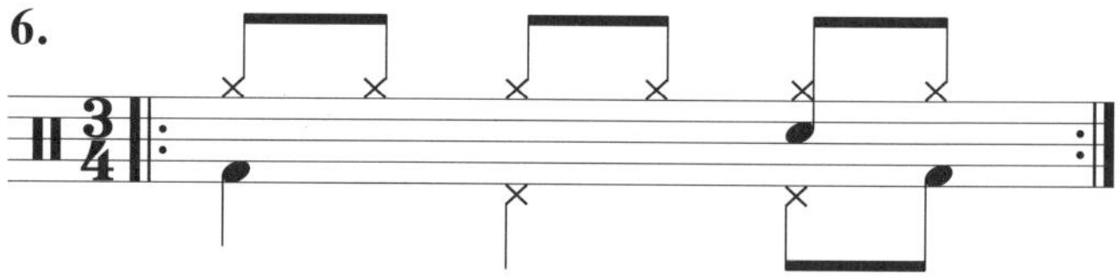

7.

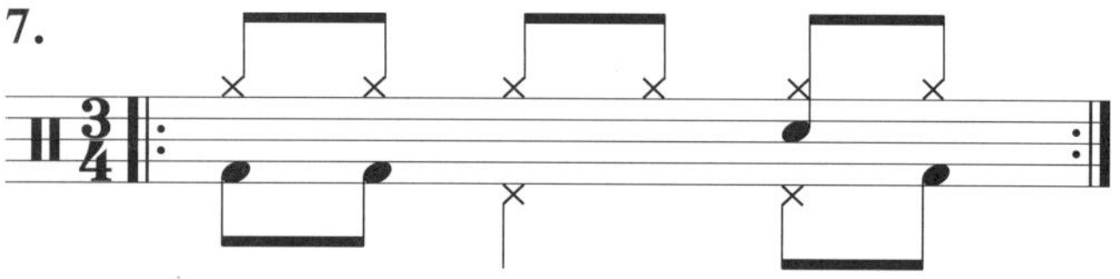

8.

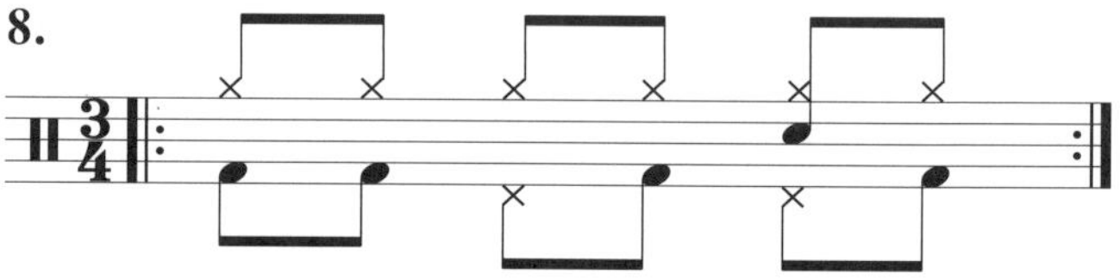

Examples 1–8 may also be played on a closed hi-hat by omitting the left foot hi-hat part.

All odd time signatures can ultimately be broken down into combinations of either 2 or 3 beats for the purpose of phrasing. This process is similar to finding a number's lowest common denominator in math class. There are fundamentally two time signature possibilities (or phrasing subdivisions): *duple* or *triple* meter. Duple means "two" (beats) and triple means "three" (beats). For example, 4/4 is two groups of two (duple meter). Five-four time (5/4), however, is an "asymmetric" meter—divisible completely neither by three or two but a combination of three and two. Therefore, 5/4 time may be divided into only two possible phrasing combinations: 2 + 3 or 3 + 2. Exercises 9–12 are examples of 5/4 time phrased as 3 + 2.

9.

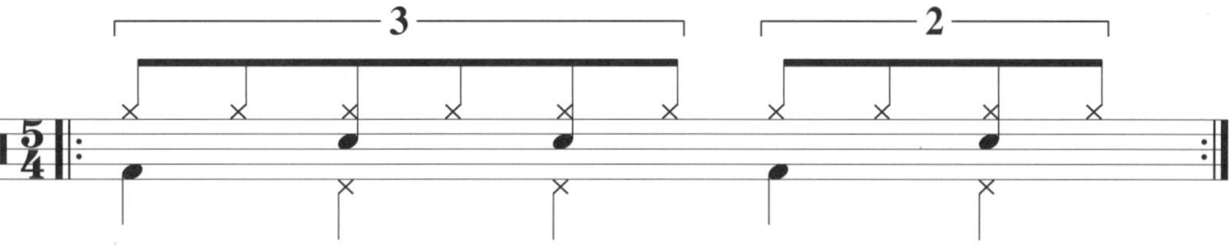

10.

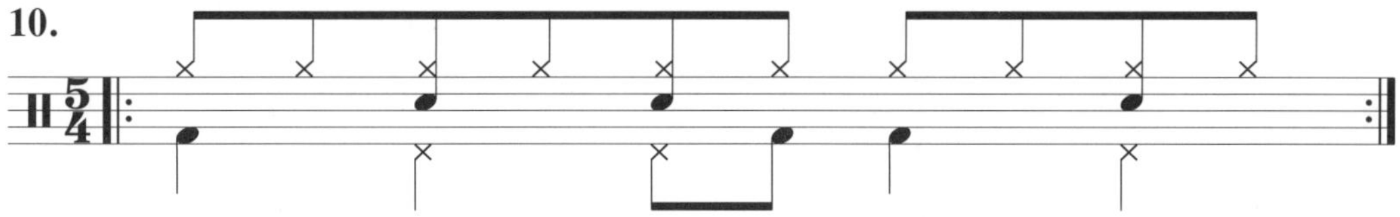

11.

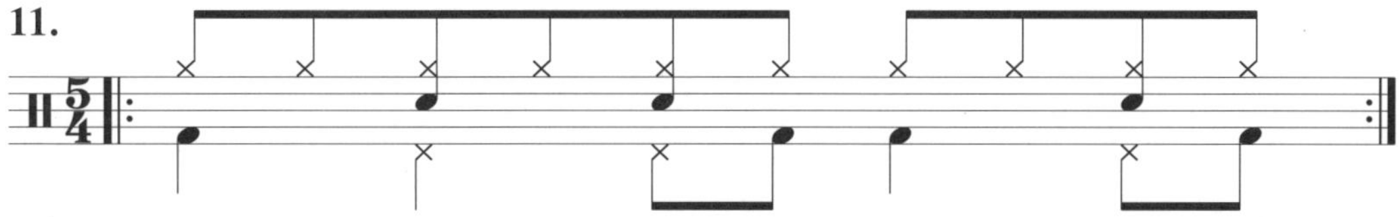

12.

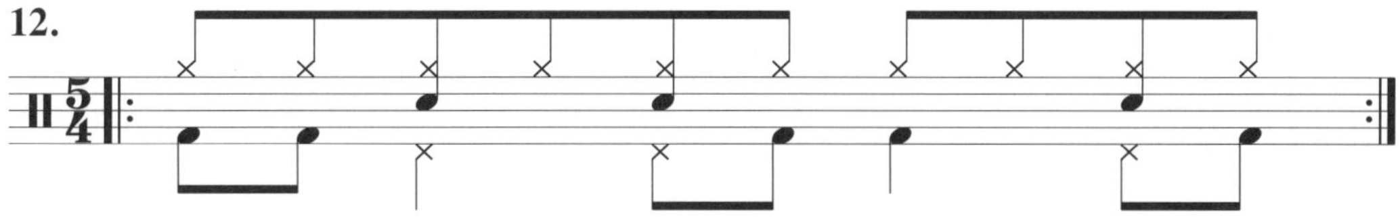

Exercises 13–18 are examples of 5/4 time phrased as 2 + 3.

13.

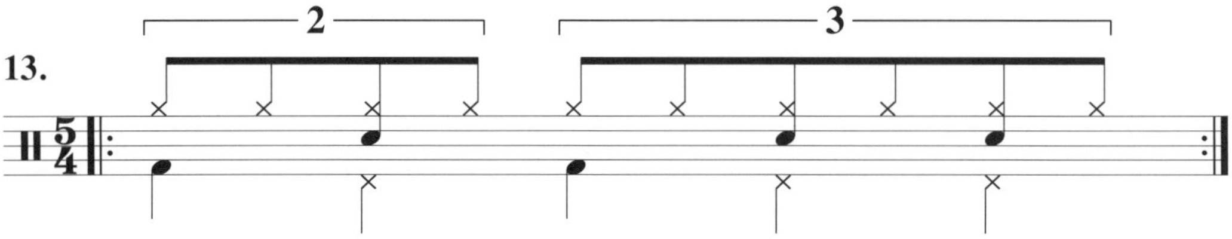

14.

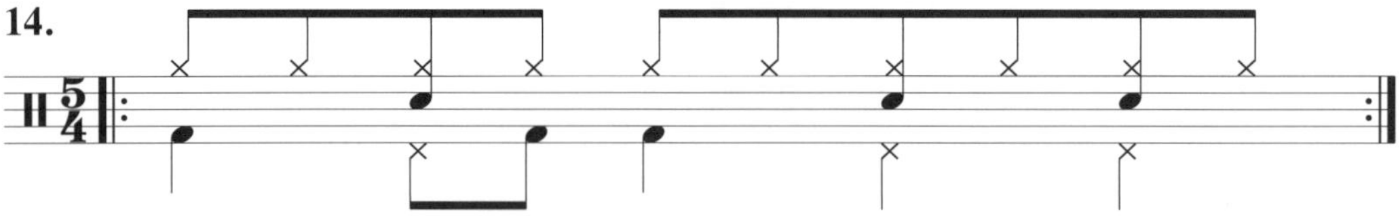

15.

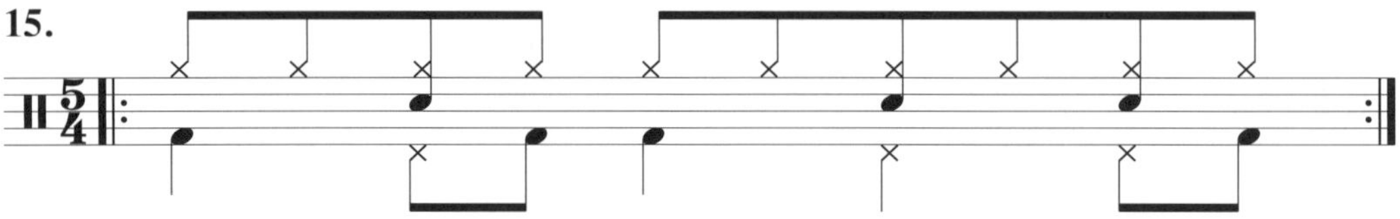

16.

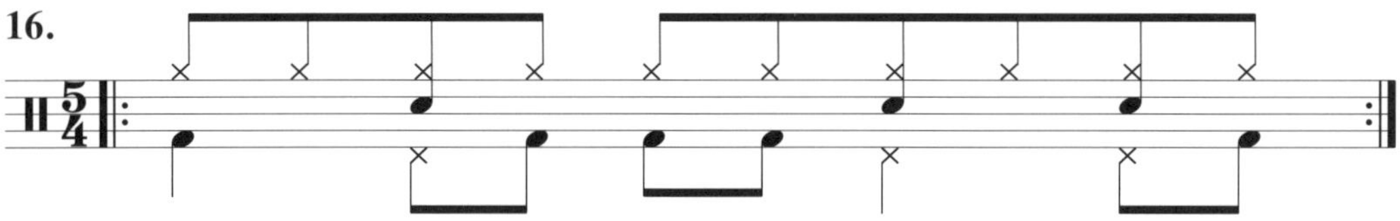

17.

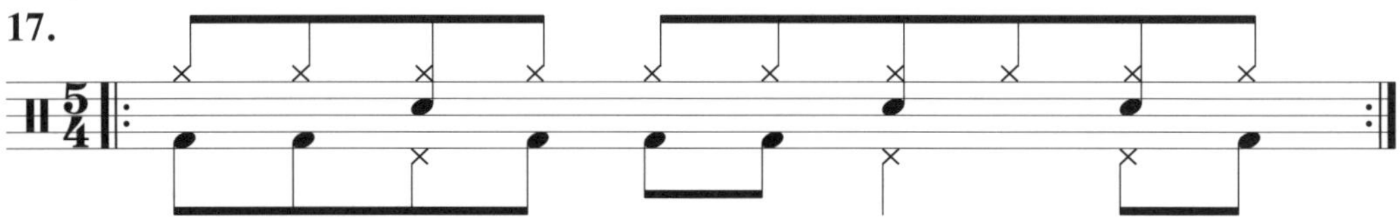

18.

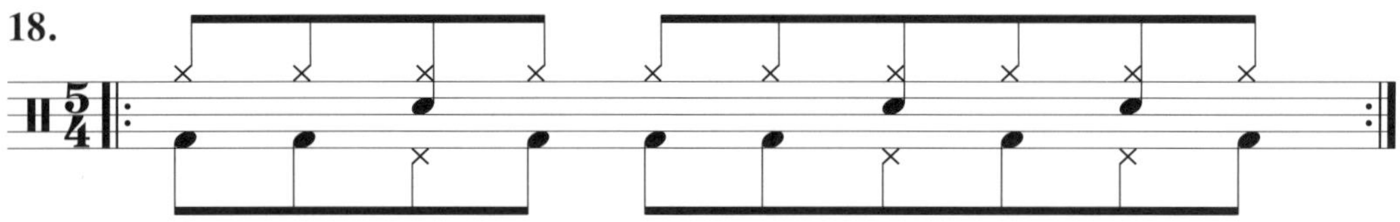

Seven-four time (7/4) is also an asymmetrical meter, and it can be phrased three ways: 2 + 2 + 3, 2 + 3 + 2, or 3 + 2 + 2. Exercises 19–36 are examples of the three ways to phrase 7/4 time.

19.

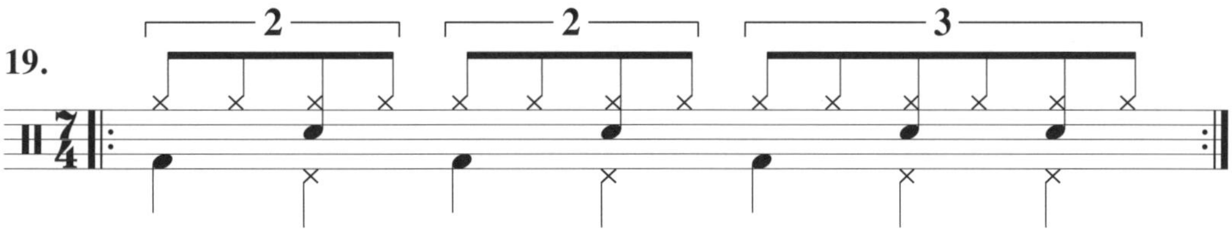

20.

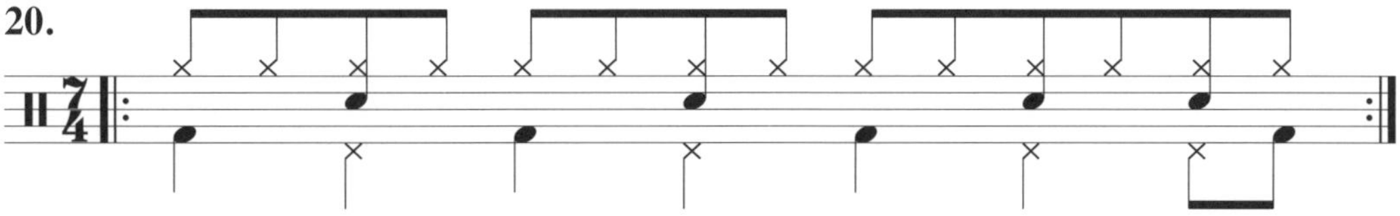

21.

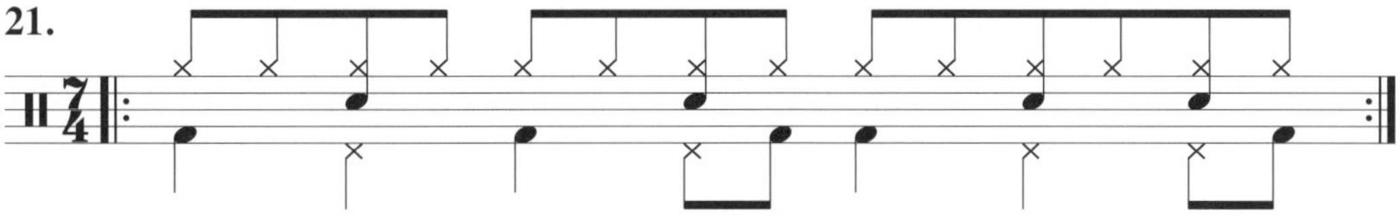

22.

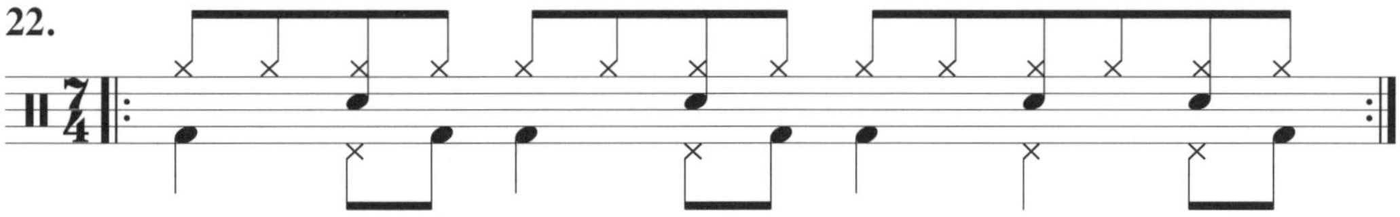

23.

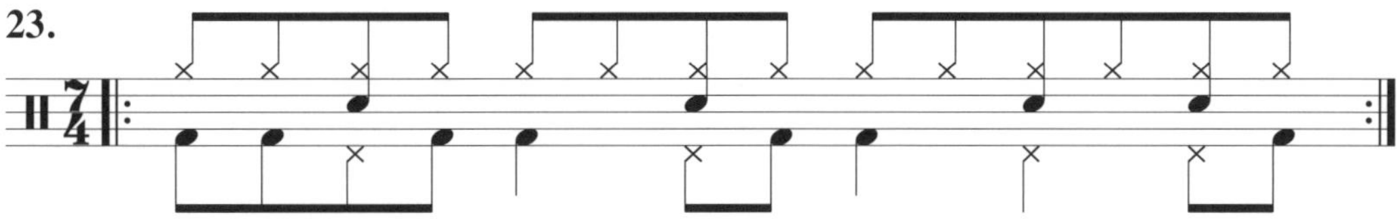

24.

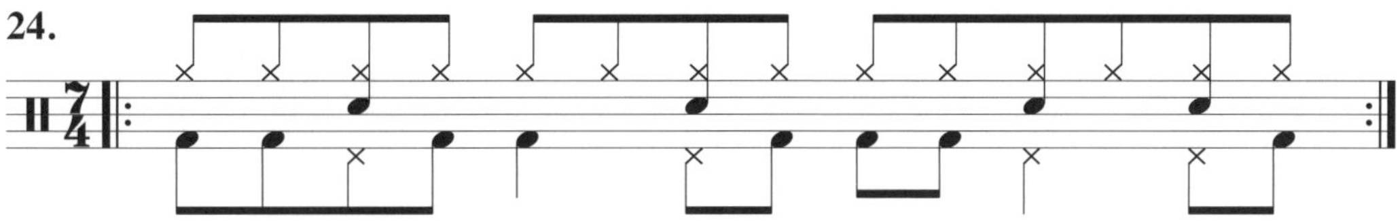

25.

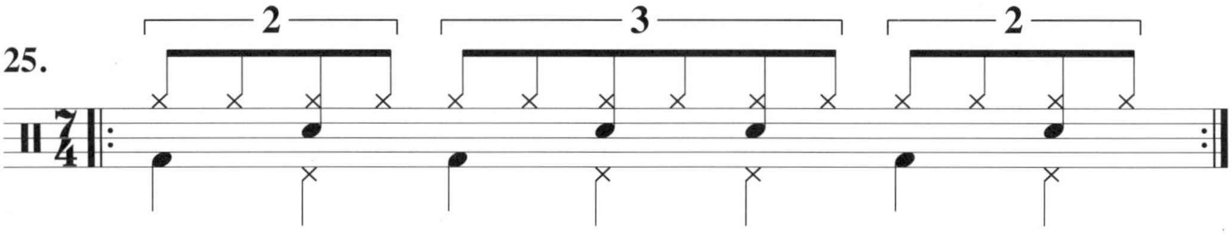

26.

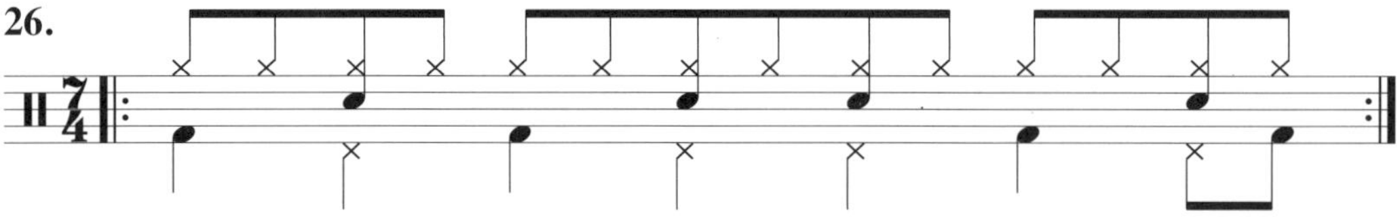

27.

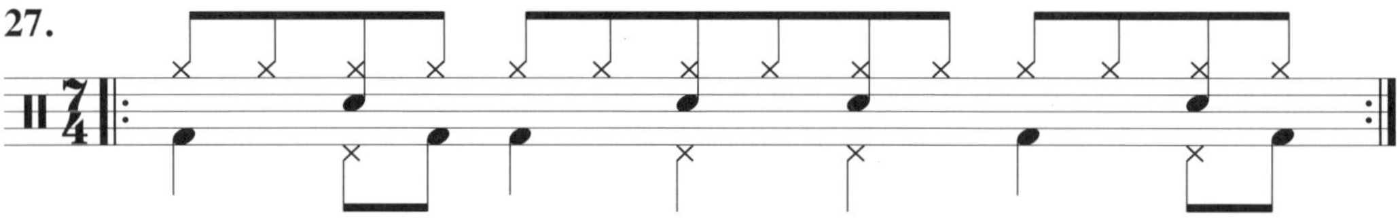

28.

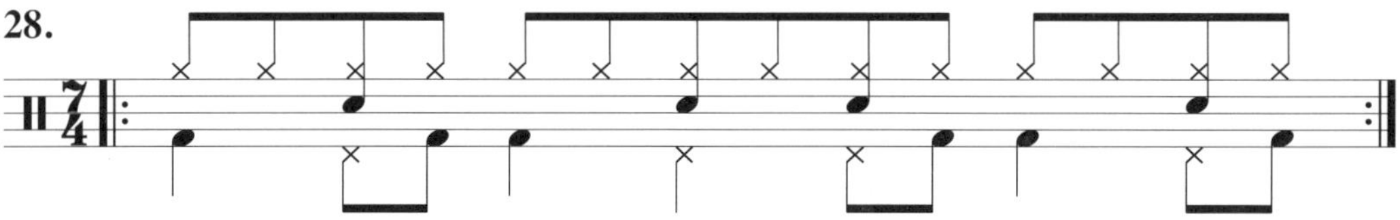

29.

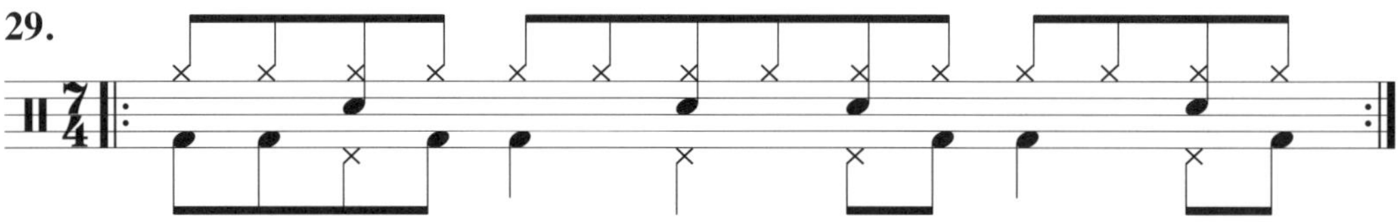

30.

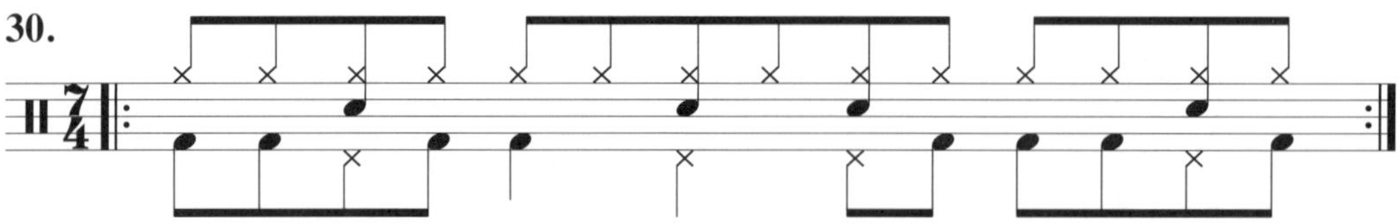

31.

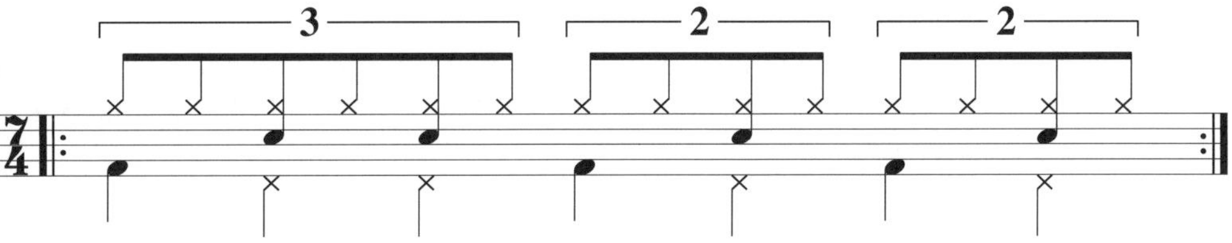

32.

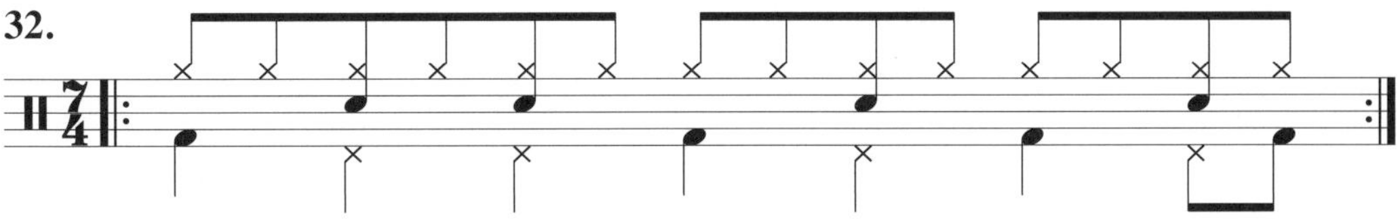

33.

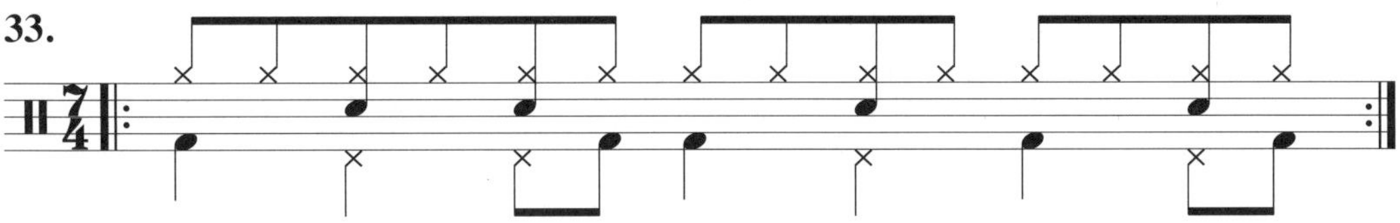

34.

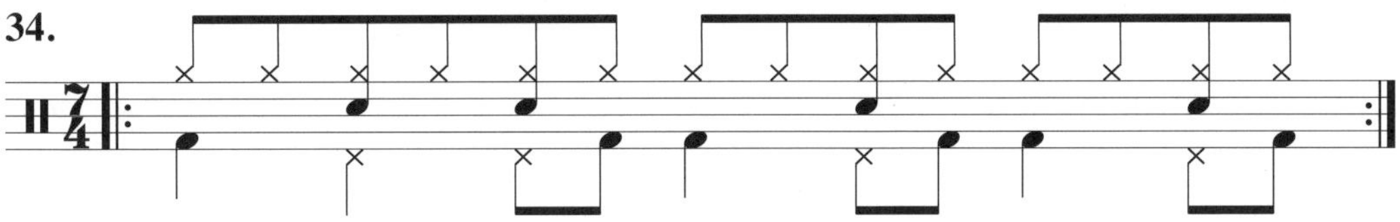

35.

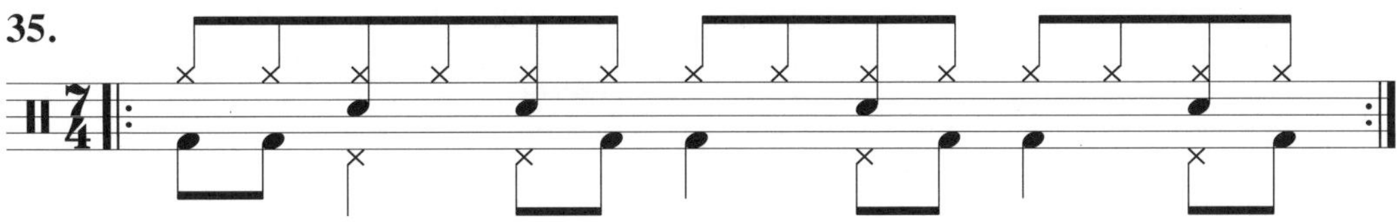

36.

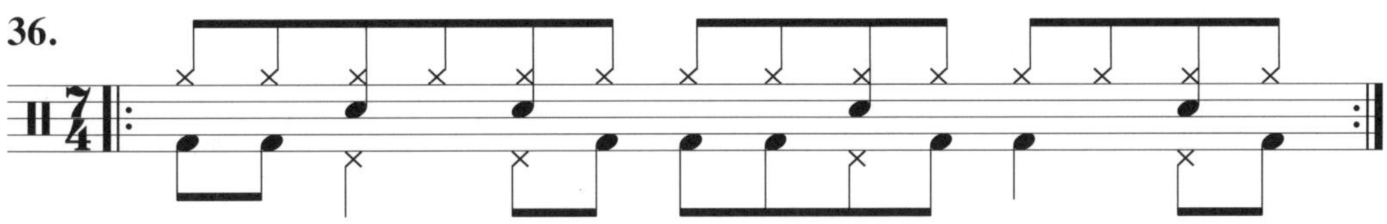

ADVANCED ODD-TIME ROCK

These exercises demonstrate advanced concepts of odd-time rock playing. For example, some songs are written in 3/4 time but are played in two-bar phrases. This means that the backbeat will actually be on beat 1 of the second 3/4 bar in each phrase, like this:

1.

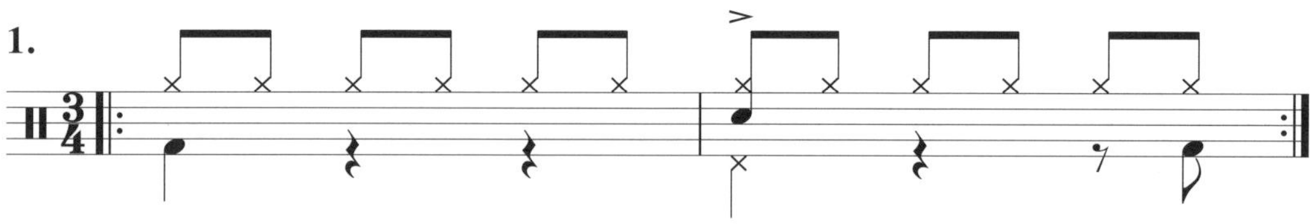

2.

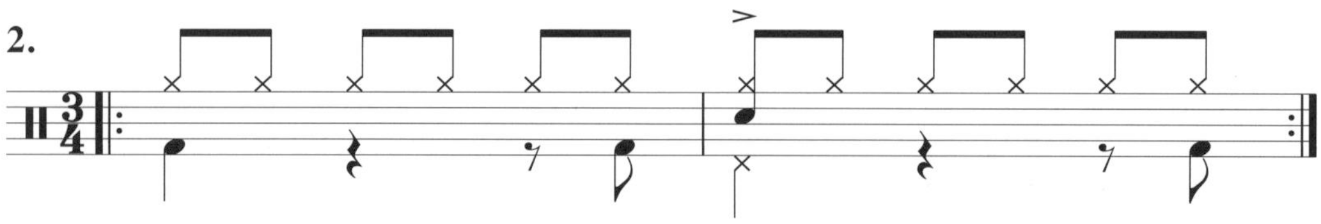

3.

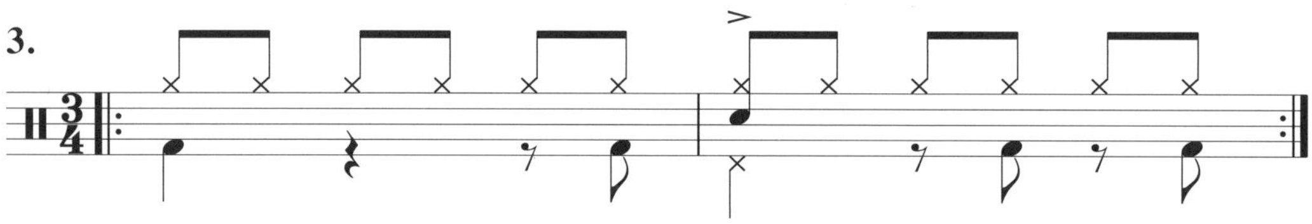

4.

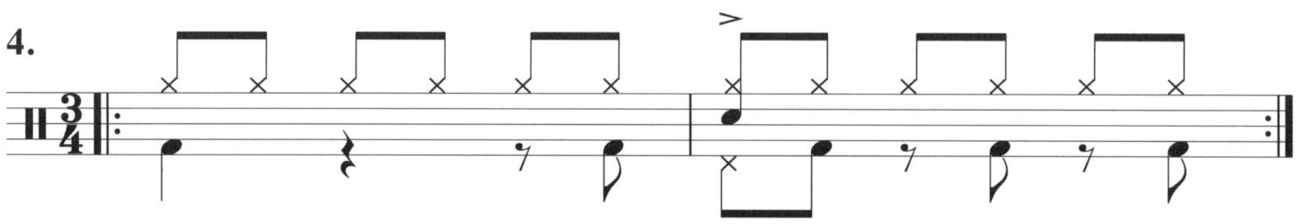

Ghost notes may also be added to these grooves to fill them out. In these exercises, play the snare drum backbeat with a strong accent and unaccented snare drum ghost notes very softly.

5.

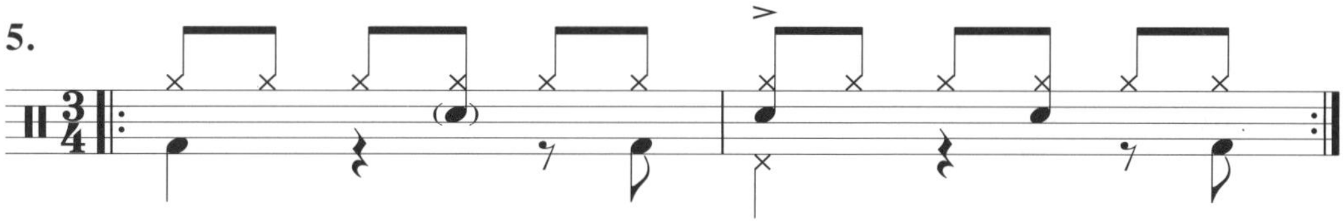

6.

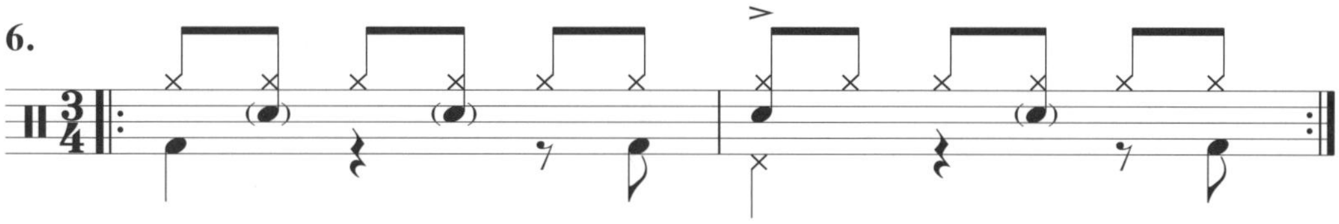

7.

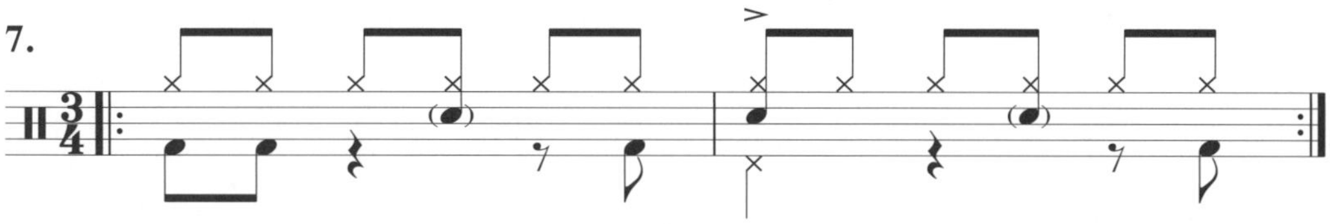

8.

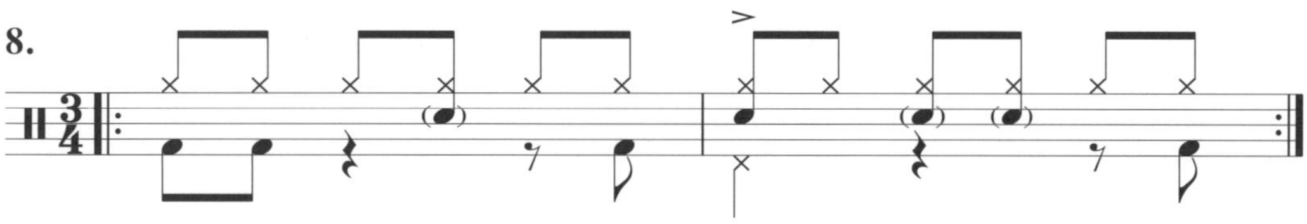

There are many different ways to interpret 5/4 measure phrasing. In many cases, however, when a 5/4 song is phrased 3 + 2, the (snare drum) backbeat is placed on beat 4, as in these examples. Hi-hat may also be played on beats 2, 3, and 5, if desired.

9.

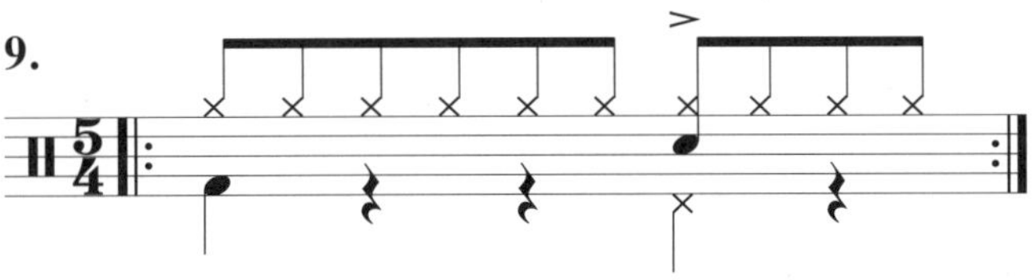

10.

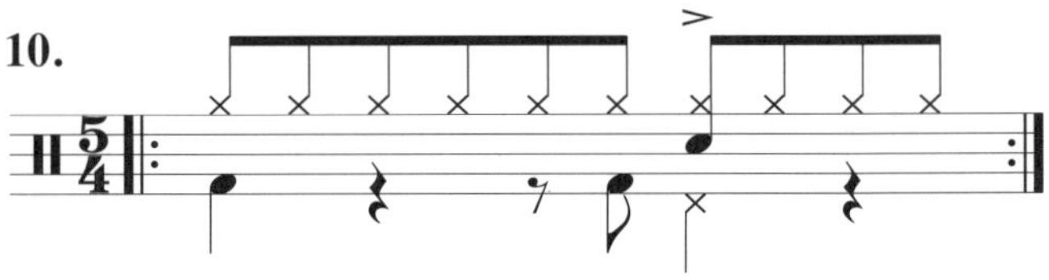

11.

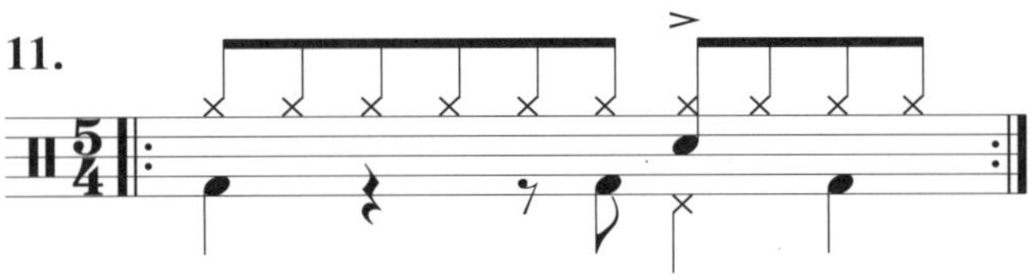

12.

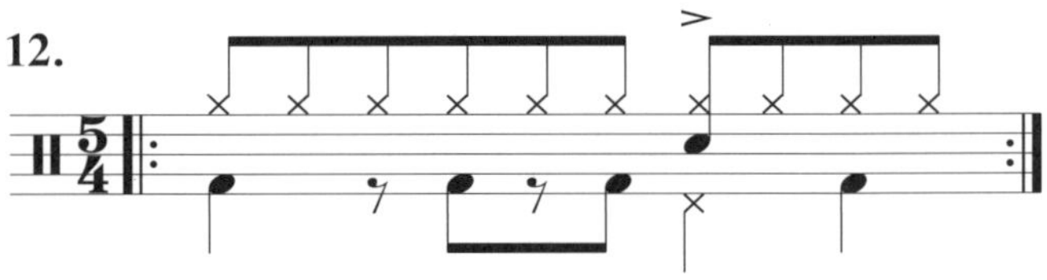

13.

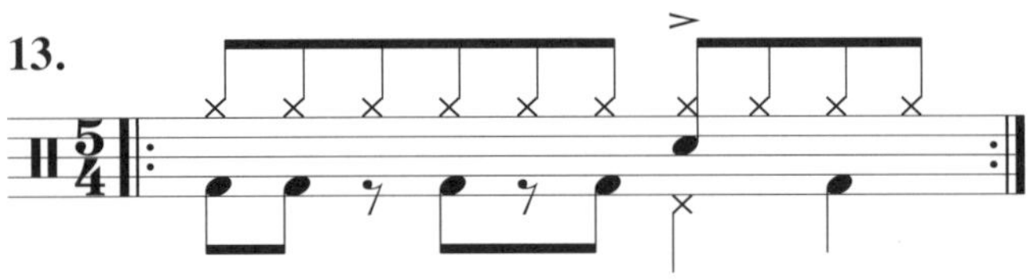

14.

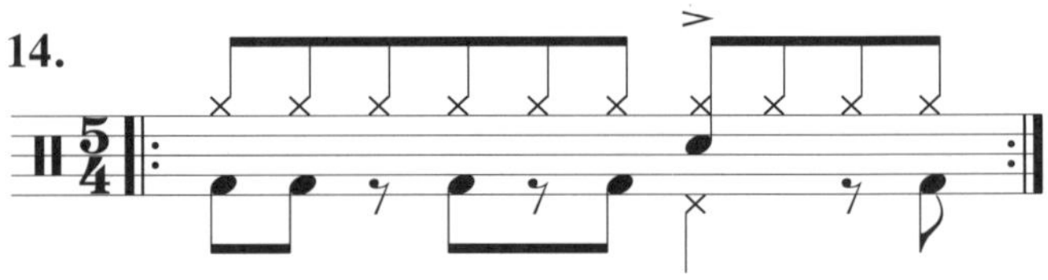

15.

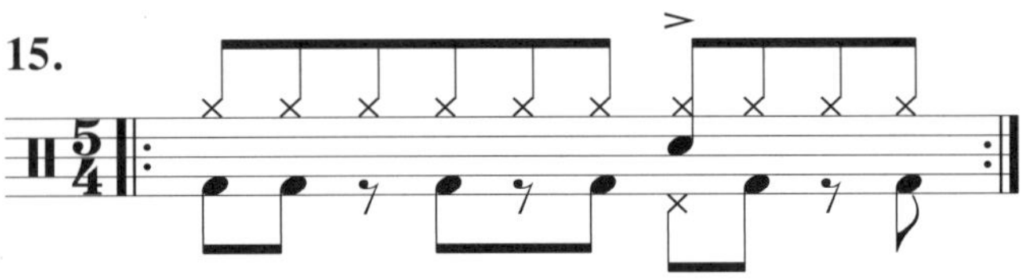

16.

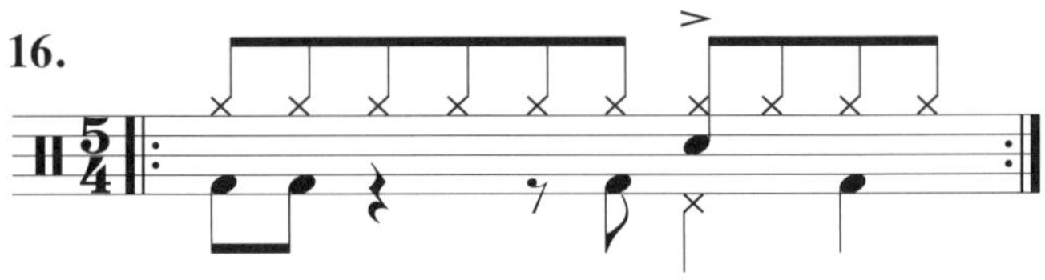

17.

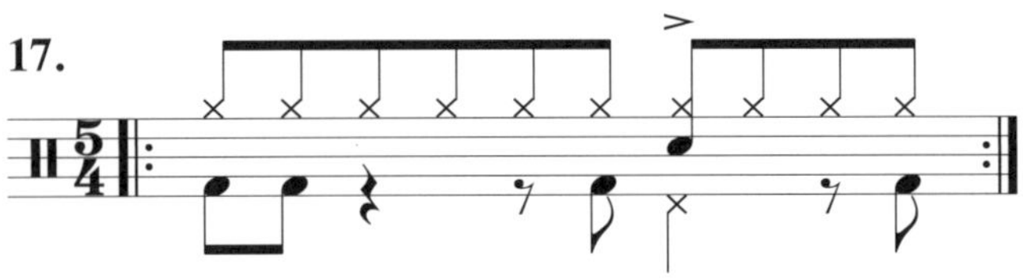

When a 5/4 song is phrased 2 + 3, often the backbeat is placed on beat 3, as in these examples. (Hi-hat may also be played on beats 2, 4, and 5, if desired.)

18.

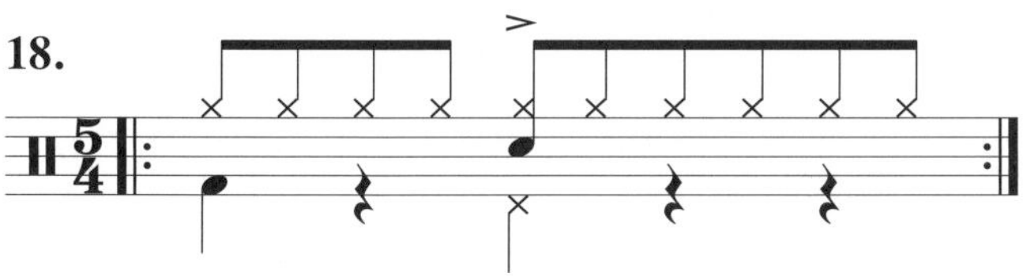

19.

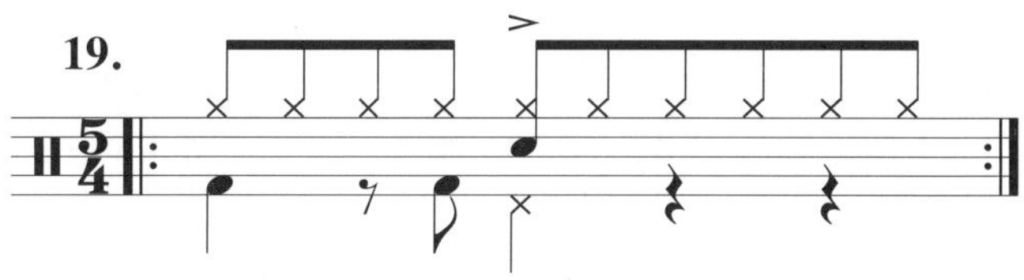

20.

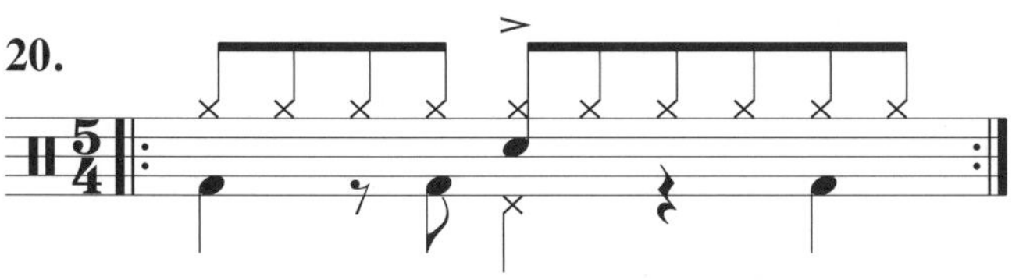

21.

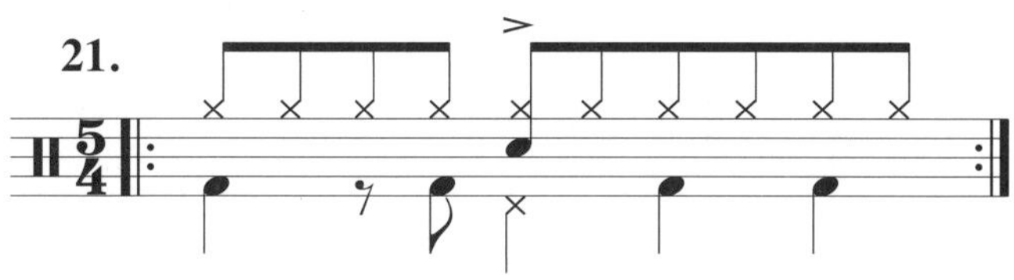

22.

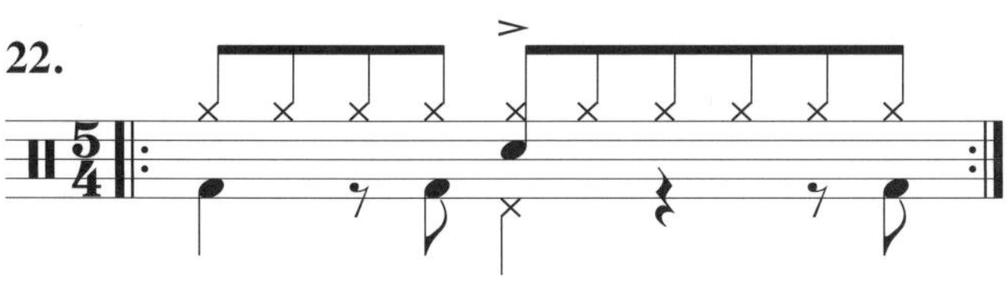

23.

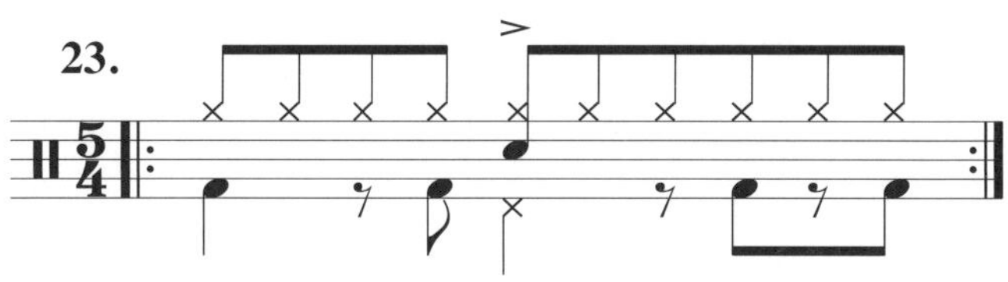

24.

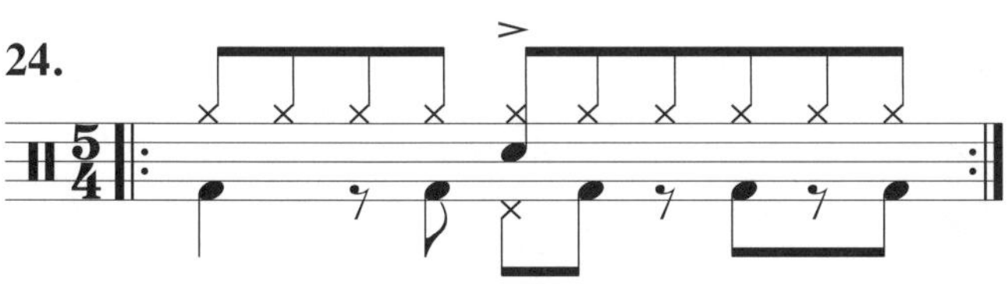

25.

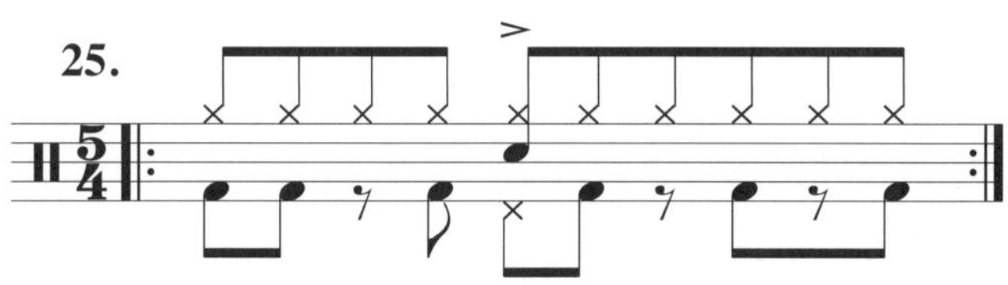

26.

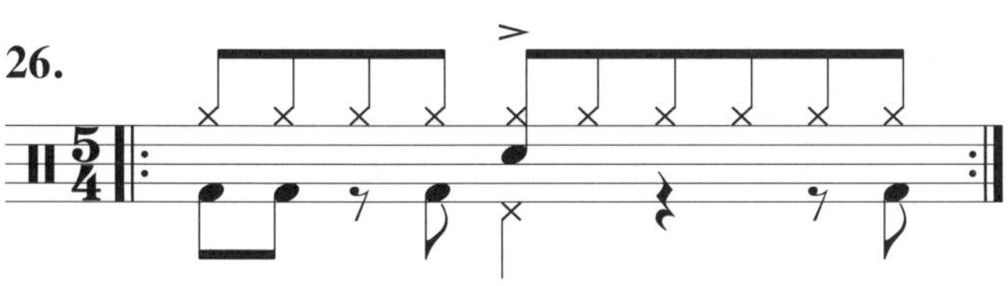

Seven-four time (7/4) may be phrased three different ways, and each way changes where the backbeats are played. Practice these exercises in order to understand where the backbeat occurs in different musical situations.

7/4 PHRASED 2 + 2 + 3

(Hi-hat may also be played on beats 2, 4, 6, and 7, or all beats.)

27.

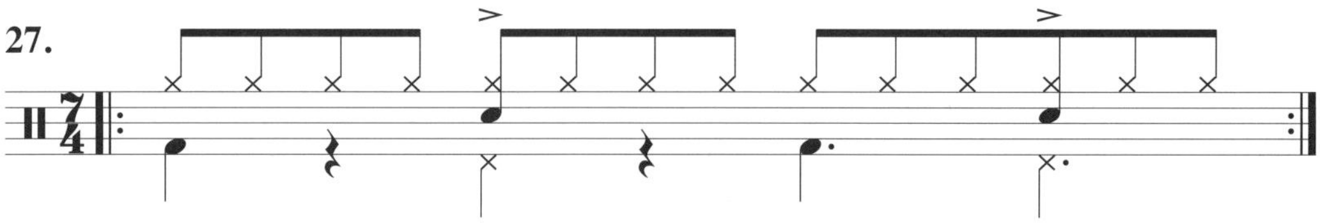

28.

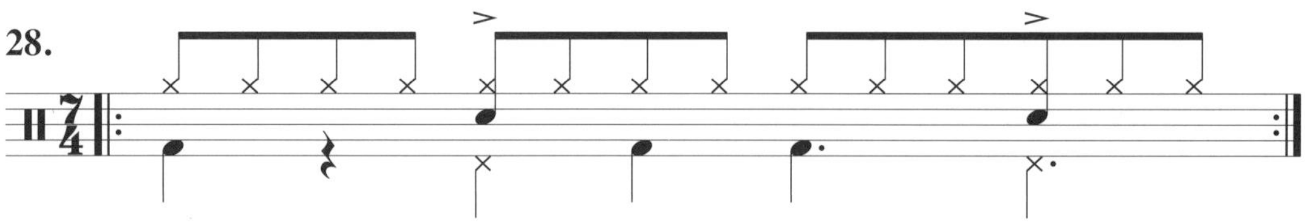

29.

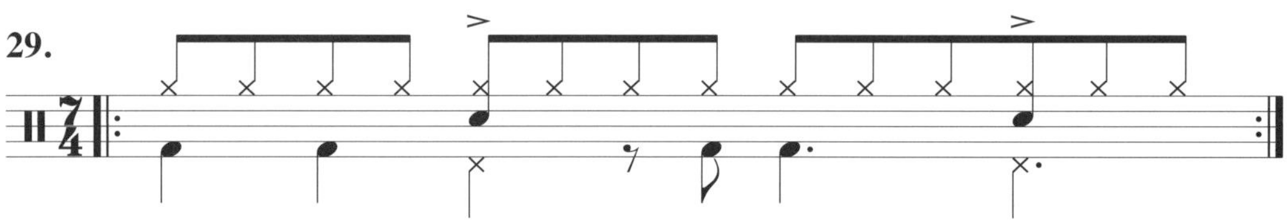

7/4 PHRASED 2 + 3 + 2

(Hi-hat may also be played on beats 2, 4, 5, and 7, or all beats.)

30.

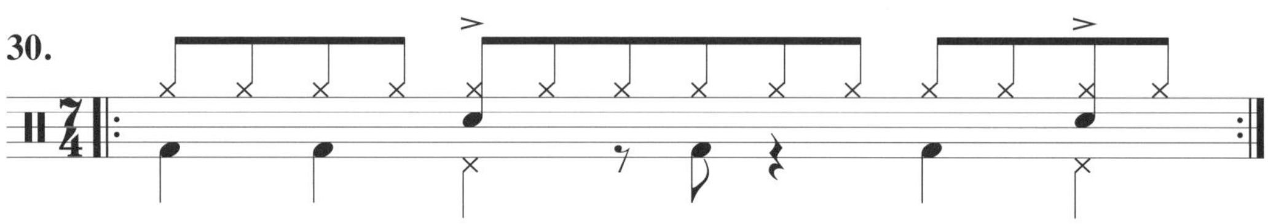

31.

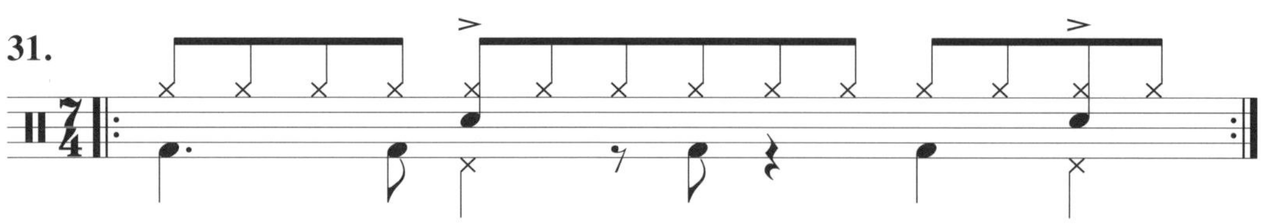

32.

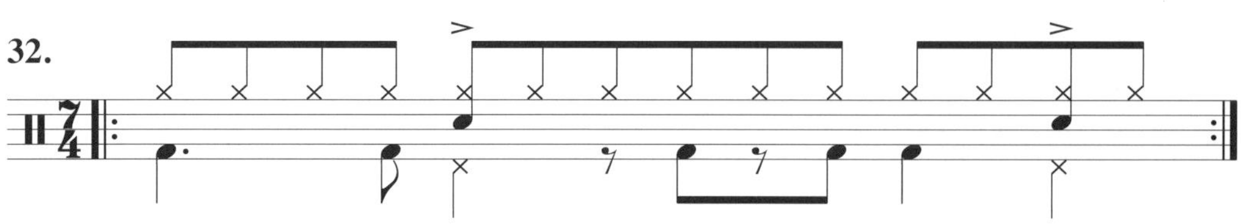

7/4 PHRASED 3 + 2 + 2

(Hi-hat may also be played on beats 2, 3, 5, and 7, or all beats)

33.

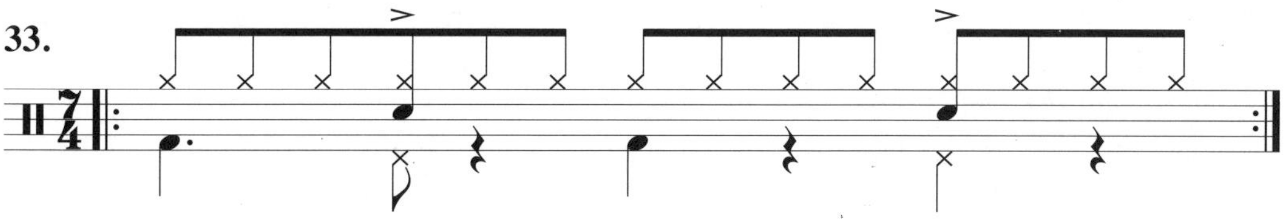

34.

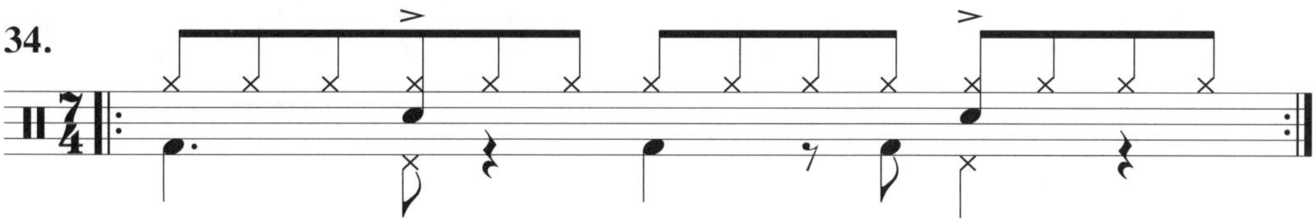

35.

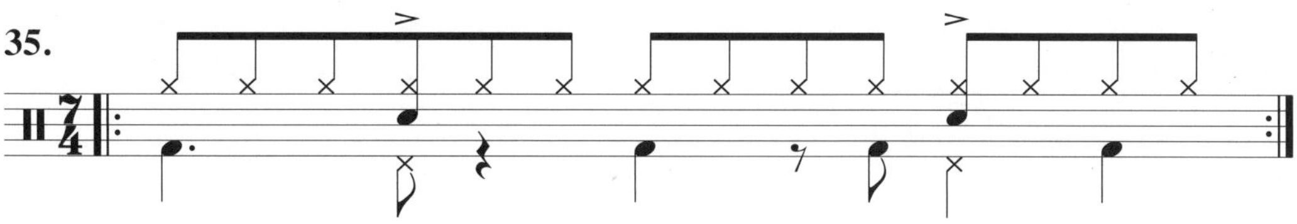

ODD-TIME EIGHTH-NOTE METERS

Songs written in eighth-note odd meters (e.g., 5/8, 7/8, 9/8, 11/8, etc.) are not uncommon and something that every drummer should understand. One of the most important aspects of working in odd meters is knowing how the meter should be counted and where to place the backbeat. Normally 5/8, for example, may be phrased either 3 (eighth notes) + 2 (eighth notes) or 2 + 3. If it's phrased 3 + 2, then the backbeat is normally played on beat 4. If it's phrased 2 + 3, then the backbeat is normally on beat 3. Practice these examples of 5/8 phrased 3 + 2, with the backbeat on beat 4. Count each eighth note of the bar: 1-2-3-4-5.

1.

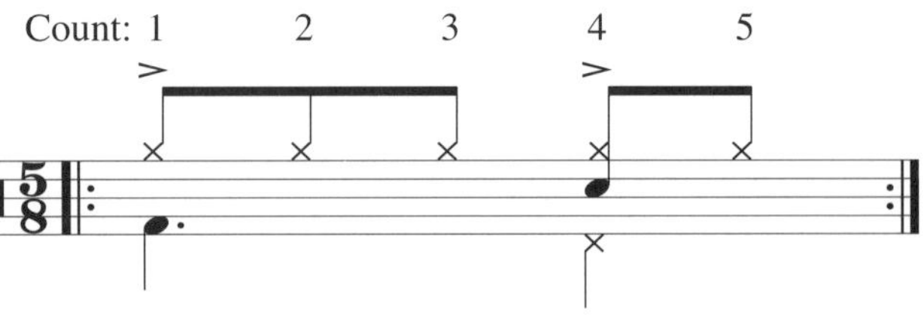

2.

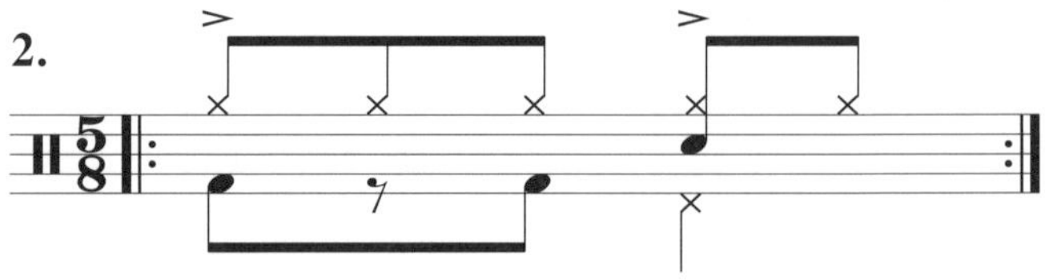

3.

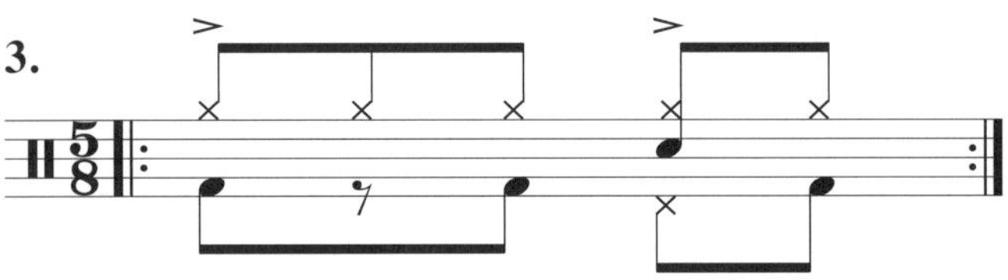

4.

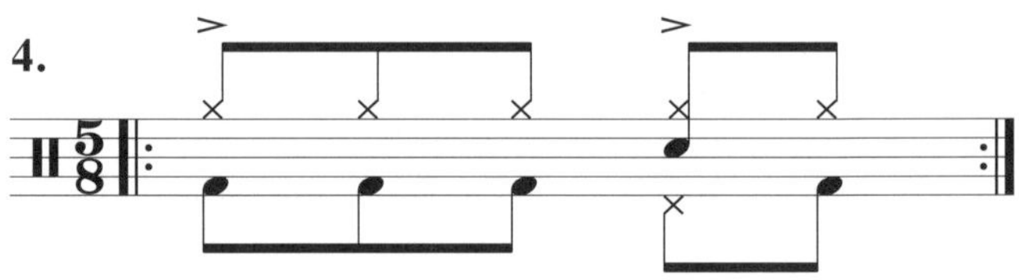

5.

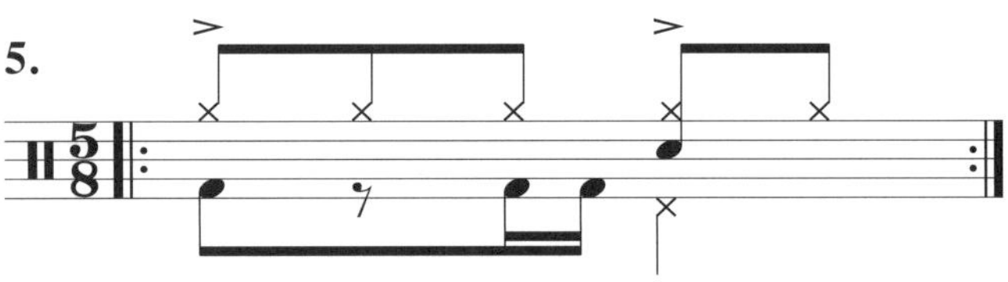

6.

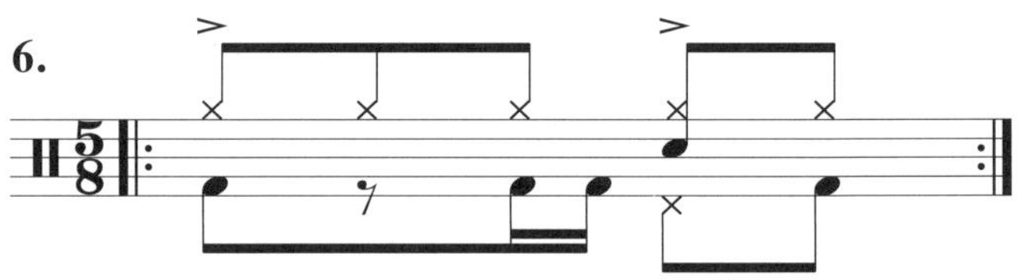

7.

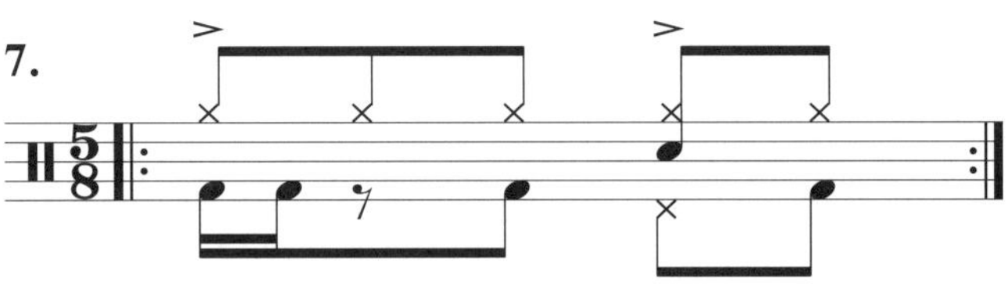

8.

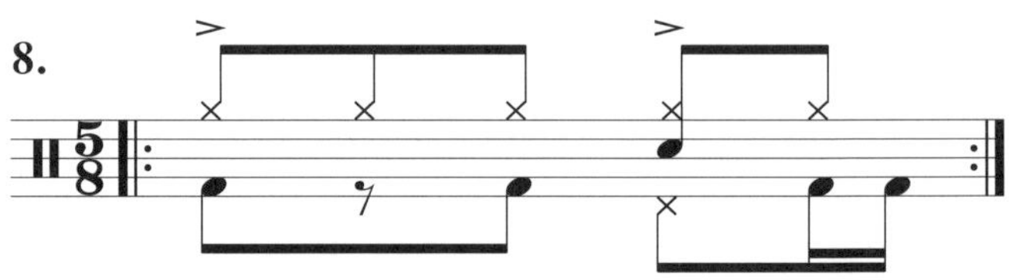

9.

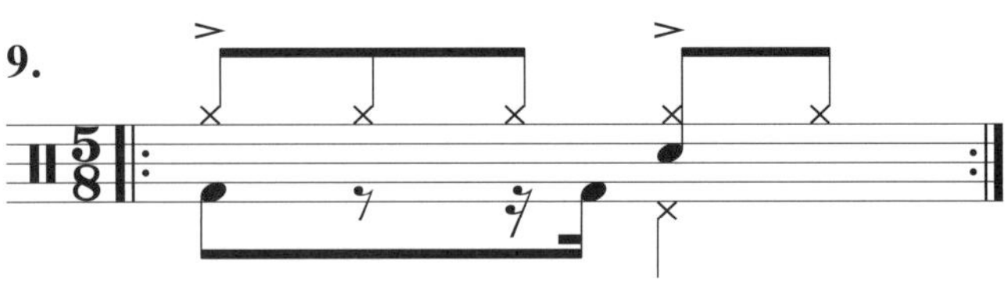

10.

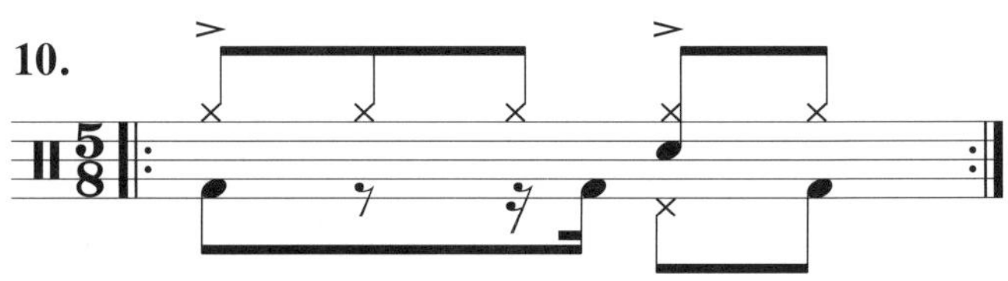

11.

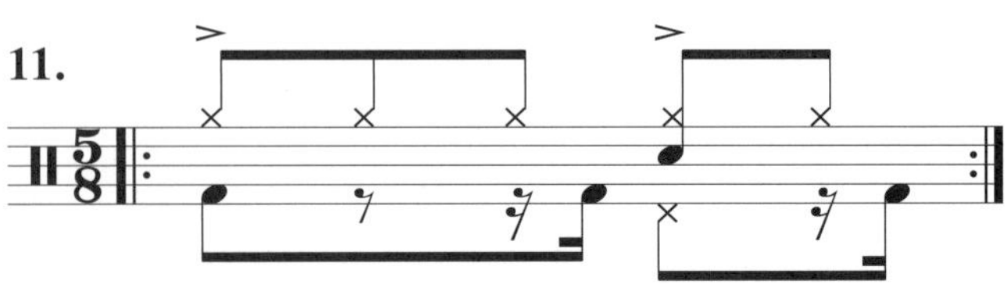

12.

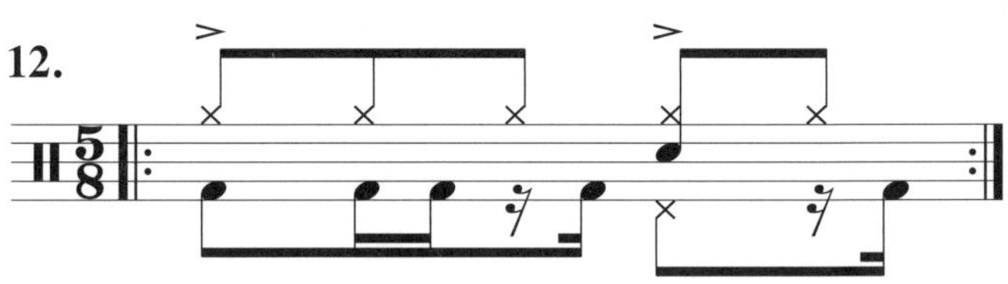

Examples 13–24 are examples of 5/8 phrased as 2 + 3, with the backbeat on beat 3.

13.

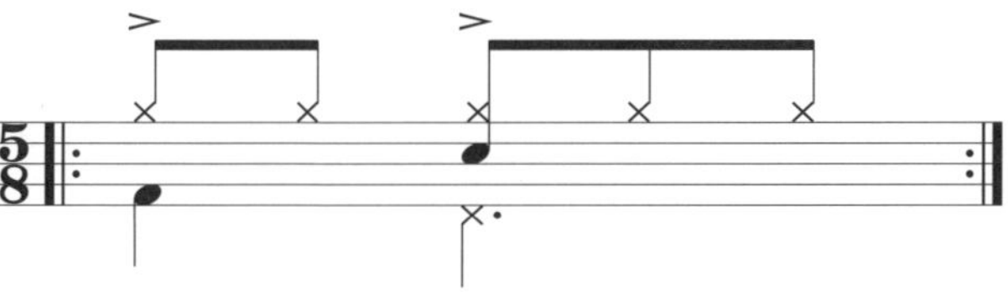

14.

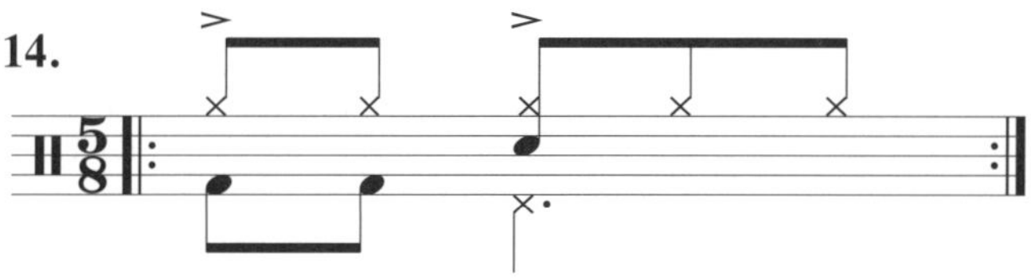

15.

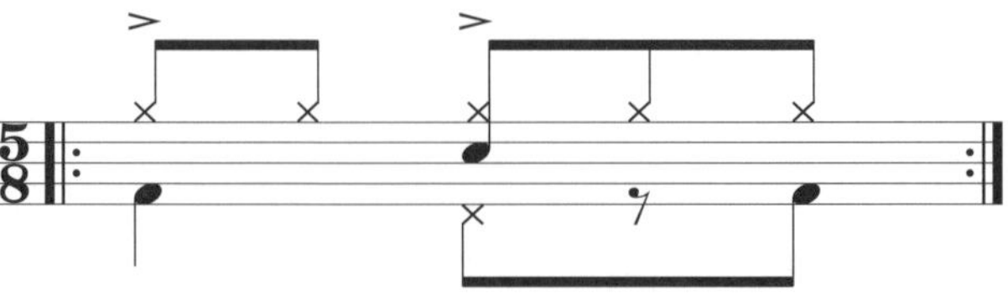

16.

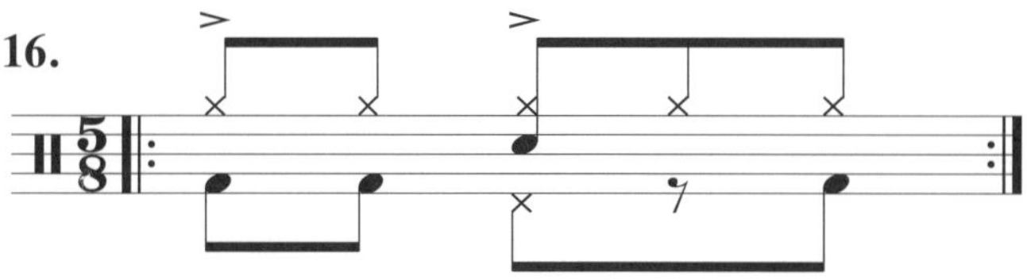

17.

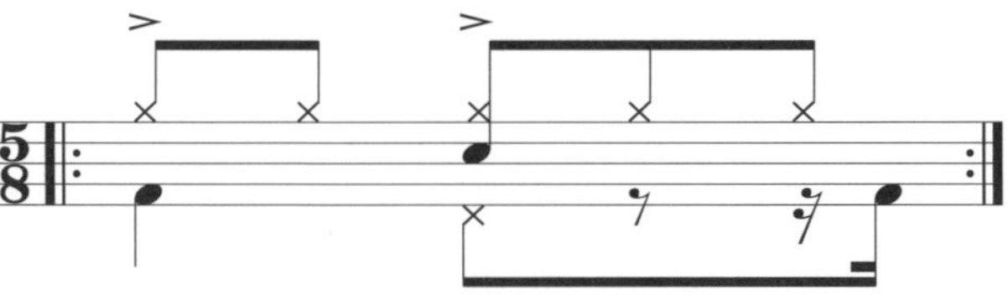

18.

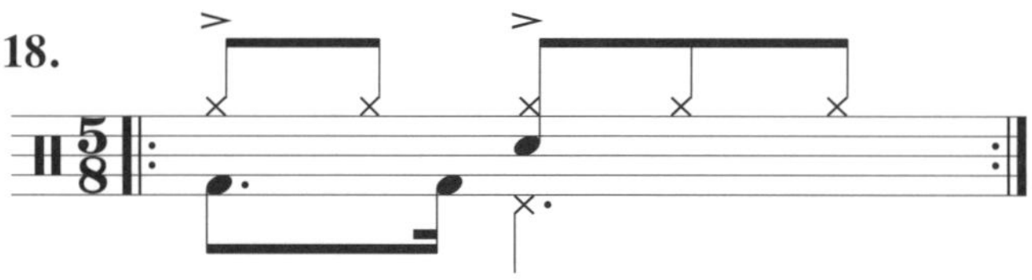

19.

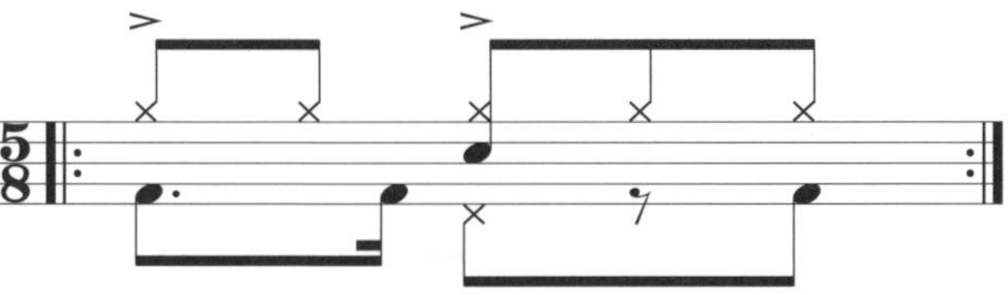

20.

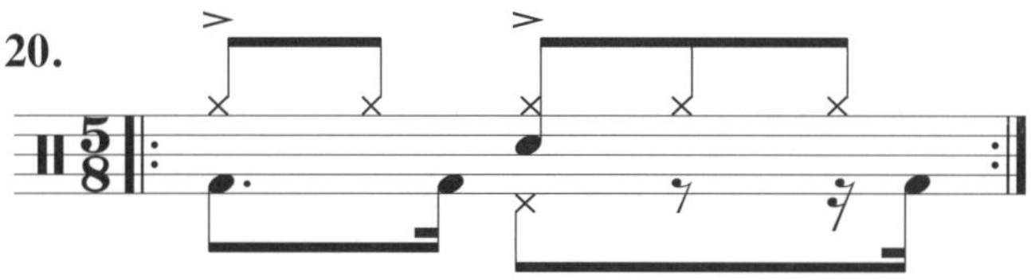

21.

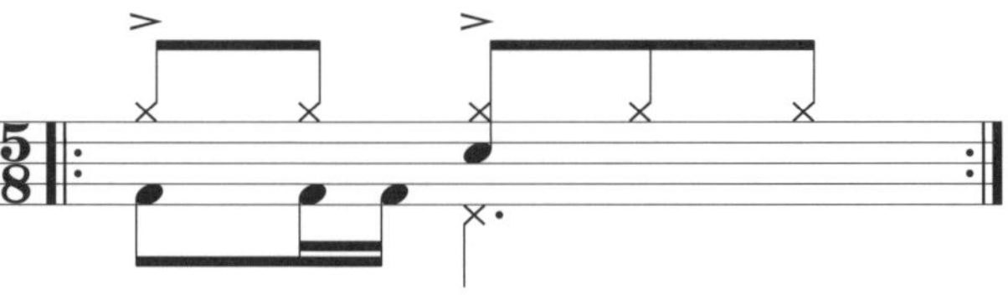

22.

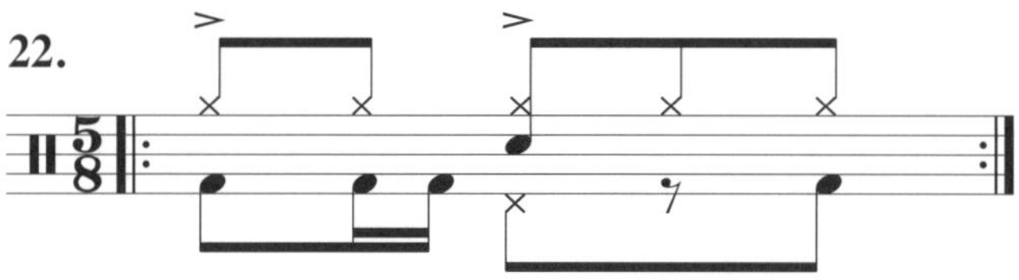

23.

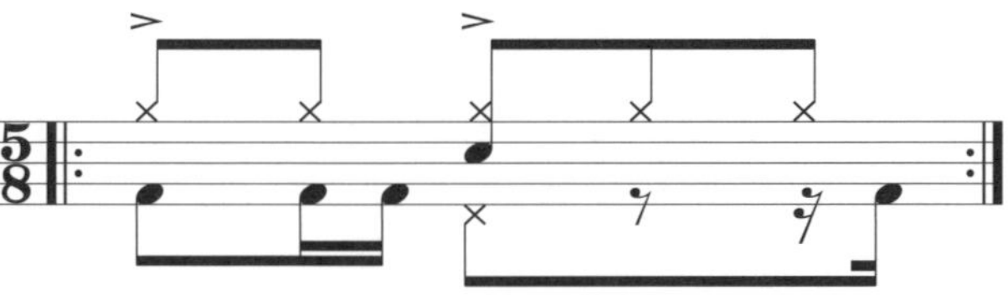

24.

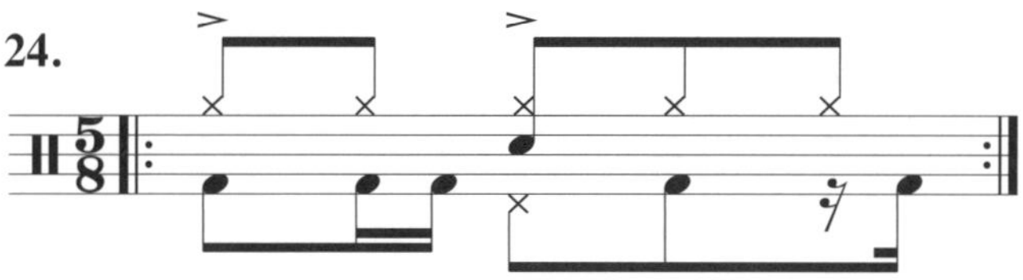

Exercises 25–48 demonstrate the phrasing possibilities in 7/8 and how the backbeat changes position depending upon the phrasing.

7/8 PHRASED 2 + 2 + 3 (BACKBEAT ON 5)

25.

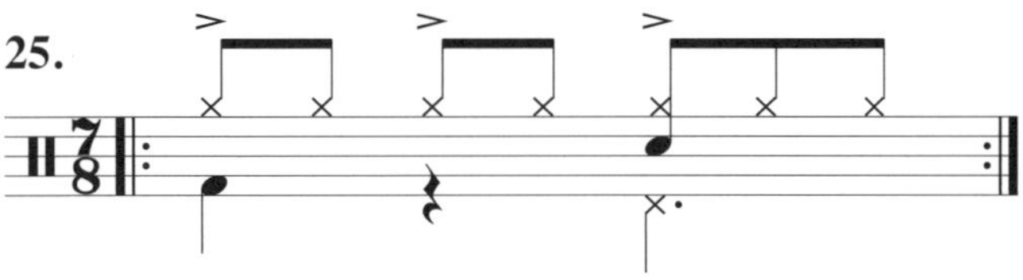

26.

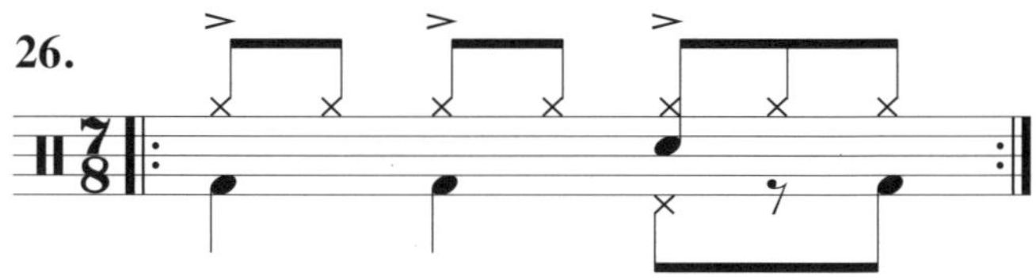

27.

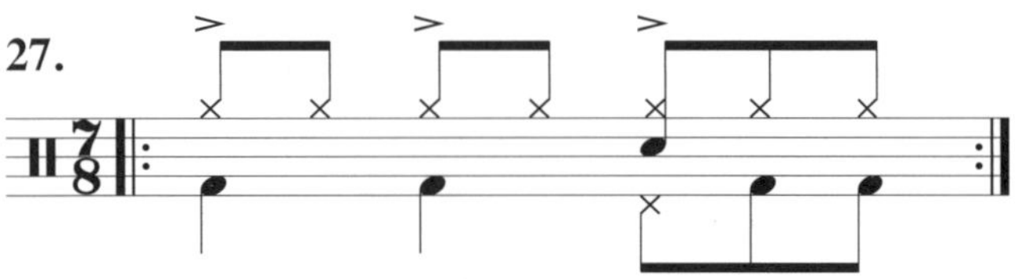

28.

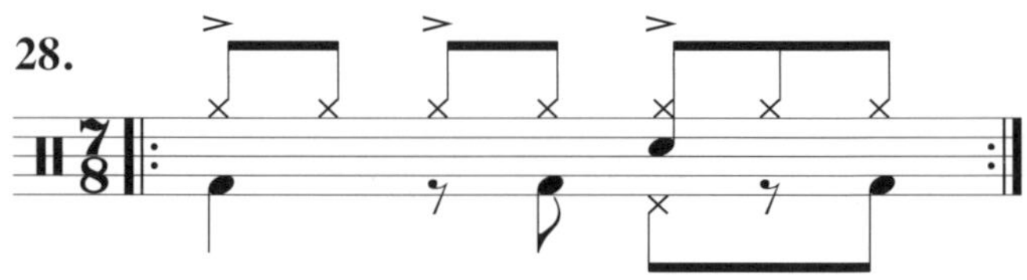

29.

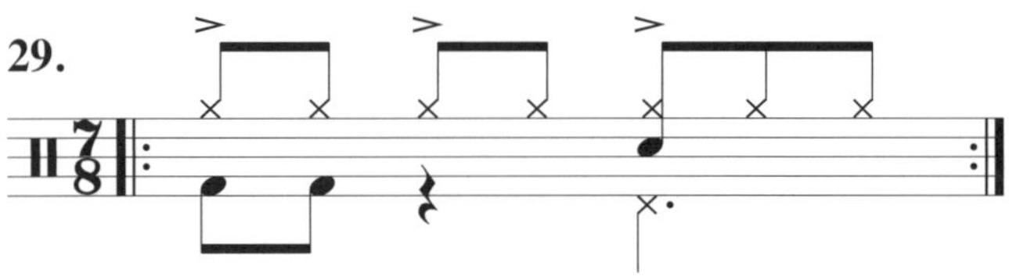

30.

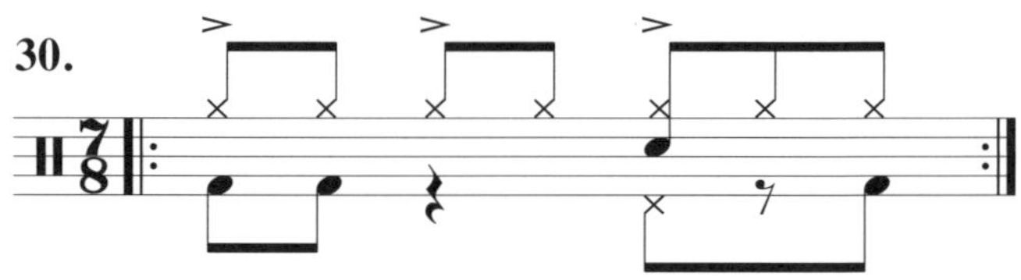

31.

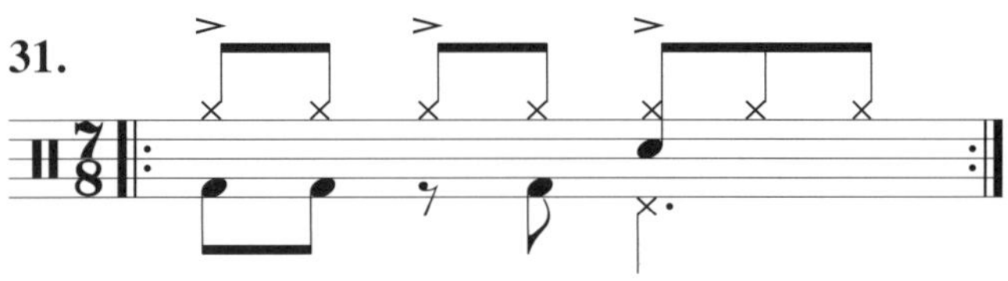

32.

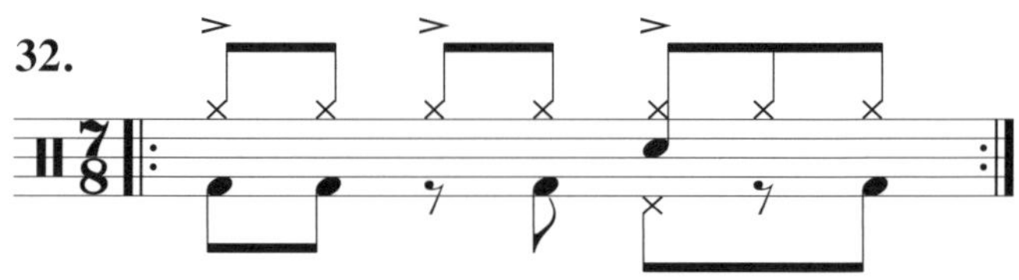

7/8 PHRASED 2 + 3 + 2 (BACKBEAT ON 3)

33.

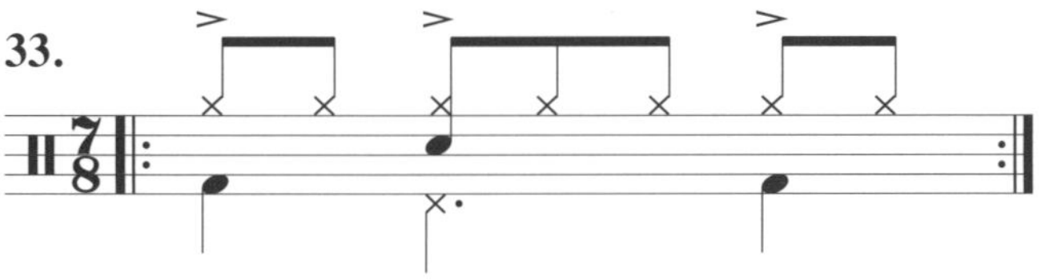

34.

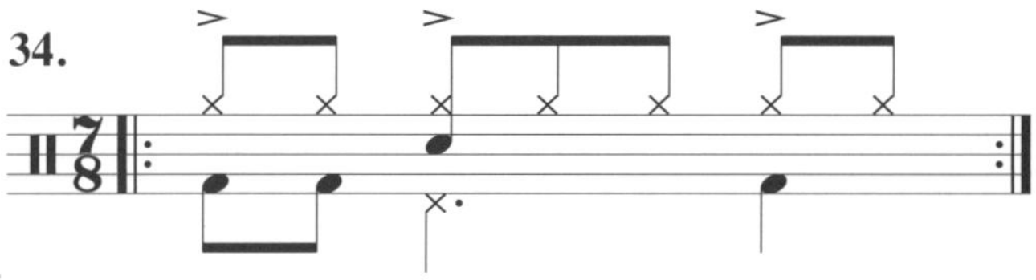

35.

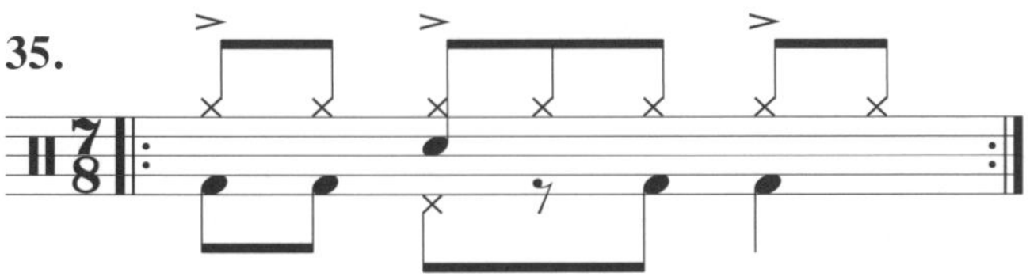

36.

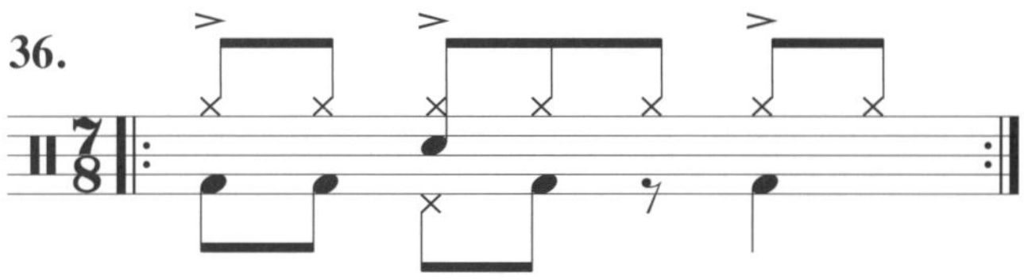

37.

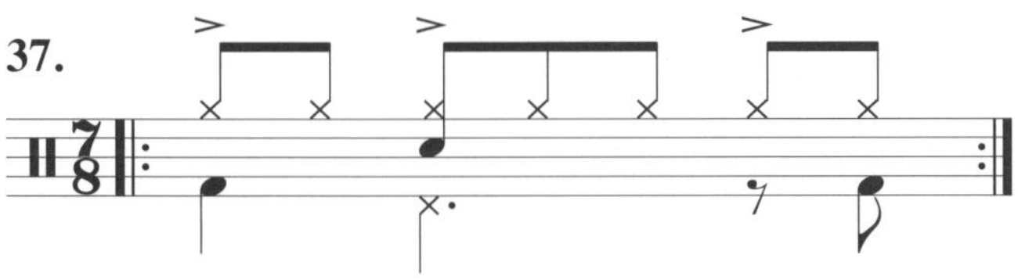

38.

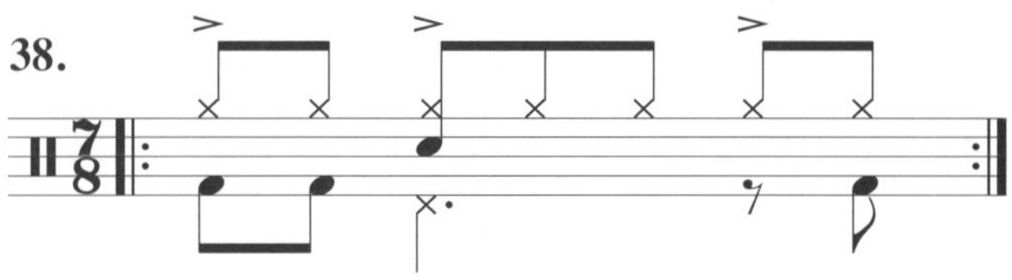

39.

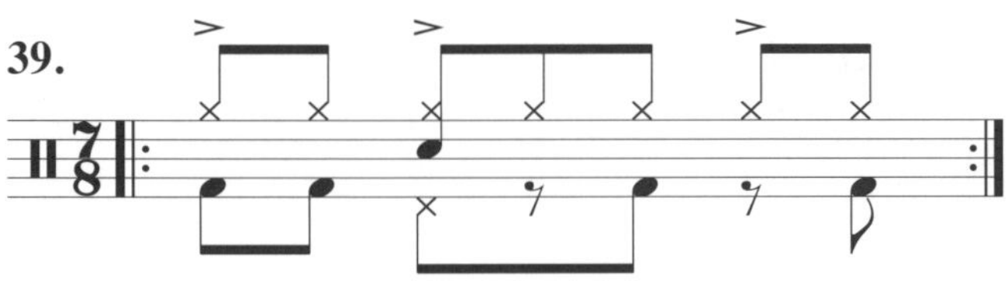

40.

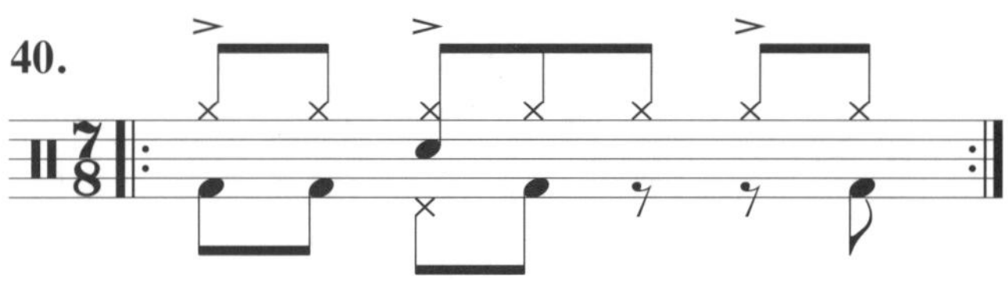

7/8 PHRASED 3 + 2 + 2 (BACKBEAT ON 4)

41.

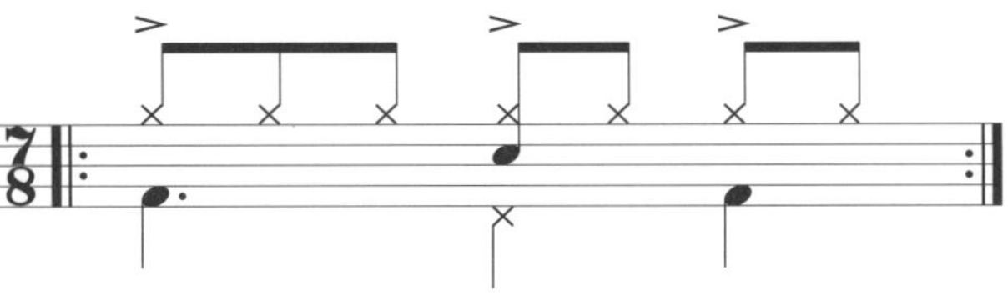

42.

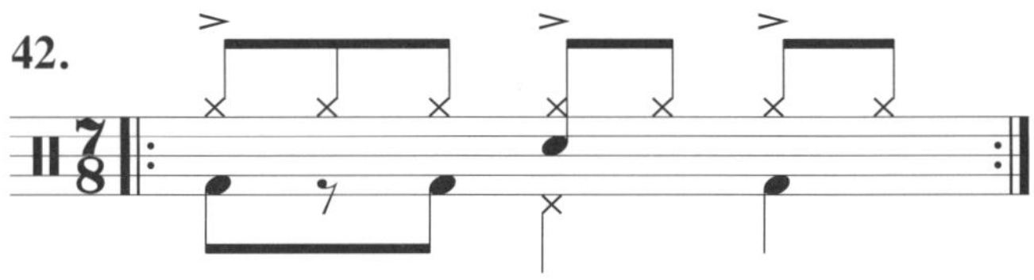

43.

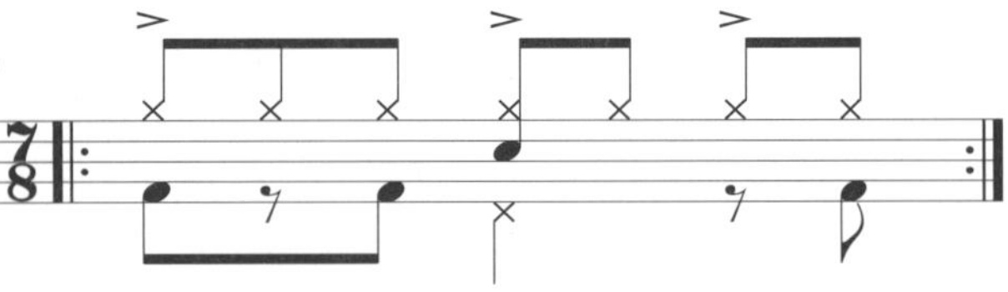

44.

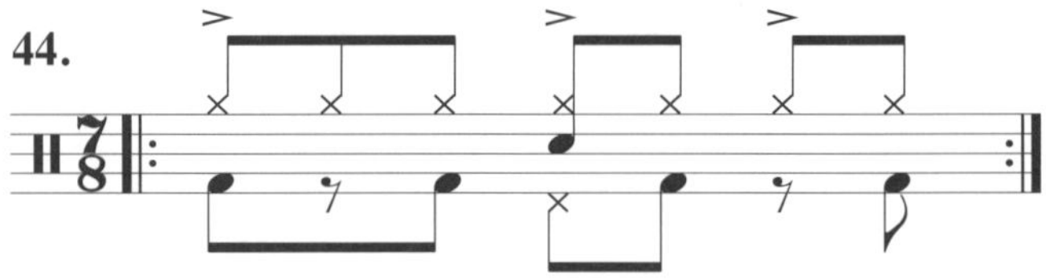

45.

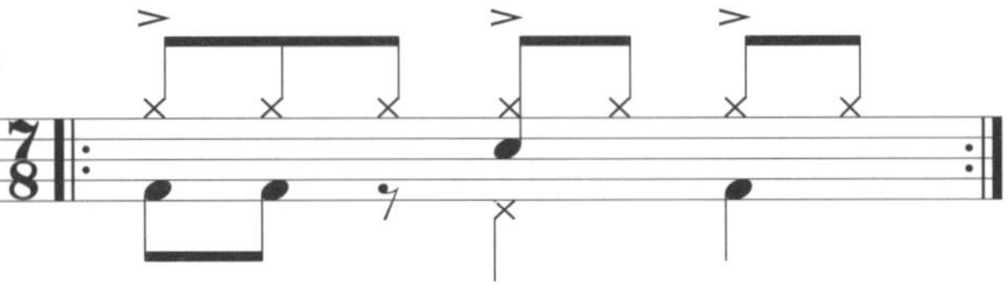

46.

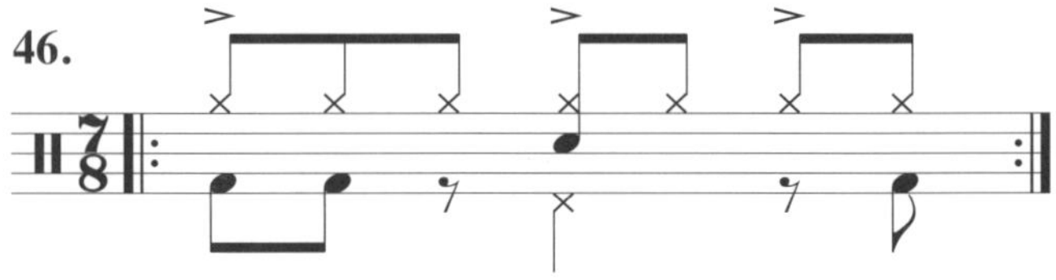

47.

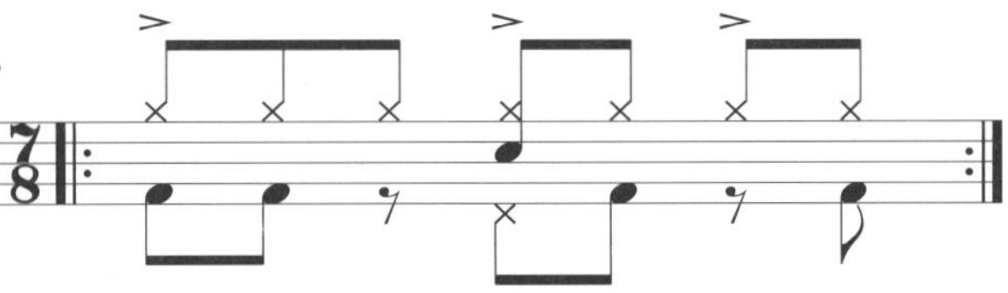

48.

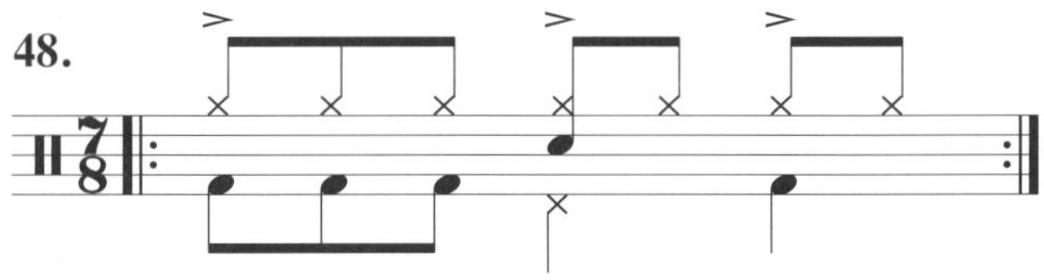

Once you're familiar with several odd meters (5/8, 7/8, etc.), it then becomes very easy to decipher any other, more advanced odd meters. For example, when encountering 9/8 phrased as 2 + 2 + 2 + 3, you could think of it as a 2/4 measure (2 + 2) plus a 5/8 measure (2 + 3). If you had 11/8 phrased as 2 + 2 + 2 + 2 + 3, it could be phrased as a 2/4 bar plus a 7/8 bar (2 + 2 + 2 + 2 + 3), or a 4/4 bar plus a 3/8 bar:

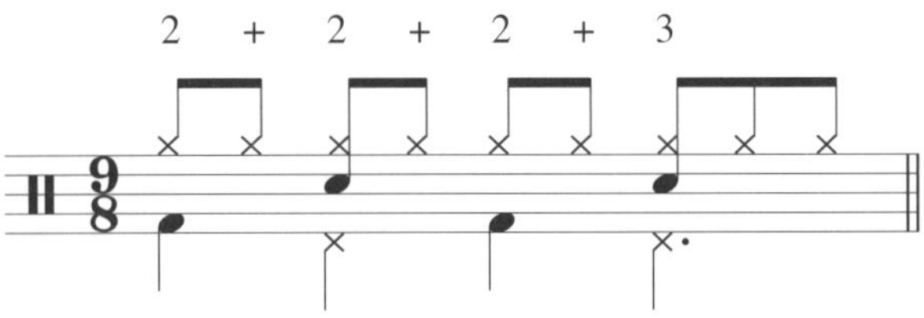

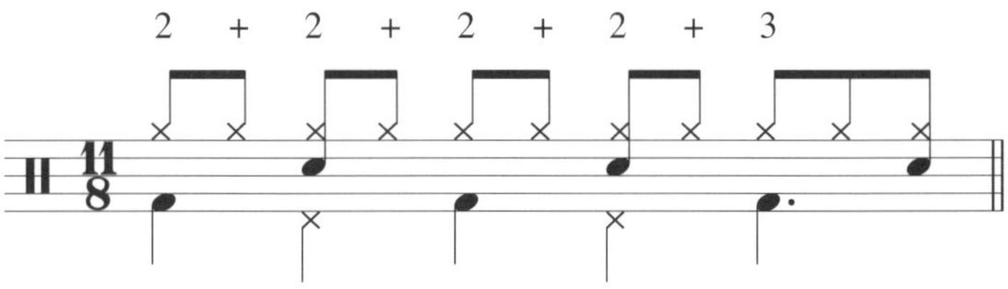

Use this last method to create your own odd meters and decipher any odd meter you encounter.

CHAPTER 2
BOSSA NOVA OSTINATOS

The Bossa Nova ostinatos are written in 4/4 (common time), which is how that rhythm is typically thought of and notated. Therefore, concentrate on the quarter-note pulse when working with these patterns. All of the rhythm studies and summary pages, however, are written in cut time, which is how the Samba and Baiao rhythms are felt. The rhythm studies and summary pages should be interpreted as 4/4 when played in conjunction with the Bossa Nova. Ostinatos 1 and 3 may be played by slightly accenting the ride cymbal or hi-hat in unison with the snare drum or cross-stick rhythms.

Tempo range: ♩ = 116–152

1.

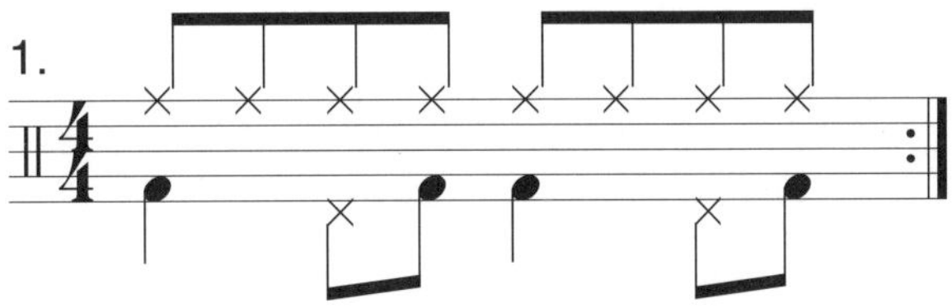

2.

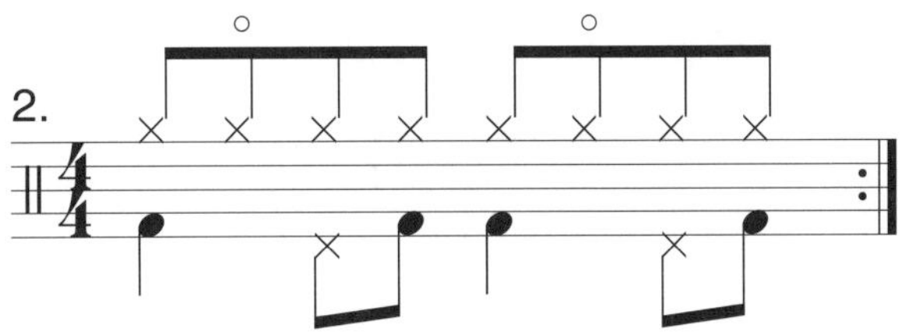

3.

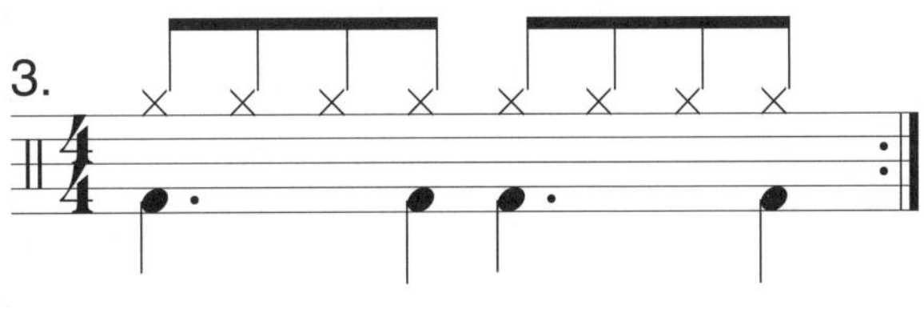

SAMBA OSTINATOS

Samba is often written in 4/4 time, but is correctly felt and played with a "two" feel, and so the ostinatos are notated here in cut time. The bass drum part written in the Samba ostinatos emulates the surdo part and should be accented on beat 2. But this should not be a heavy accent; rather, the beat should simply be stressed.

Tempo range: 𝅗𝅥 = 80–120

1.

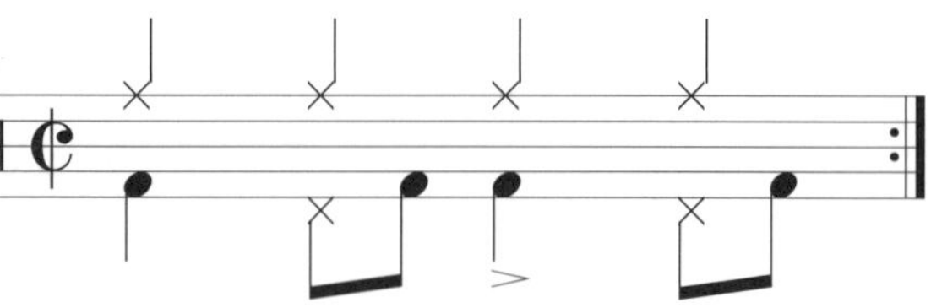

2.

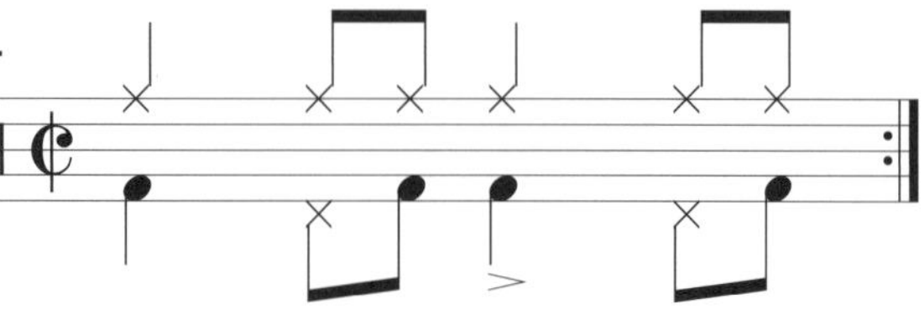

3.

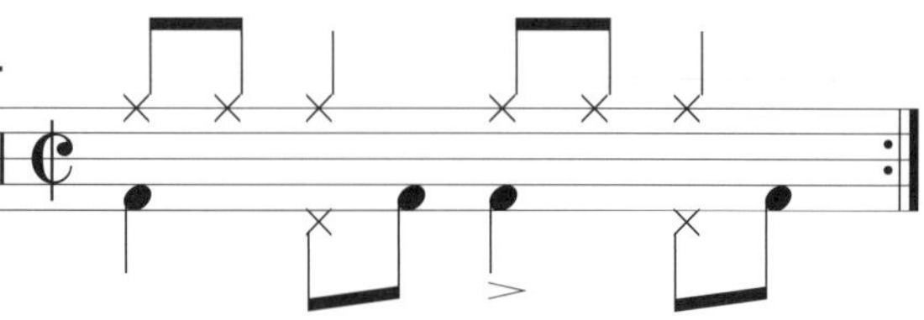

4.

5.

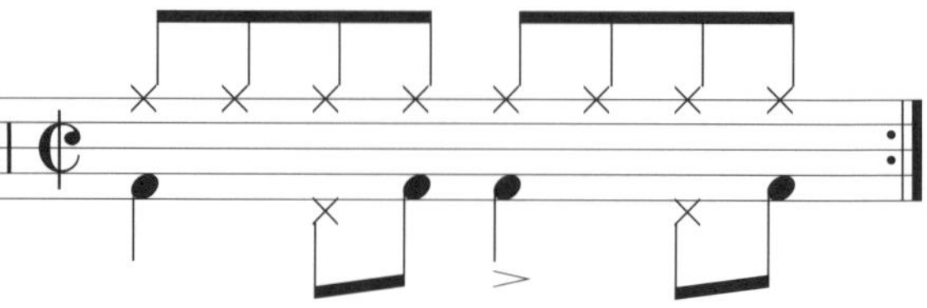

6.

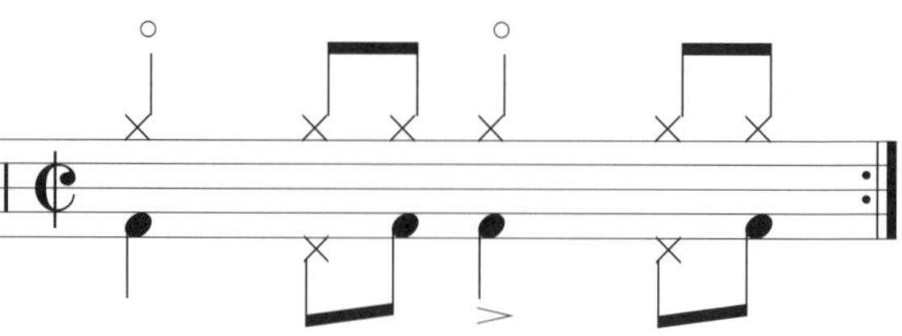

7.

BAIAO OSTINATOS

Although Baiao and Samba have different underlying pulses, they are both felt and played with a "two" feel, and so the Baiao ostinatos are notated in cut-time. The bass drum in these ostinatos emulates the rhythm played by the zabumba, a type of surdo drum used in the Baiao musical style. Be sure to accent the bass drum slightly on the "and" of two, as indicated.

Tempo range: 𝅗𝅥 = 100–120

1.

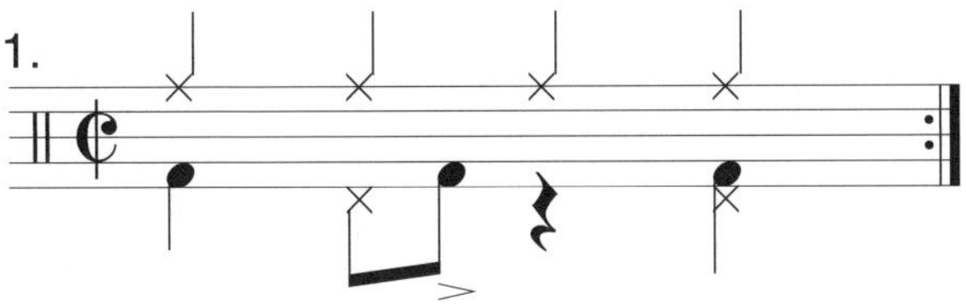

2.

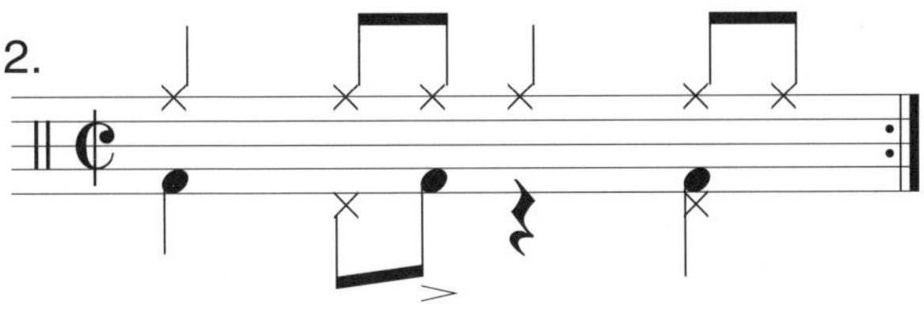

3.

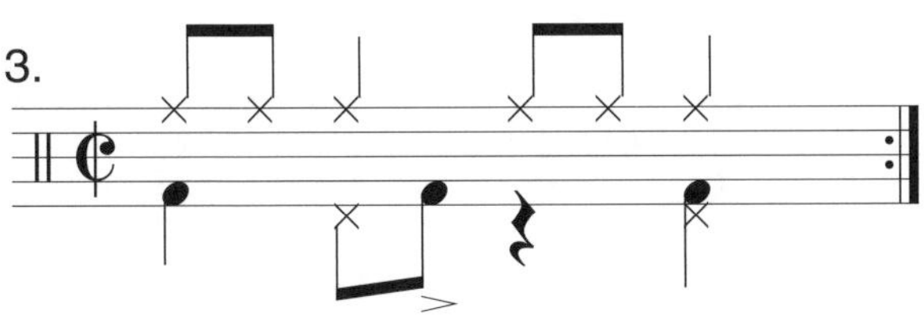

4.

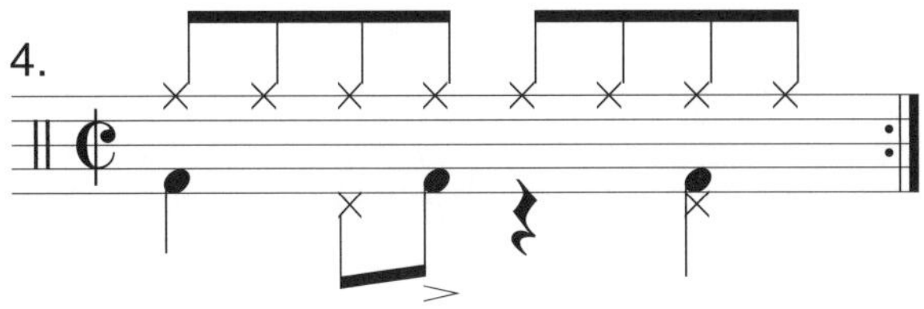

5.

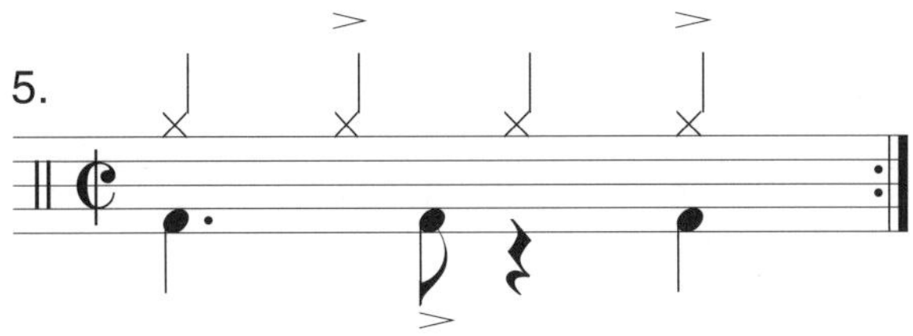

6.

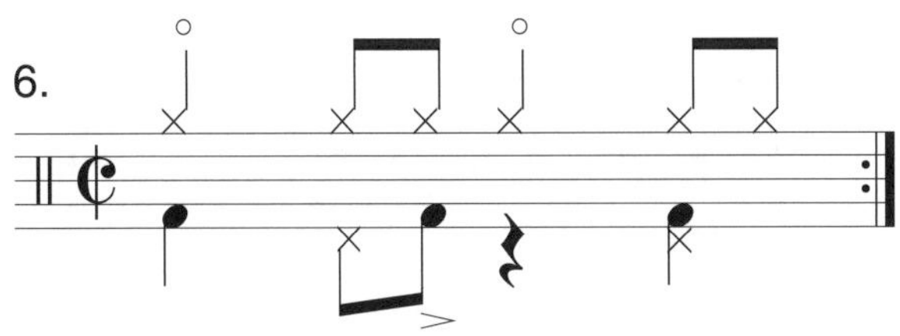

7.

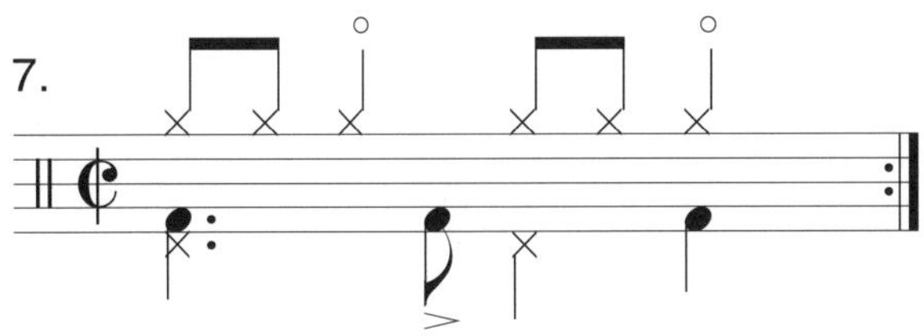

RHYTHM STUDIES

PART I: RHYTHM STUDIES

1.

2.
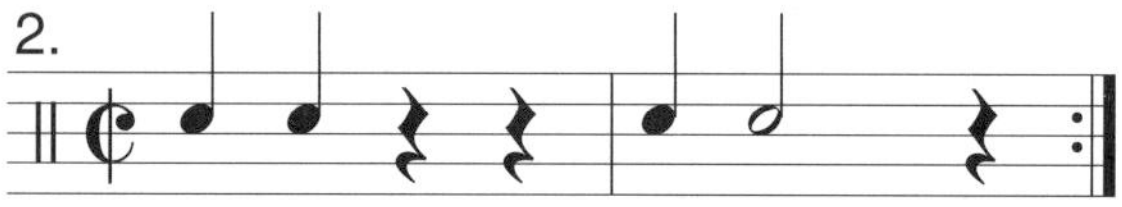

3.

4.
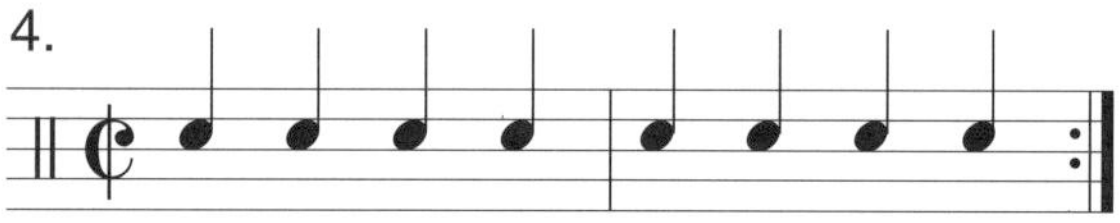

5.
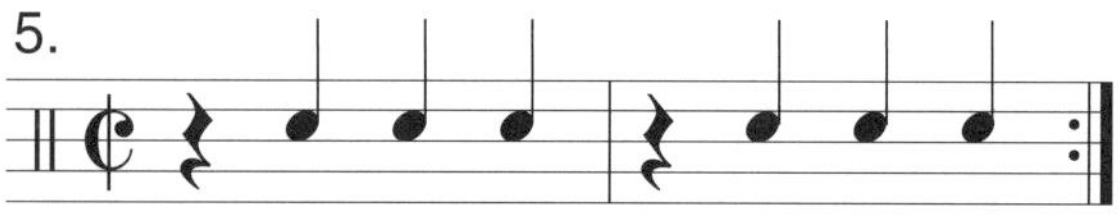

6.
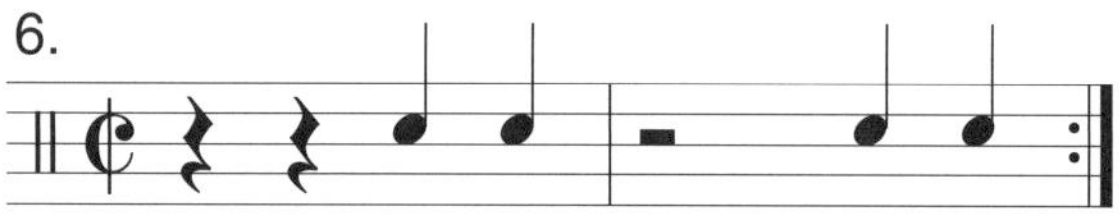

7.
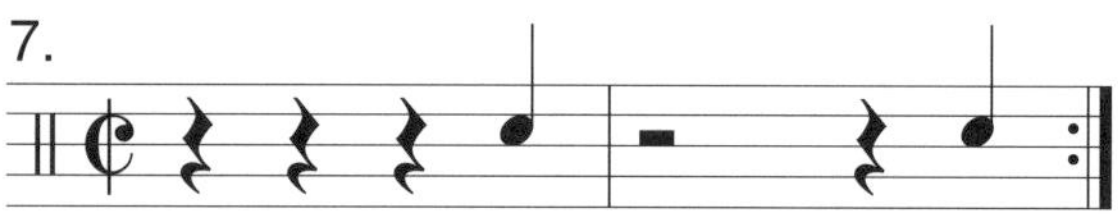

8.
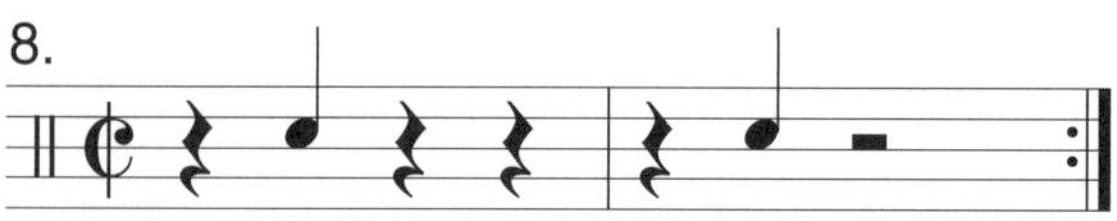

9.

10.
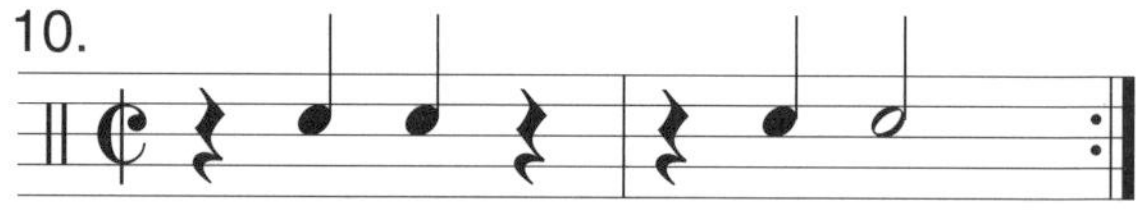

11.

12.

13.
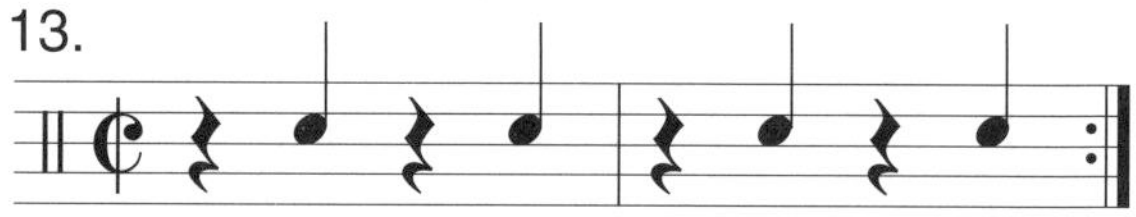

14.
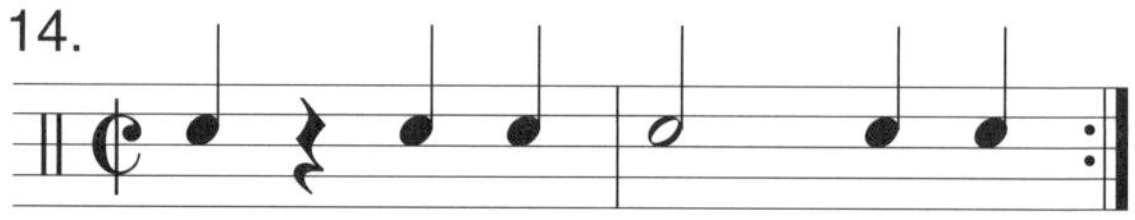

15.
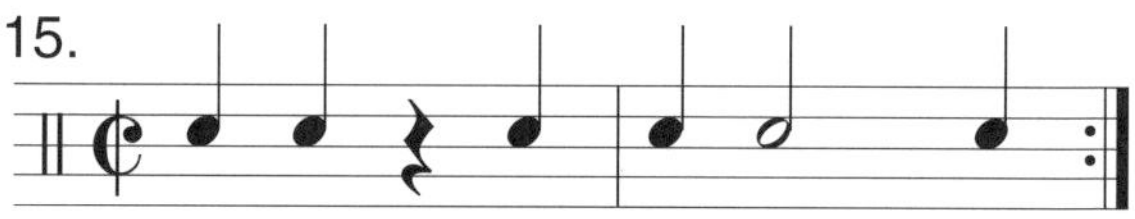

PART II: RHYTHM STUDIES

PART III: RHYTHM STUDIES

1.

2.

3.

4.

5.
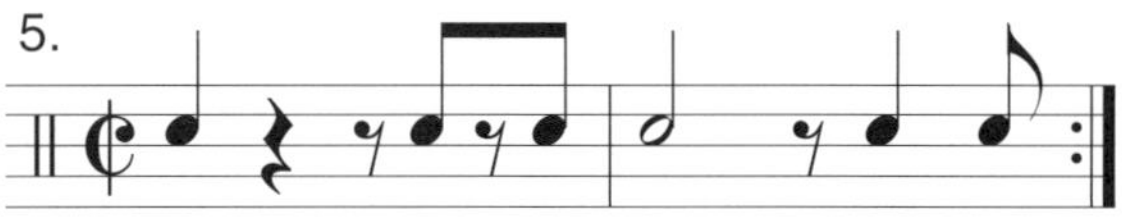

6.
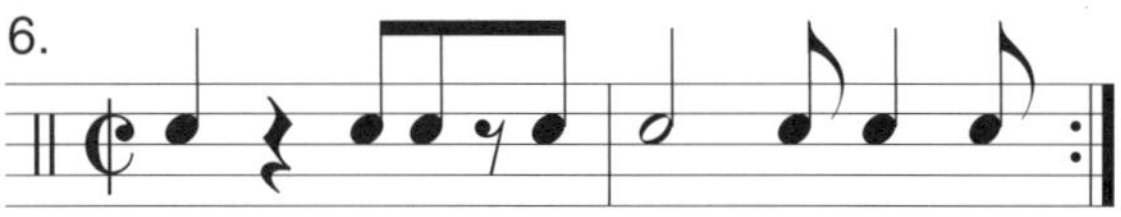

7.

8.
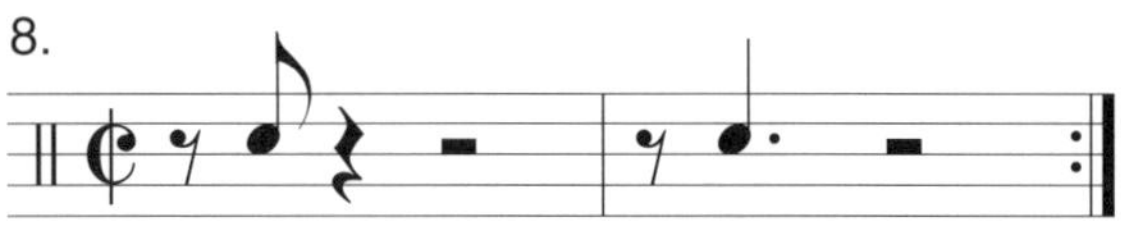

9.

10.

11.
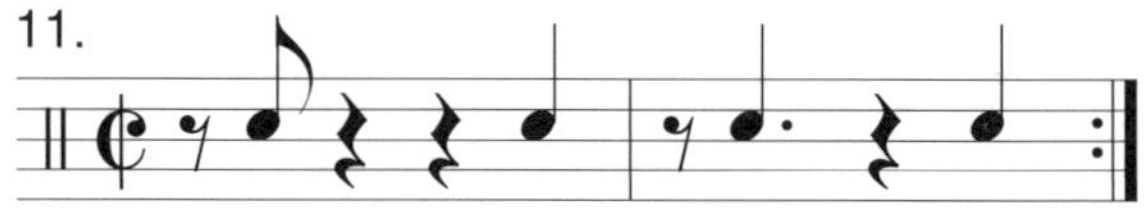

12.

13.

14.

15.

16.

17.

18.
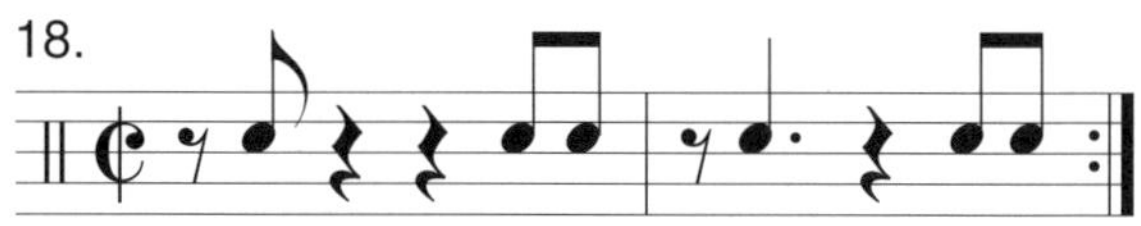

19.

20.

PART III: RHTYHM STUDIES, continued

21.

22.

23.

24.

25.

26.

27.

28.

29.

30.

31.

32.

33.

34.

35.

36.

37.

38.

39.

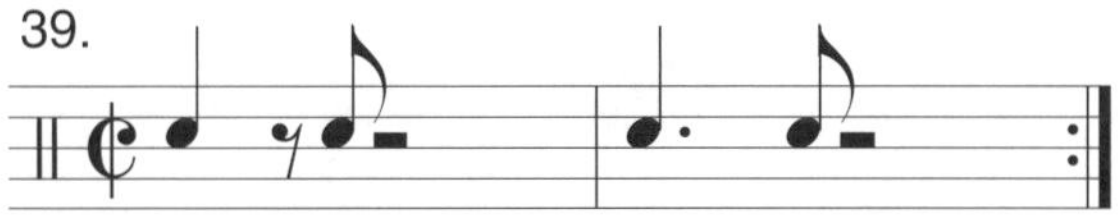

40.

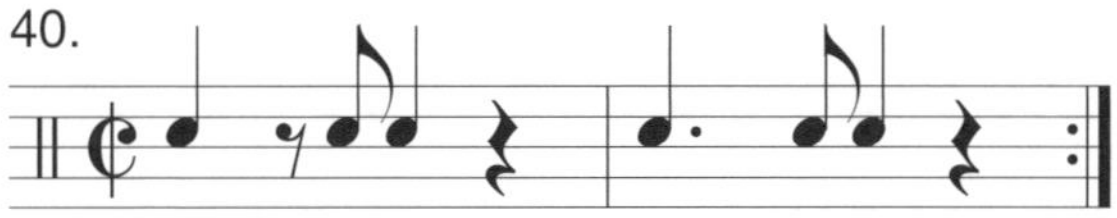

41.

42.

43.

44.

45.

46.

47.

48.

49.

50.

51.

52.

53.

54.

55.

56.

57.

58.

59.

60.
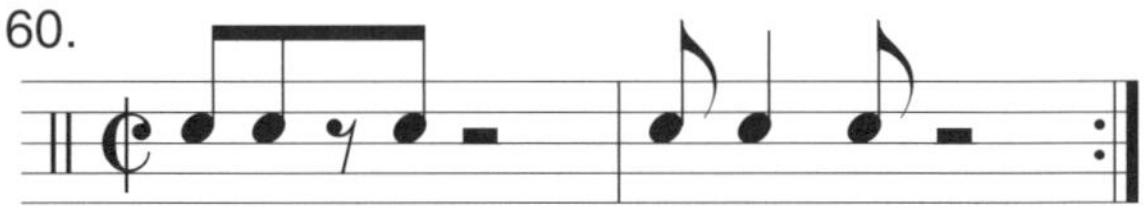

1.

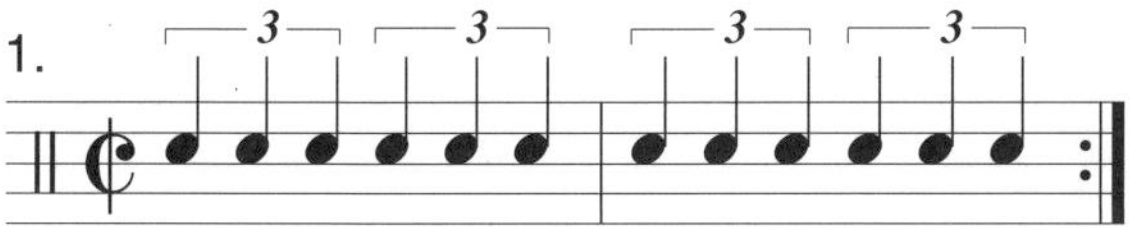

2.

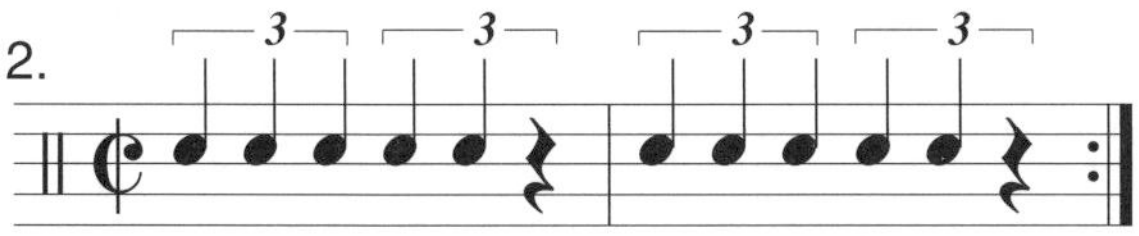

3.

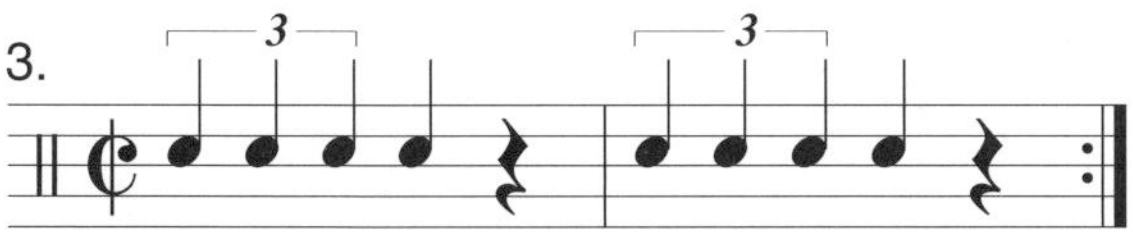

4.

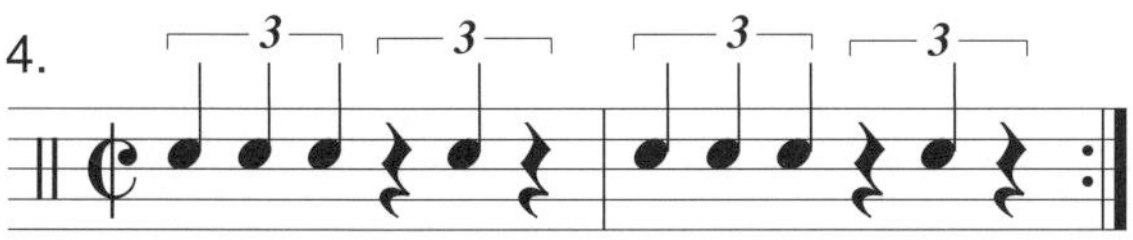

5.

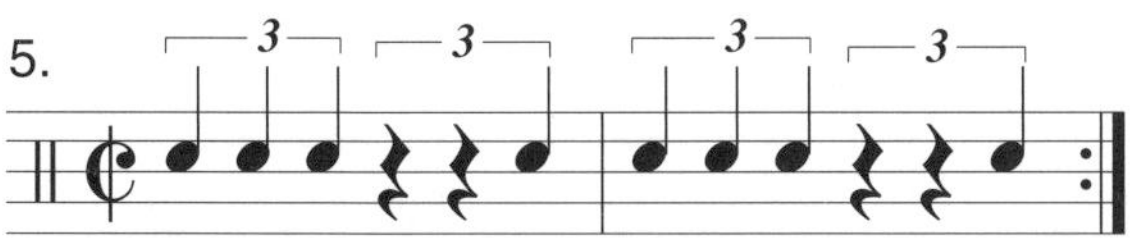

6.

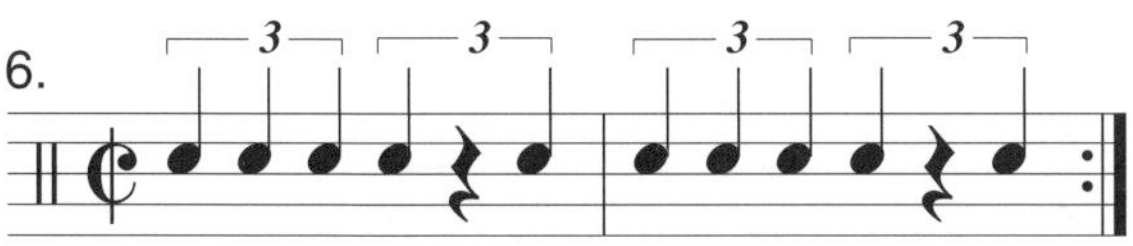

7.

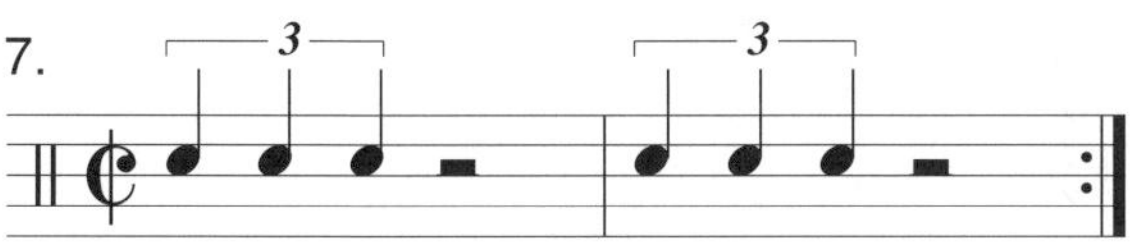

8.

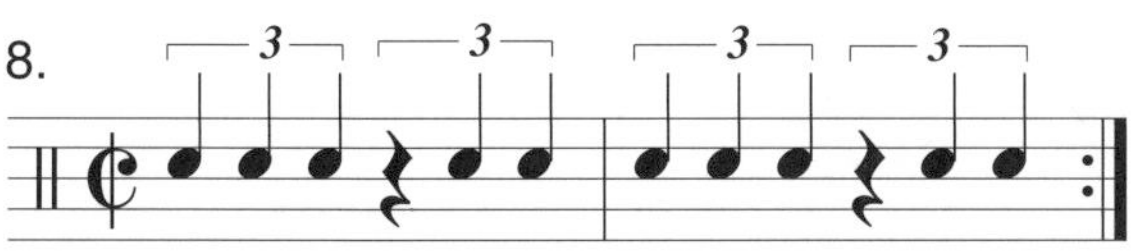

9.

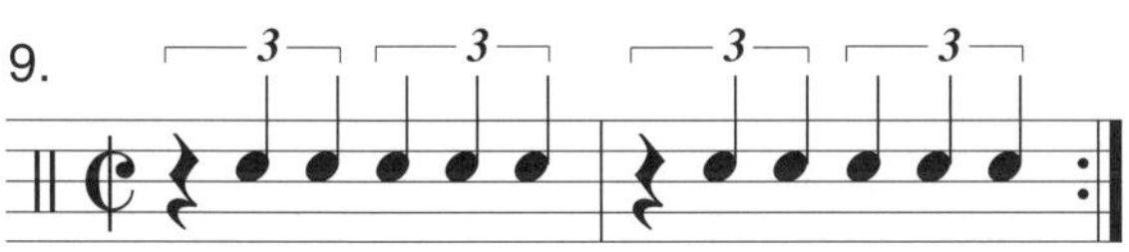

10.

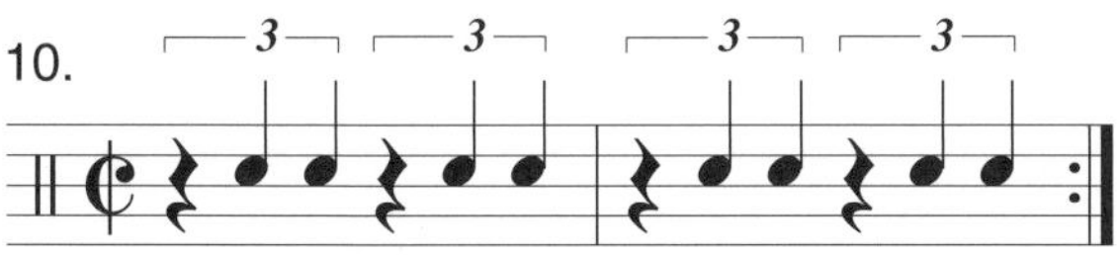

11.

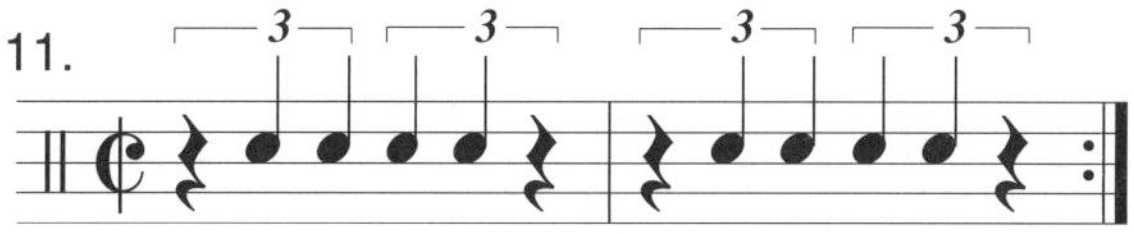

12.

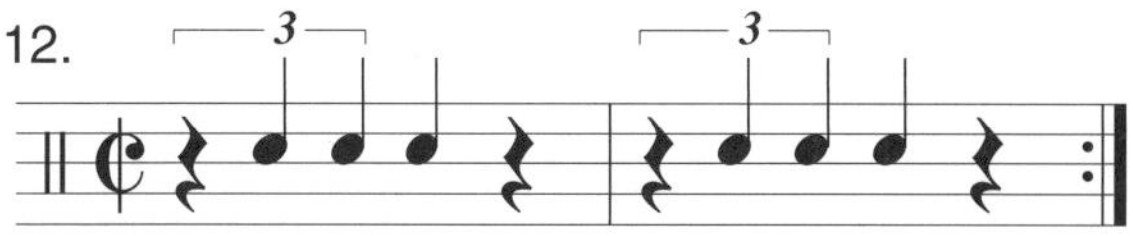

13.

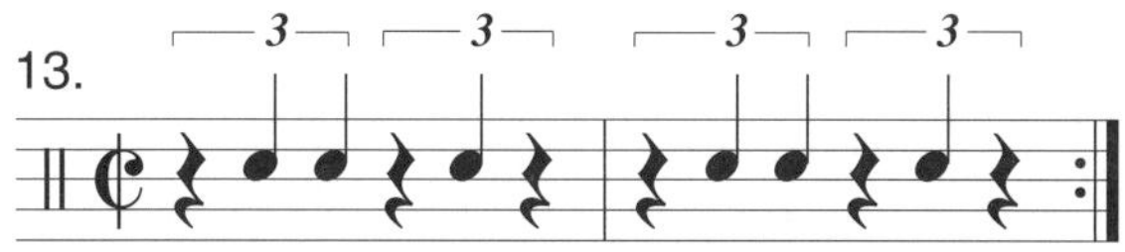

14.

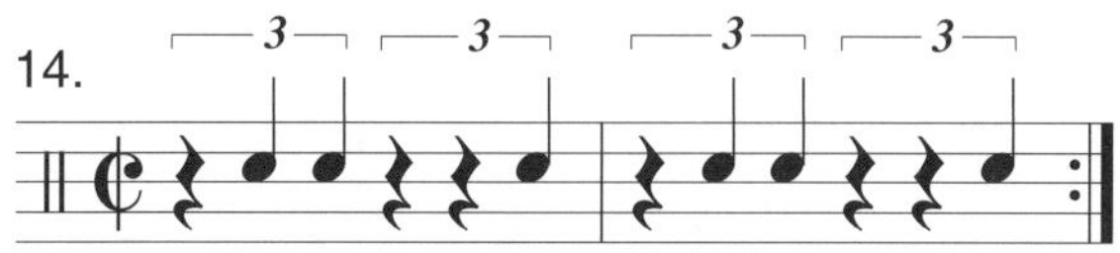

15.

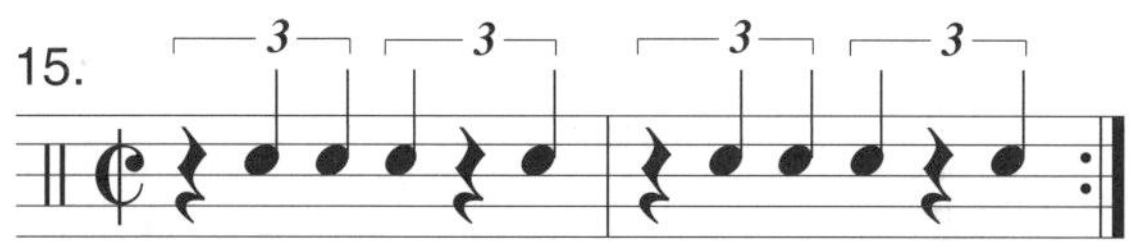

16.

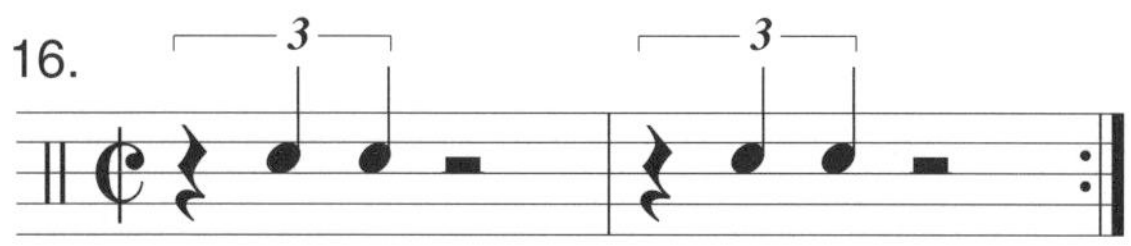

17.

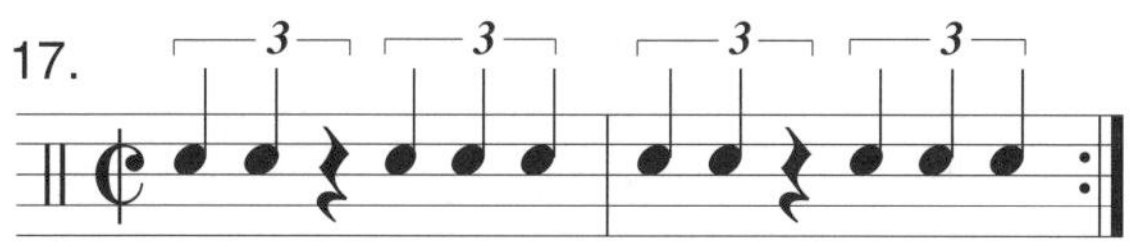

18.

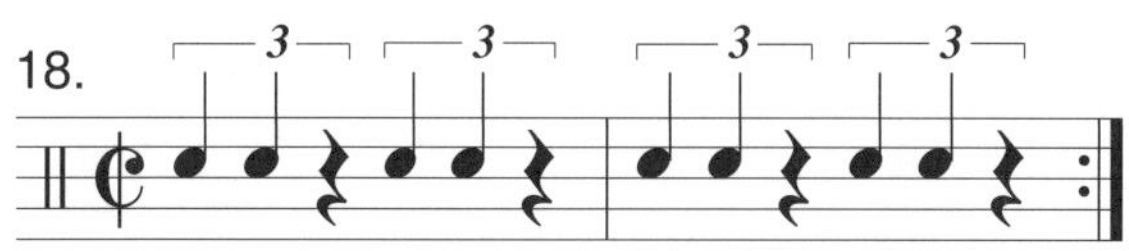

19.

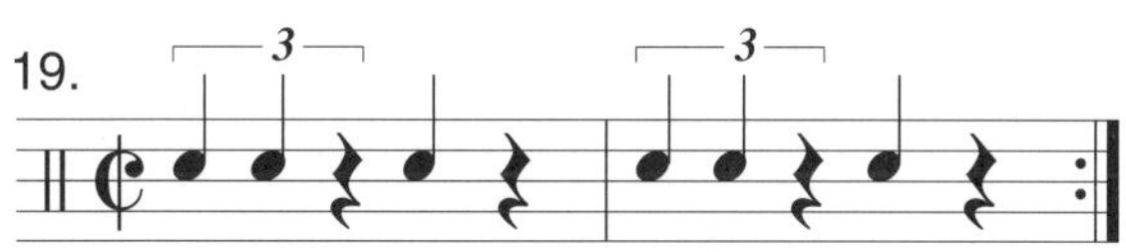

20.

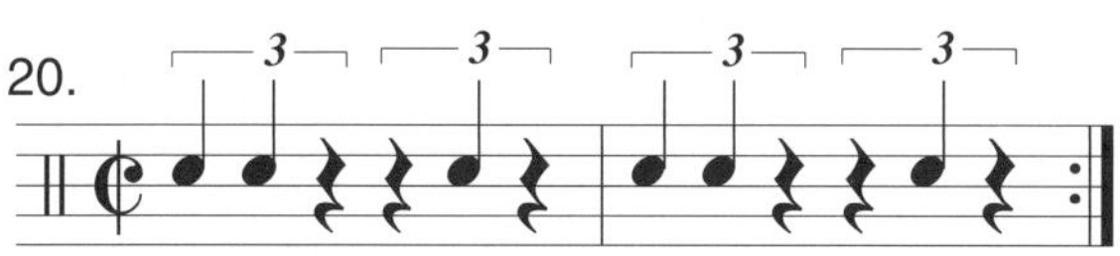

PART IV: SUMMARY A FROM PARTS I–IV

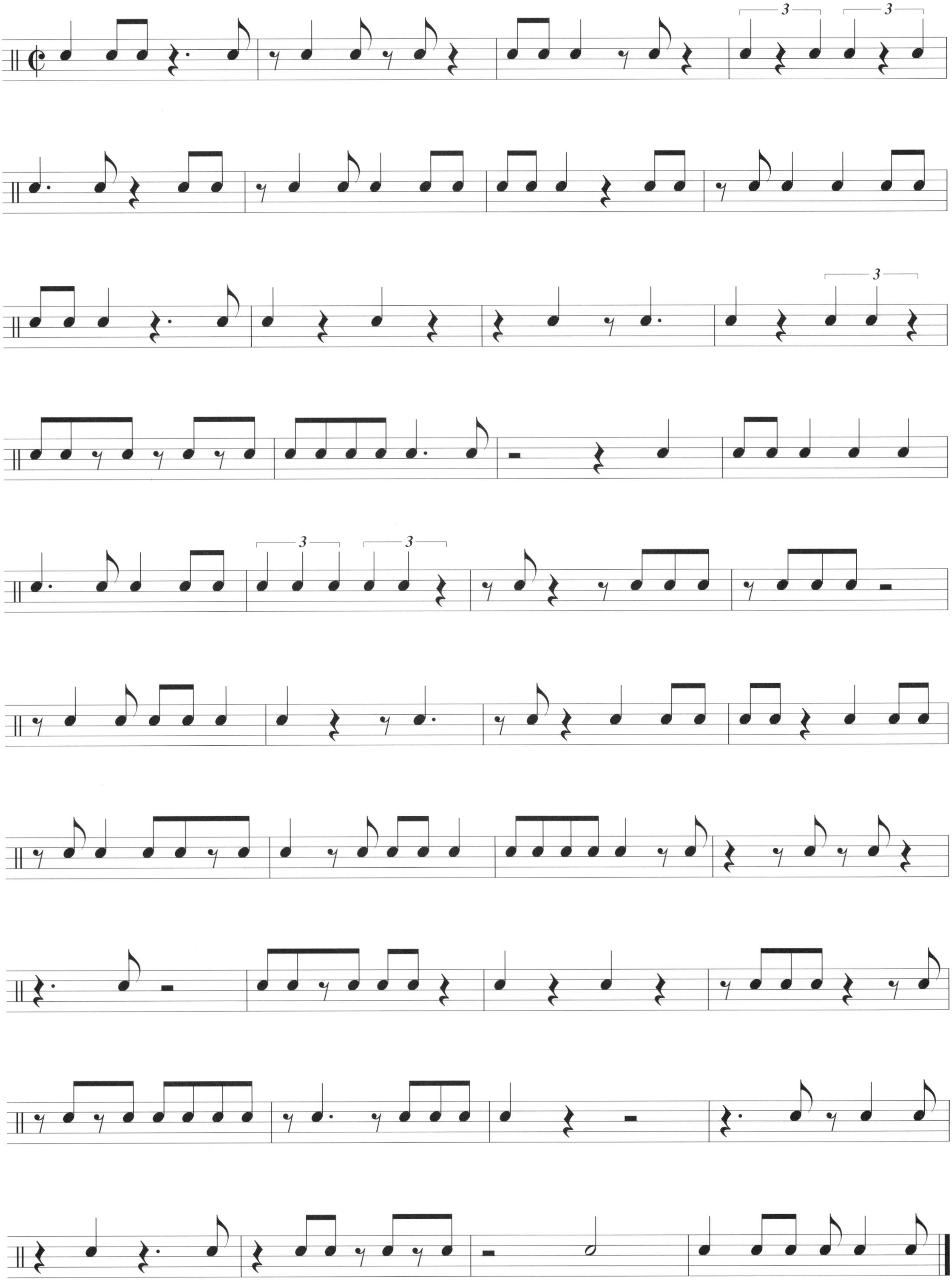

CHAPTER 3
PROG METAL

Prog (progressive) metal is a musical style that began in the U.K. in the 1970s. A combination of progressive rock and heavy metal, it's a diverse style that often utilizes musical concepts from other genres (classical music, jazz fusion, etc.) and combines it with aggressive drumming, lightning-fast riffs (melodic phrases), and a guitar-driven sound. In addition to the traditional drumming patterns in 4/4 time, prog metal is often performed in odd meters (5/8, 7/8, 5/4, 7/4, etc.) or with mixed meters (combinations of different meters).

Exercises 1–6 are four-measure examples of prog metal-style grooves and fills in various odd meters.

1.

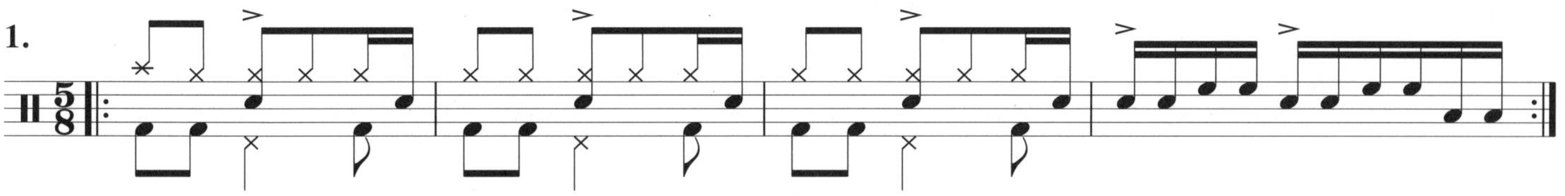

2.

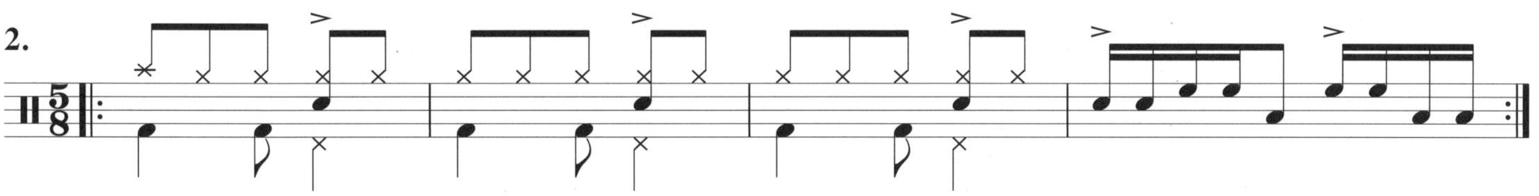

3.

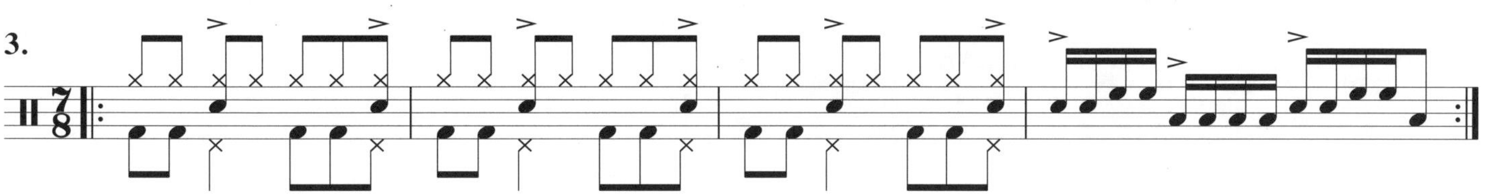

4.

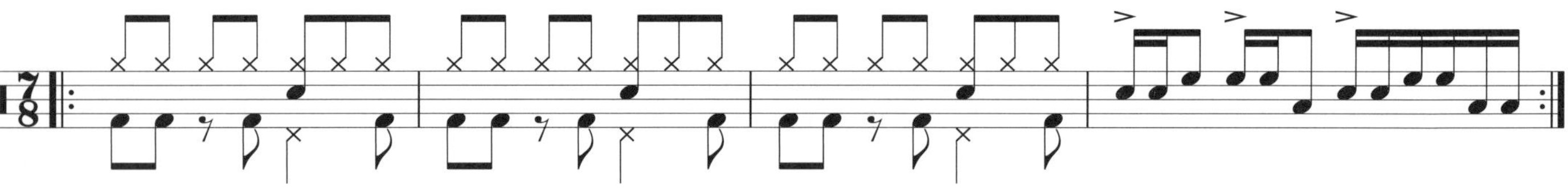

5.

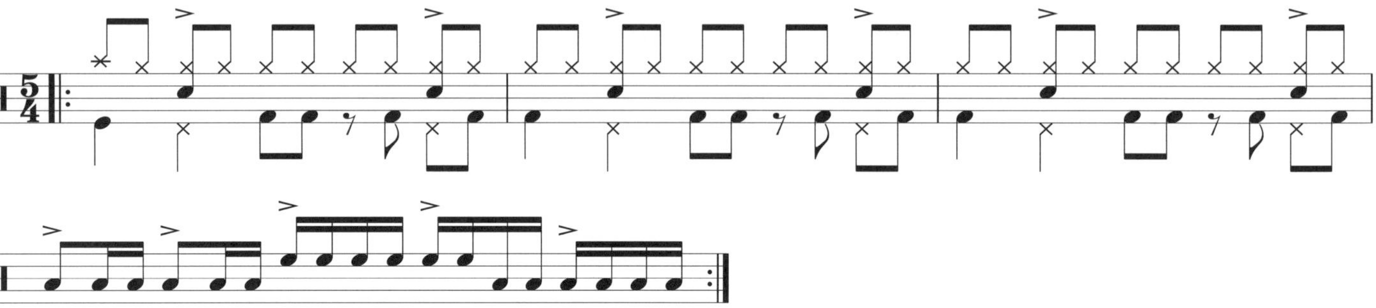

6.

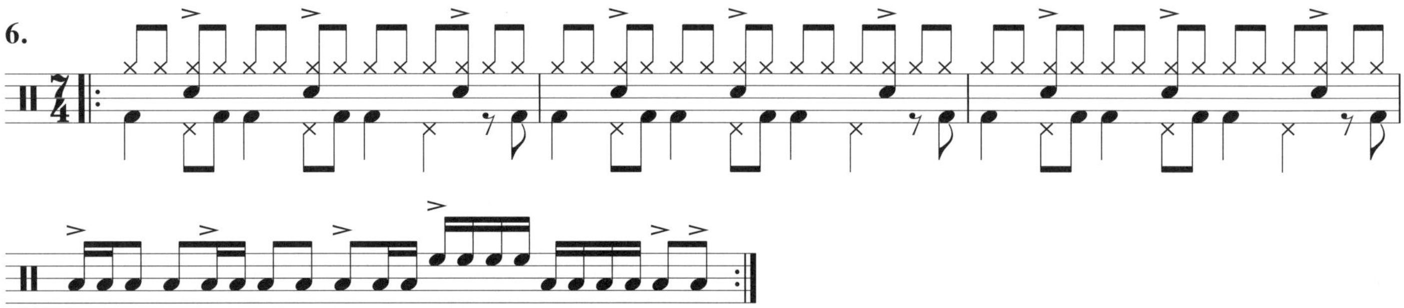

Prog metal also frequently includes combinations of different meters in one song. Any two meters may be used when mixing meters (4/4 and 7/8, 5/4 and 3/8, 7/4 and 5/8), but the most common use of mixed meters in prog metal involves alternating 4/4 time and odd meters with an eighth pulse (5/8, 7/8, or 9/8). When mixing meters, the speed of the eighth note normally stays the same. Notice that eighth note odd meters may be phrased in different ways, which changes where the snare drum backbeat is played (see Exercises 7 and 8, etc.).

7.

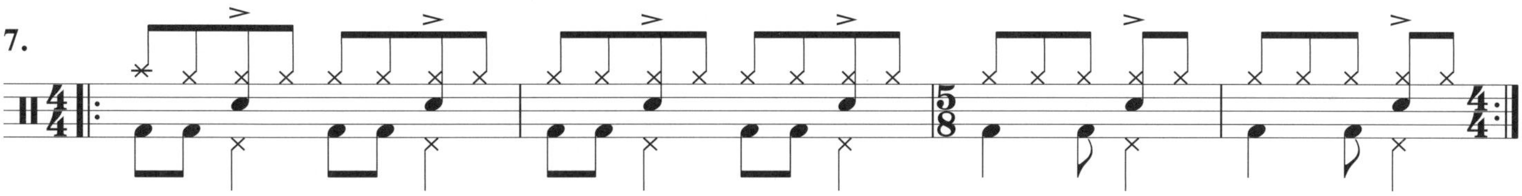

8.

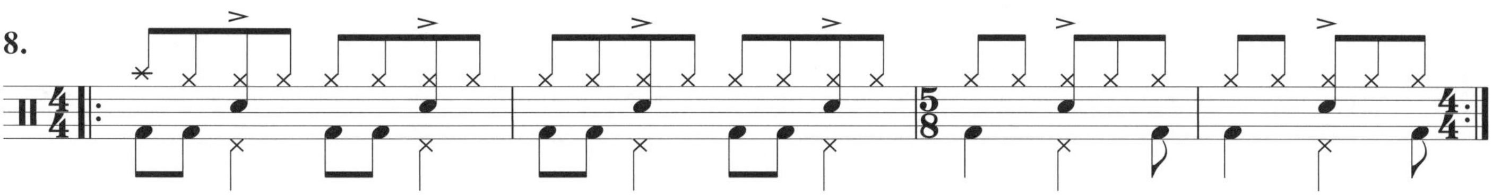

9.

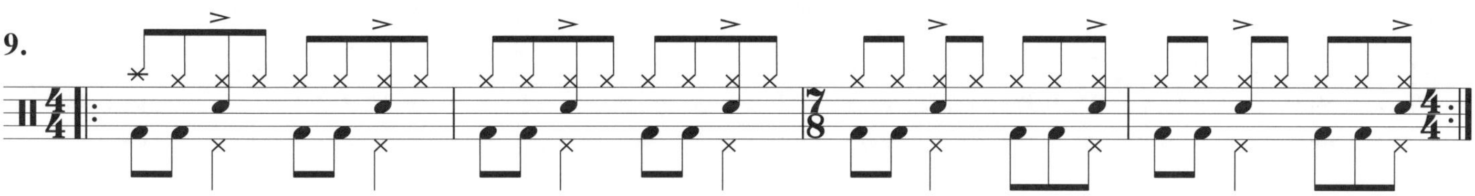

10.

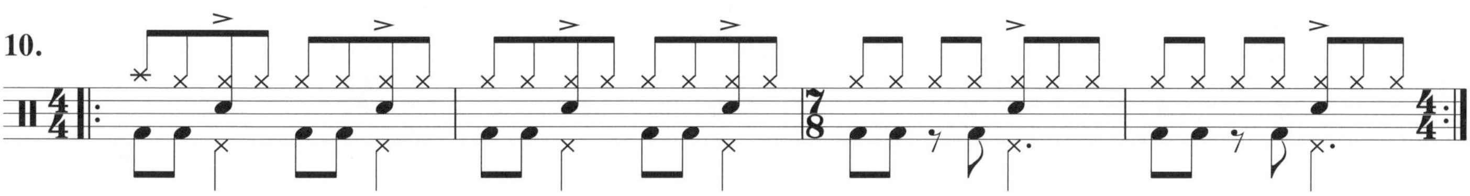

11.

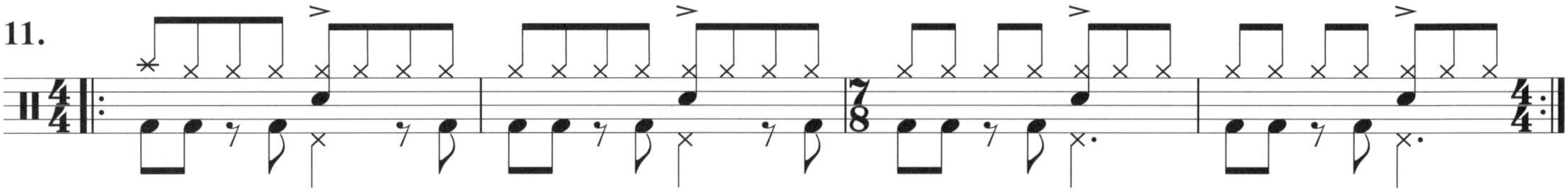

12.

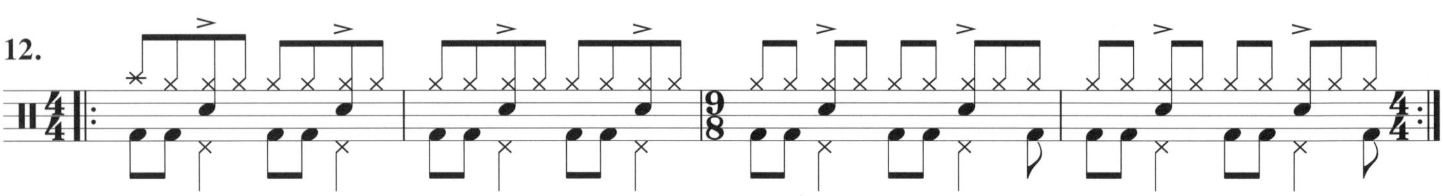

13.

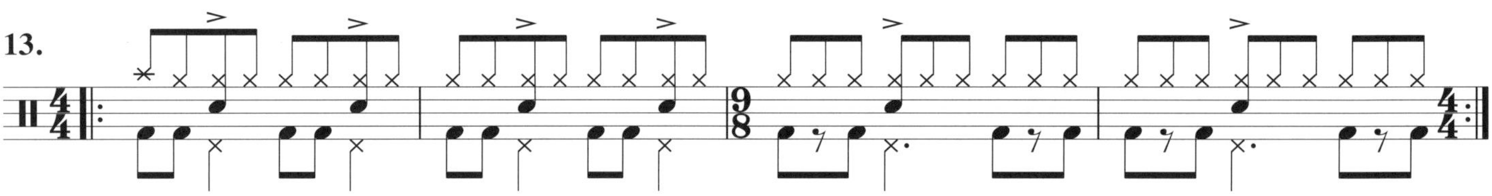

14.

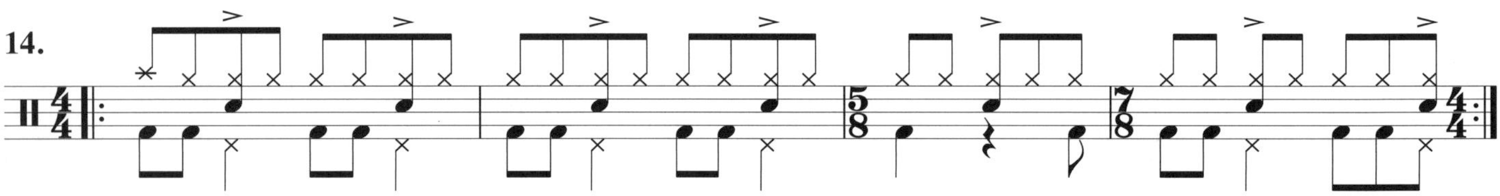

REGGAE

Originating from the island of Jamaica, reggae is now a musical style heard around the world. Bob Marley was the most well-known reggae artist, having brought reggae to the attention of the world in the 1970s, and listening to some of his recordings is a prerequisite in understanding the reggae style.

There are a number of different drum grooves associated with reggae. One of the most common is known as "one-drop," which got its name from the one loud bass drum note on beat 3 of each measure. Notice that some variations use a different accent pattern in the hi-hat part to create a different feel. More variations can also be created by substituting a cross-stick for each snare drum note.

1.

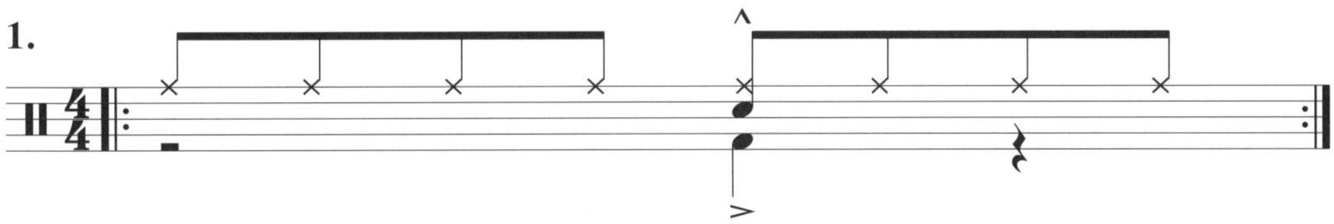

2.

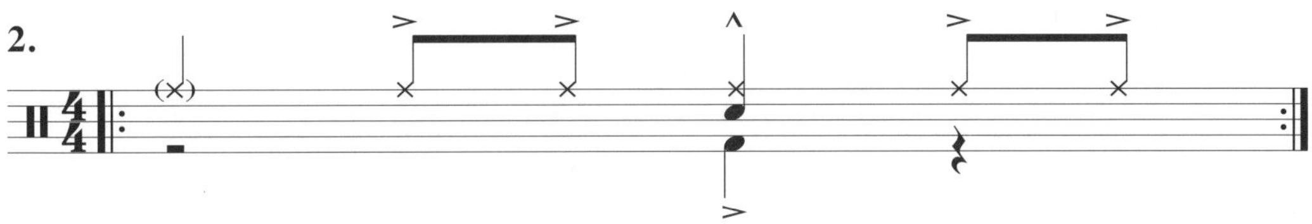

3.

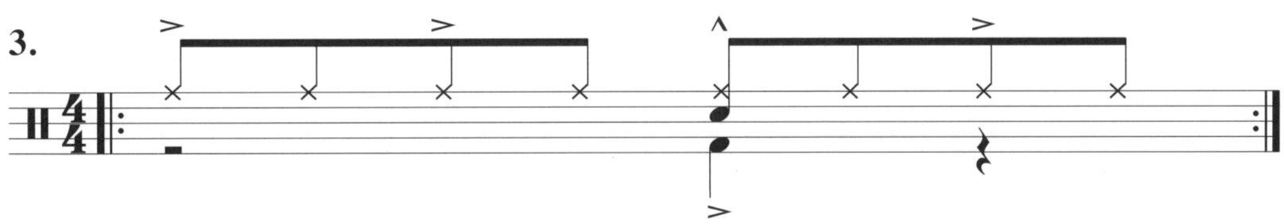

Another important aspect of reggae is its tendency to avoid playing a strong downbeat (beat 1 of each bar), so often the first beat of the drum groove will be omitted, as in this example.

4.

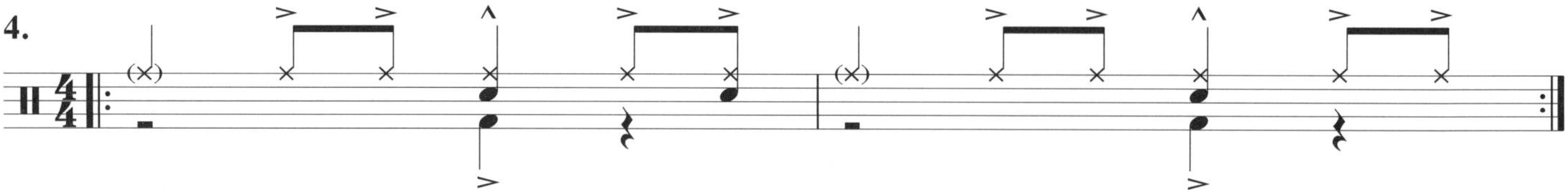

"Four-drop" is another reggae style, and its name is based on the four bass drum notes in each measure.

5.

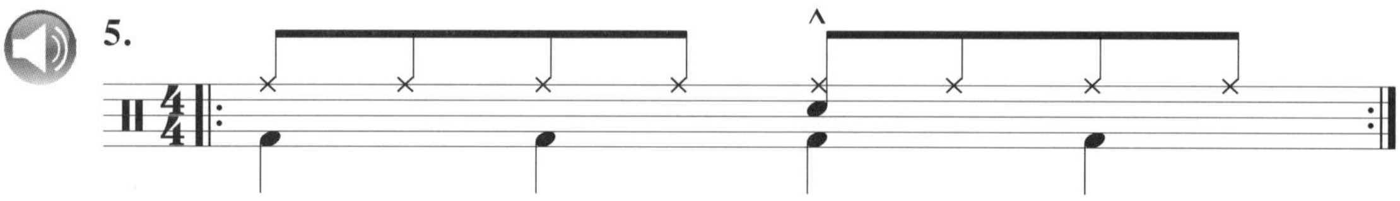

6.

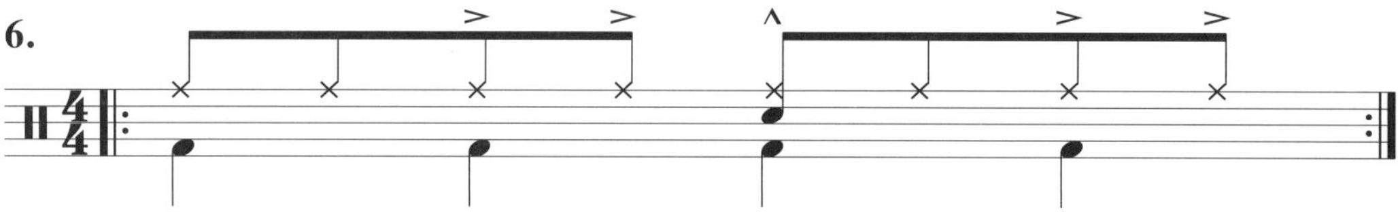

7.

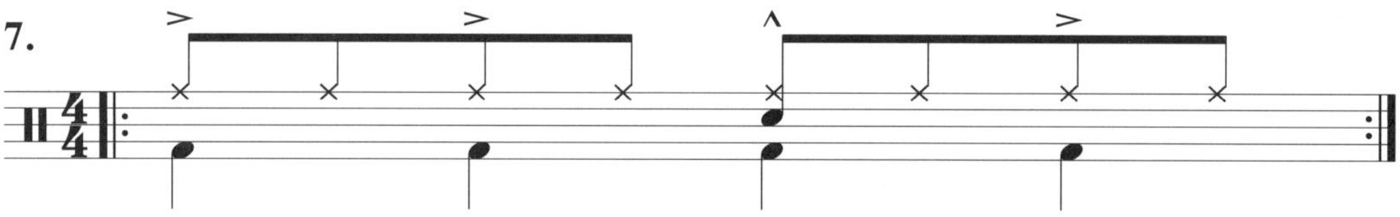

"One-drop" and "four-drop" reggae styles may also be played with a shuffle feel on the hi-hat.

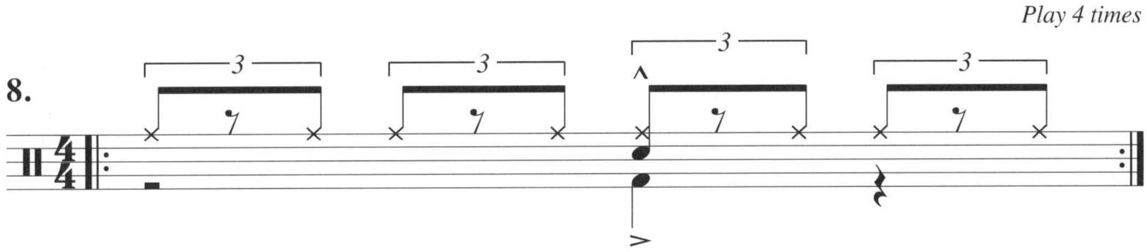

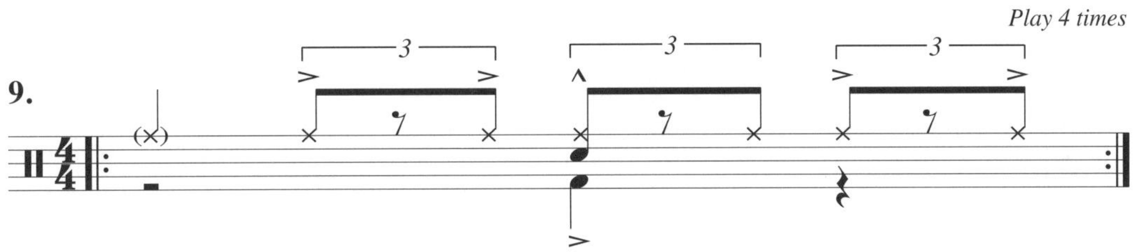

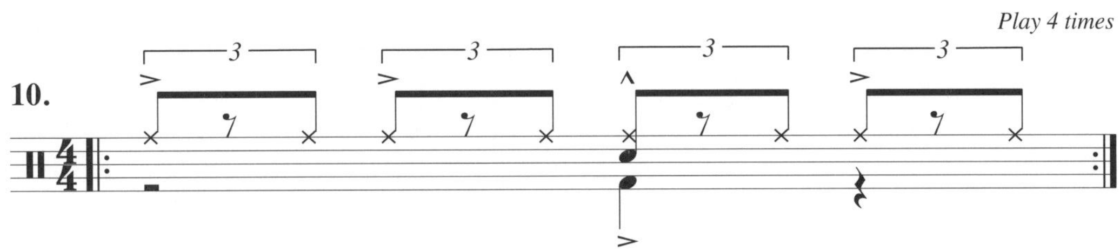

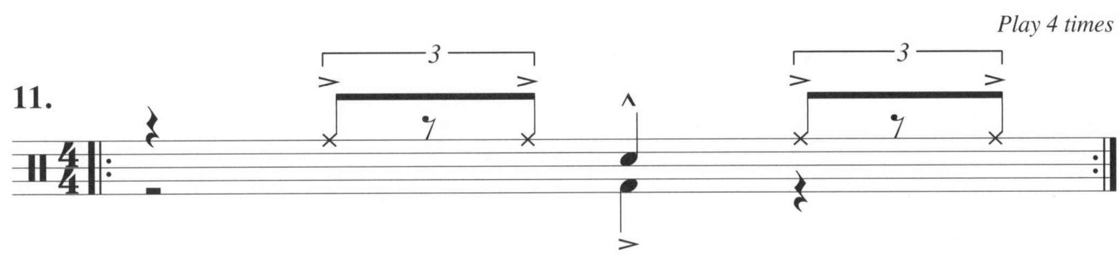

12.

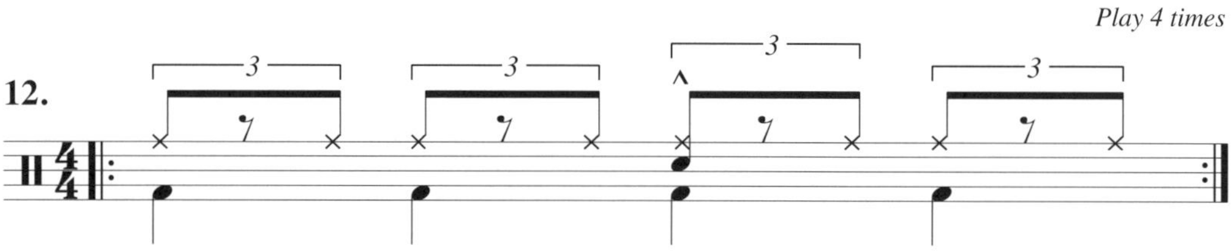

13.

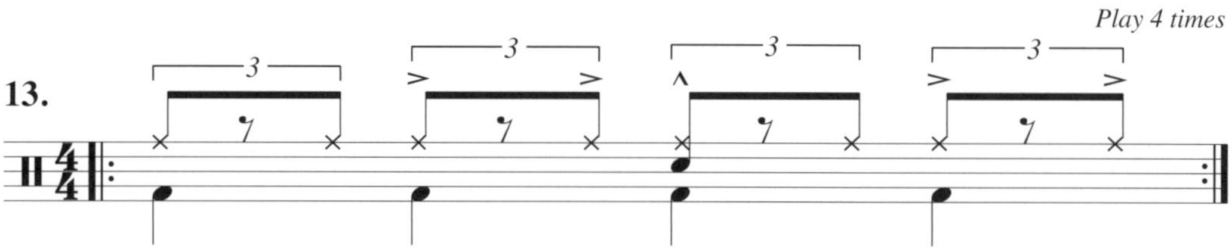

14.

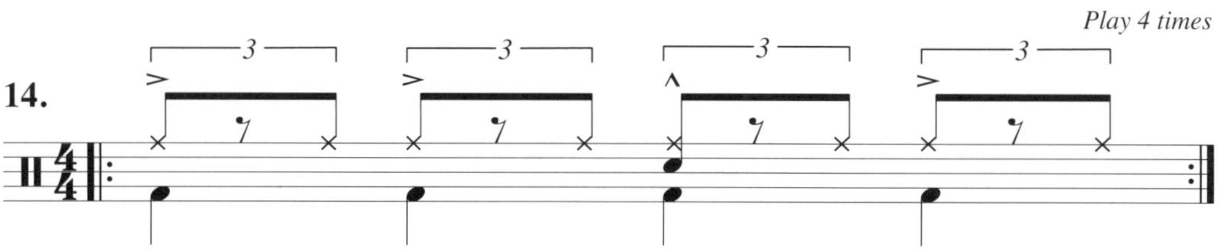

15.

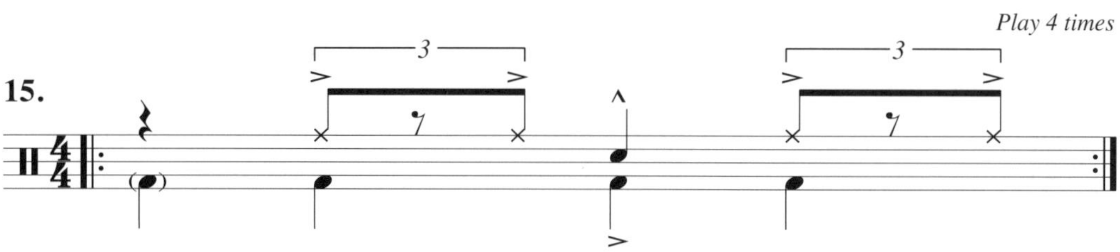

Reggae fills often end differently than fills in other types of music. In reggae, fills often end with a crash cymbal/snare drum unison on beat 4 of the fill measure. Fills often include the use of quarter-note triplets, which provides a momentary sense of rhythmic tension. These fill examples will make your reggae playing sound more authentic.

16.

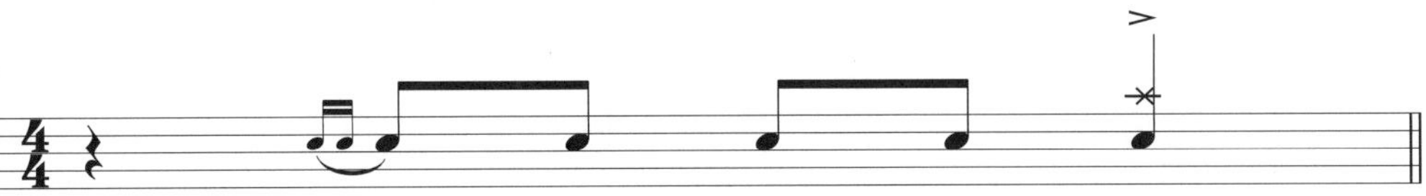

17.

18.

19.

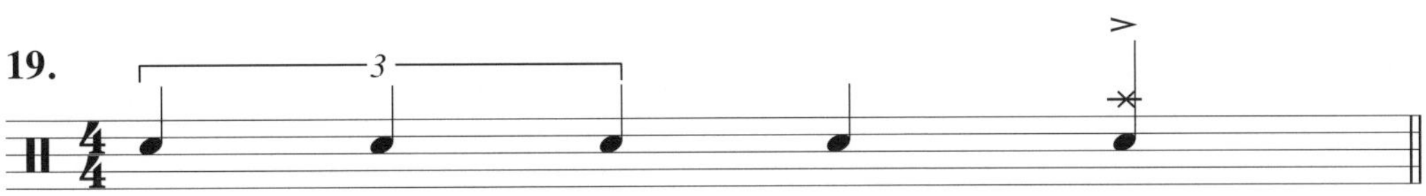

20.

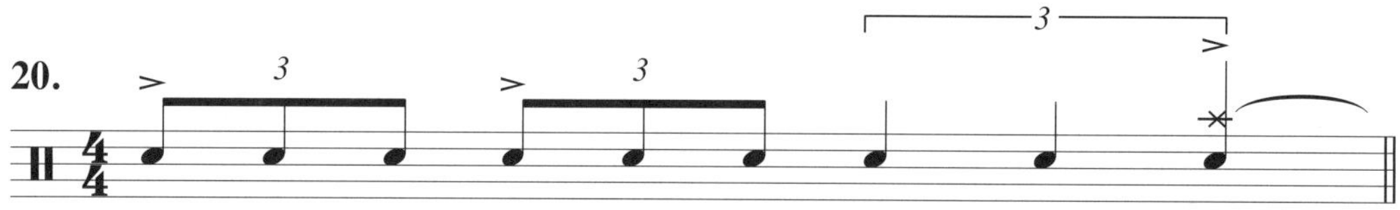

21.

22.

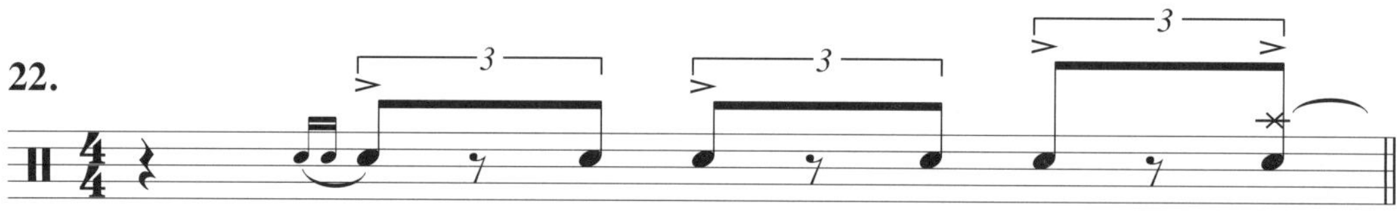

23.

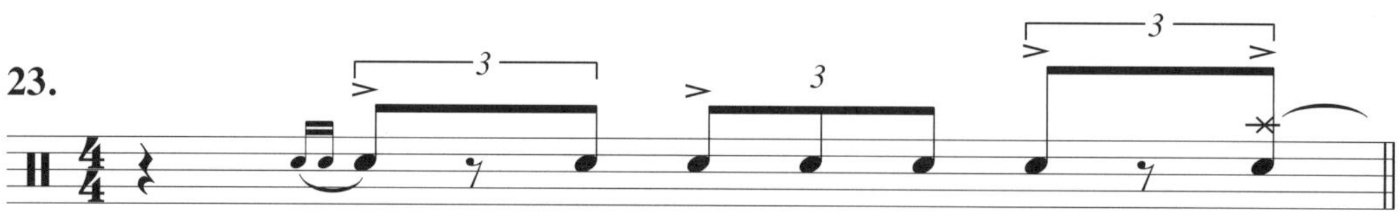

Use these exercises to practice different styles of reggae. Play-Along Tracks

One-Drop Straight 8th-Note Reggae

24.

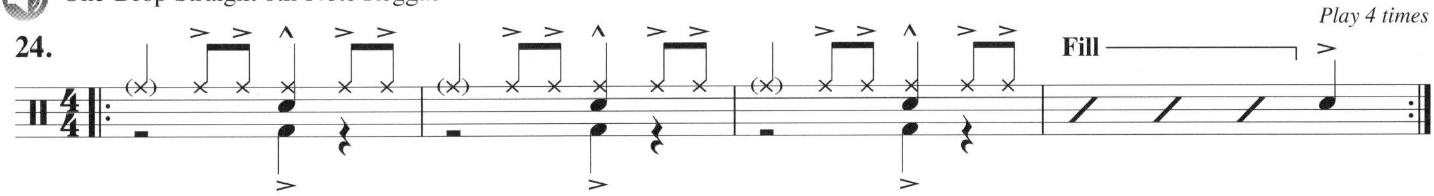

Four-Drop Straight 8th-Note Reggae

25.

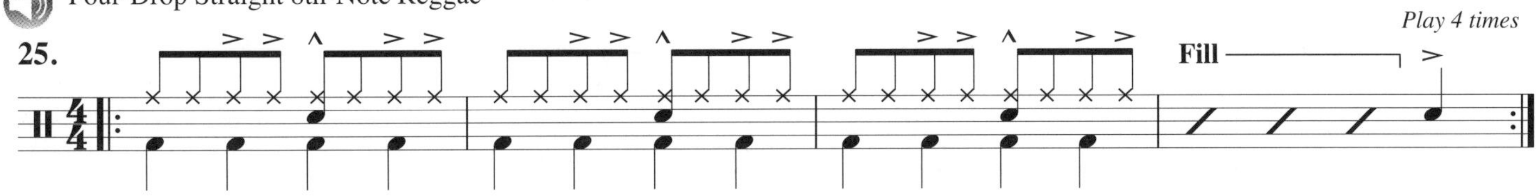

One-Drop Shuffle Reggae

26.

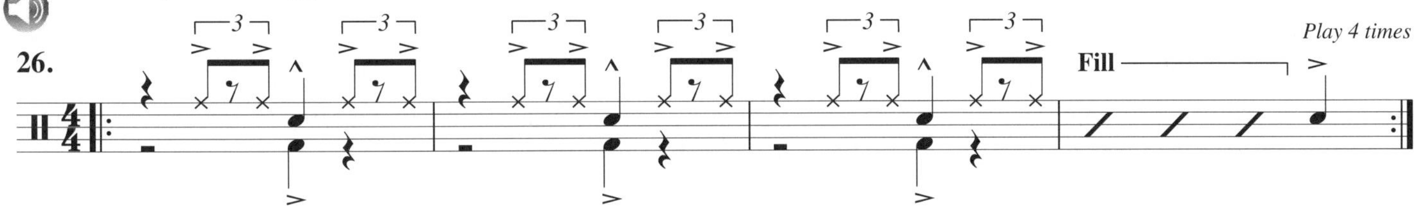

Four-Drop Shuffle Reggae

27.

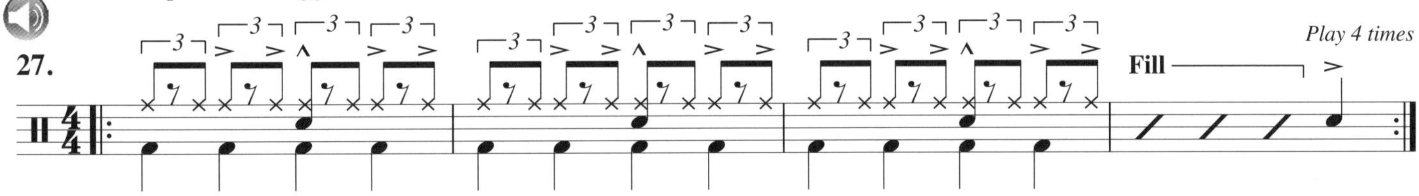

NEW ORLEANS DRUMMING

New Orleans holds an important place in the history of popular music in North America. Styles and approaches begun in New Orleans can still be heard in the jazz, rockabilly, rock, R&B, soul, funk, and pop music of today. Understanding New Orleans drumming requires knowing its history. Early New Orleans musical groups often included both a snare drummer and a bass drummer (who also frequently played the suspended cymbal).

New Orleans bands would play a variety of different musical styles—marches, ragtime tunes, blues, and popular songs of the day—so the drummers often had to be able to improvise in many different styles. *Ragtime* was a popular style from the late 1890s to the 1920s, and the two drummers would play rhythms similar to this when playing in a ragtime band:

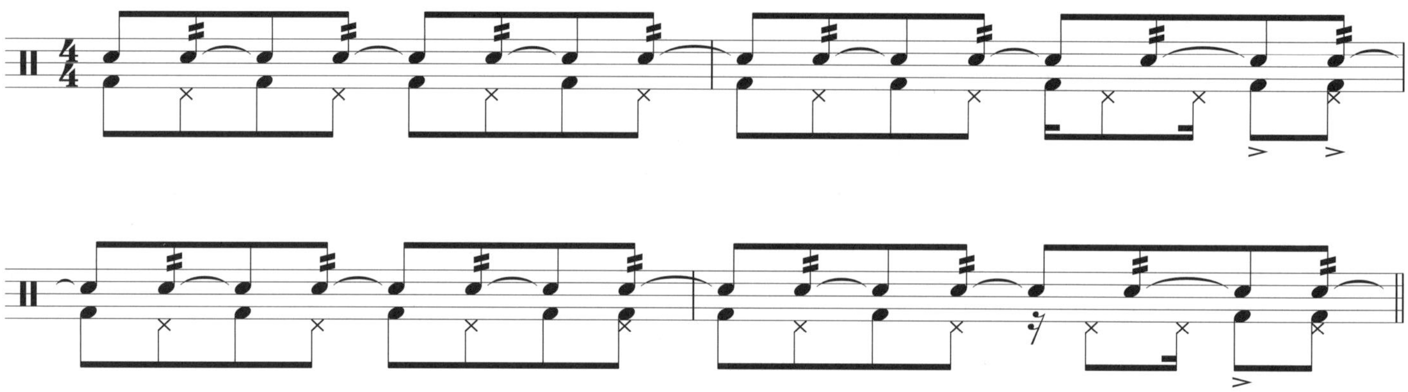

In the early part of the 20th century, drummers also marched in funeral processions and played a slow drumbeat on the snare drum to accompany the funeral procession to the cemetery, known as a *dirge* (or *durge*).

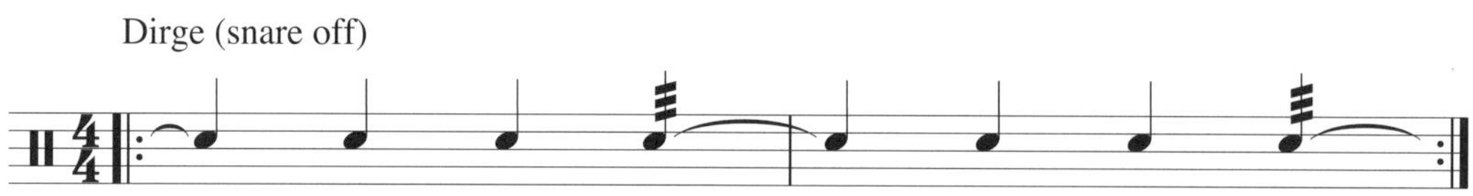

After the deceased person was buried, however, the drummers would play a lively, swinging version of a march as the mourners marched/danced back to the *wake* (a gathering following a funeral). The musicians were known as the "second line" in the funeral procession because they were in a group behind the mourners, so the drumming style became known as "second line drumming." Both the snare drum and bass drum part were largely improvised, but it was often loosely based on the 2-3 Cuban clave rhythm.

These are some variations on a second line pattern for snare drum and bass drum. Depending on the situation, the eighth notes may be played straight, swung (like triplets), or "in the cracks." New Orleans musicians use the term "in the cracks" to describe eighth notes played somewhere in between a straight and swung feel. They must be heard to be understood. An open, "splashed" hi-hat sound may be substituted for the suspended cymbal part if played on drumset.

1.

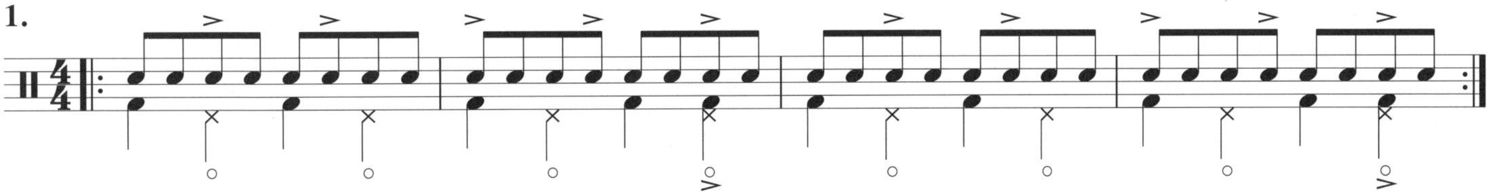

2.

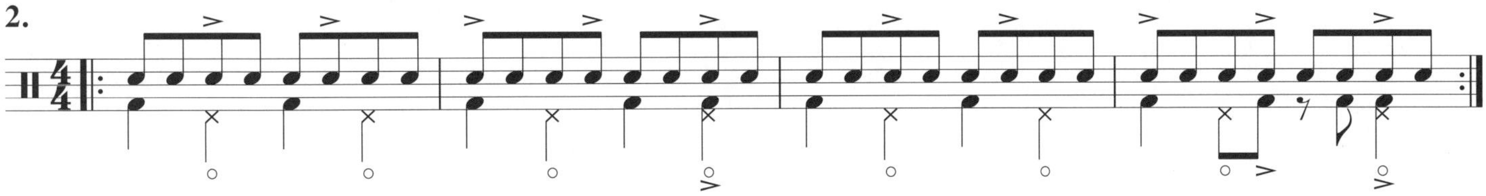

Another important aspect of New Orleans second line drumming is the use of *buzz strokes* (multiple bounce strokes or "buzz-es"). Buzz strokes are what you use in a "closed roll" on snare drum. New Orleans drummers often play with their snares loosened to create a very buzzy, continuous sound, so tune accordingly for a more authentic sound. These buzz strokes can substituted for almost any of the eighth notes in a two-bar second-line phrase:

3.

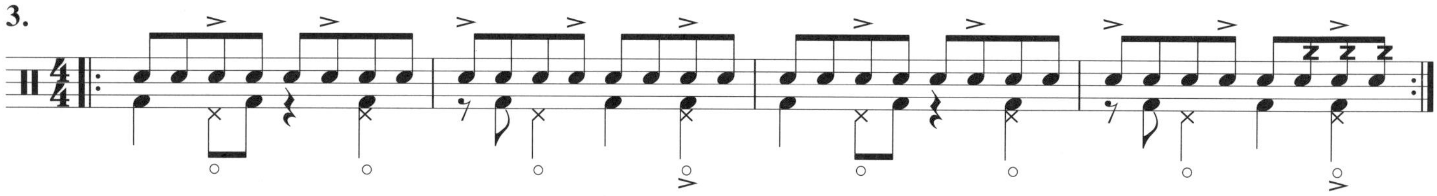

4.

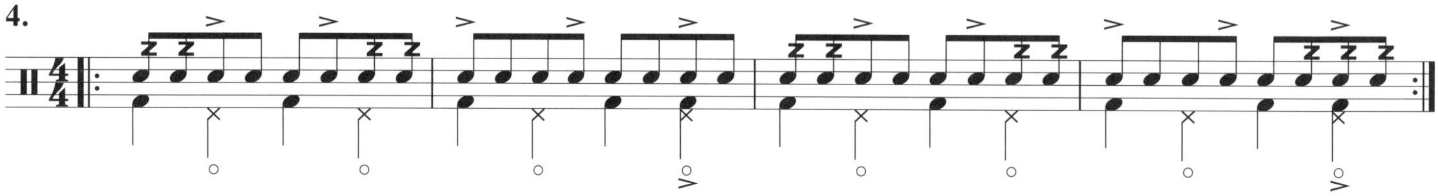

5.

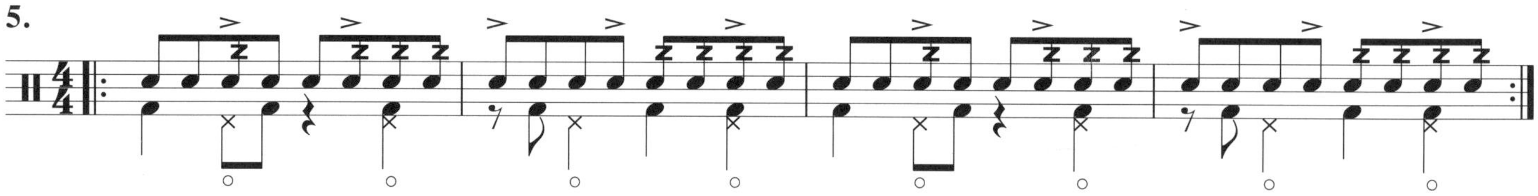

6.

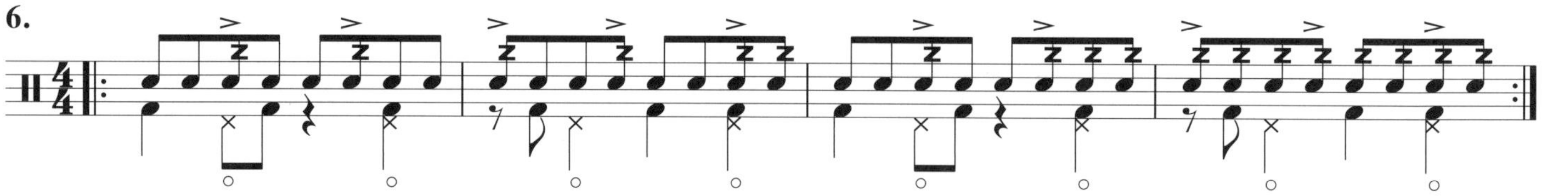

The fourth beat in the second bar of the two-bar second-line phrase is one of the most important places to accent and is often the loudest note of the phrase. Some jazz drummers today have developed their own interpretations of second line drumming. It has the flavor of second line drumming—with the buzz strokes, general clave accent pattern, accent on beat 4 in the second bar, and syncopated style—but is adapted for the whole drumset. This is an example of a drumset second-line feel used in a jazz context.

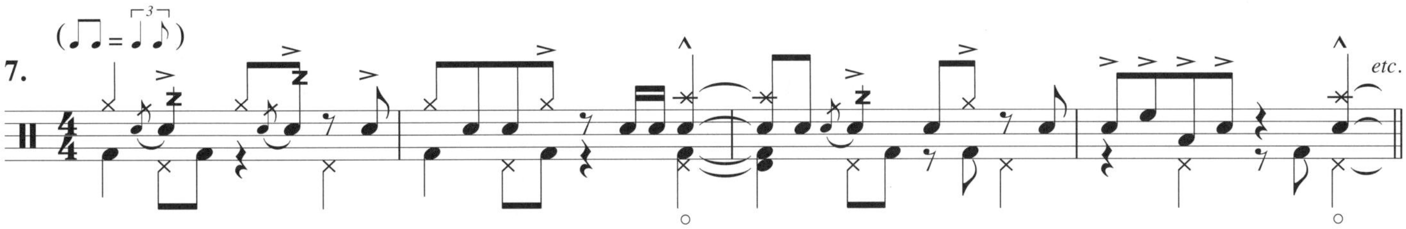

For a more in-depth study, listen to and study the styles of such influential New Orleans drummers as Warren "Baby" Dodds, Zutty Singleton, Vernel Fournier, Ed Blackwell, Earl Palmer, Joseph "Zigaboo" Modeliste, Idris Muhammad, Herlin Riley, Johnny Vidacovich, and Stanton Moore. Experiment and create your own interpretations of second line drumming.

BASIC AFRICAN GROOVES

Africa is a continent with many countries—each with their own rhythmically rich musical traditions. As with other musical cultures, the grooves presented in this lesson are drumset adaptations of complex patterns normally played by numerous percussion instruments (hand drums, cowbells, shakers, etc.) or drumset patterns that are frequently augmented by a battery of percussion instruments. To fully appreciate the music from which these grooves are derived, you will need to explore African percussion more fully through recordings. It is important to remember that all of these styles continue to evolve, so the grooves presented here are the basic patterns, with new variations constantly emerging.

Bikutsi, from Cameroon, is an interesting style that uses a 3:4 (or 3 against 4) cross-rhythm that is typical of African music. Written in 4/4 time, the hi-hat (or ride) is playing triplet subdivisions phrased in groups of four (thus implying a half-note triplet—the "3" in the 3:4 cross-rhythm). This is set against the quarter-note pulse in the bass drum, which is the "4" in the 3:4 cross-rhythm. Notice that only the first three notes of triplet groups in 4 are being played; the fourth note of the phrase is a rest. This gives the groove some space. Listen to artists such as Les Têtes Brûlées, Lady Ponce, and K-Tino for more examples of this music.

1.

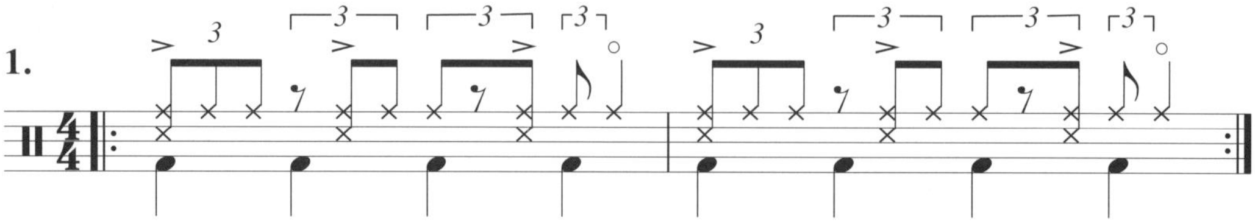

2.

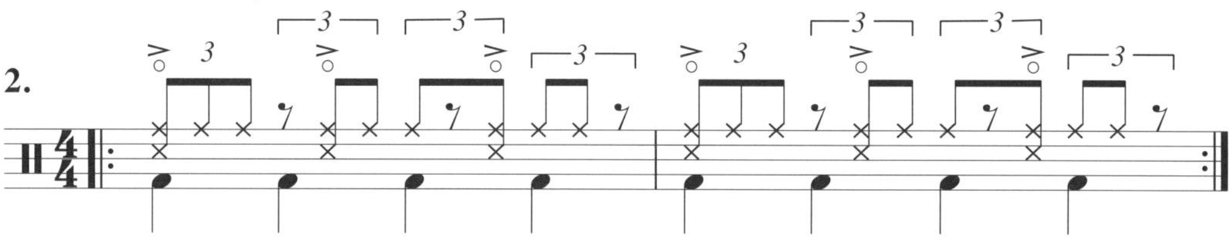

Mangambe (Examples 3 and 4), also from Cameroon, is another triplet-based groove

3.

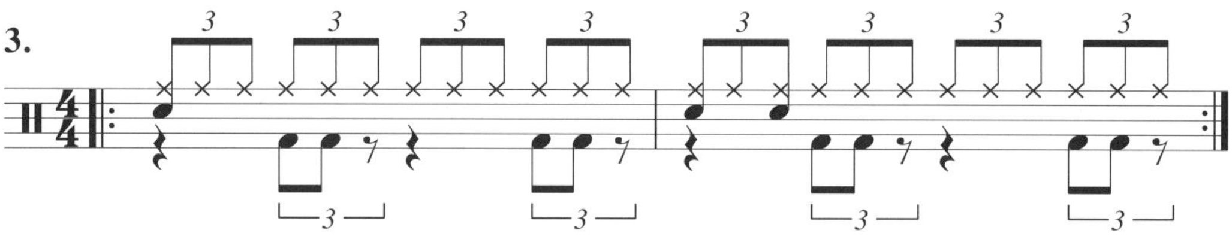

4.

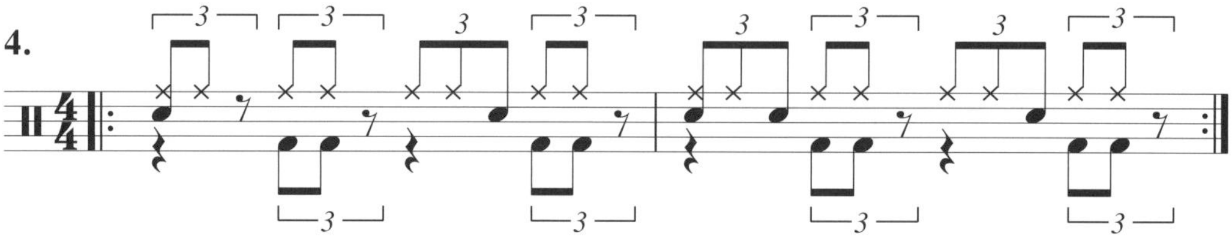

From Nigeria, *Afrobeat* is a popular dance groove that was championed by singer/political activist Fela Kuti. In Example 6, the bell part may be played on either a cowbell or bell of the cymbal.

5.

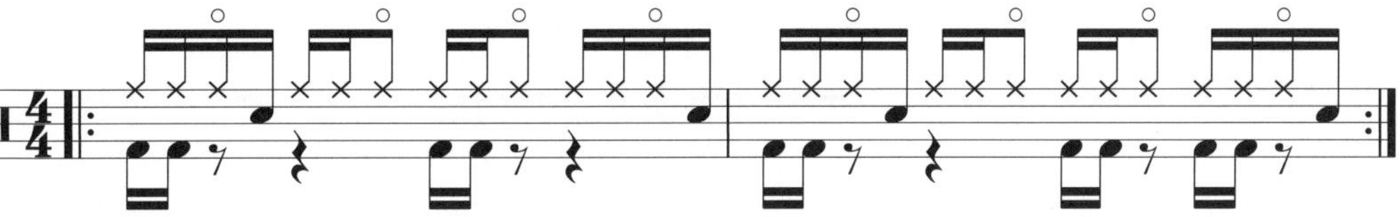

6.

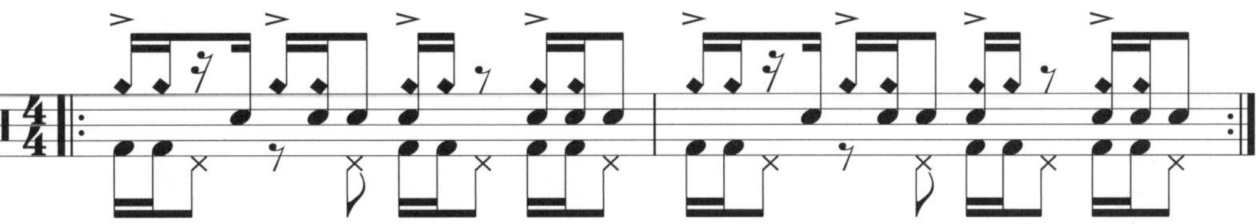

Soukous, originally from the Congo, is a lively dance groove that is rhythmically based on the dotted-eighth/dotted-eighth/eighth rhythm (or the "3" side of the Cuban clave). This rhythm is normally played by a variety of instruments (hi-hat, cross-stick, cowbells, etc.). Listen to Zaiko Langa Langa, Pepe Kalle, and Kanda Bongo Man for examples of soukous.

7.

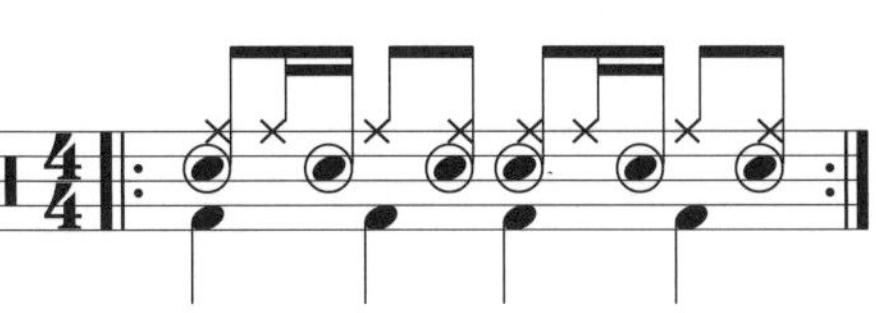

8.

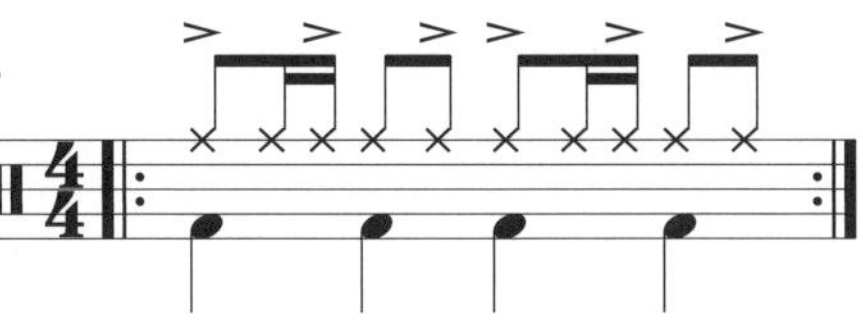

9.

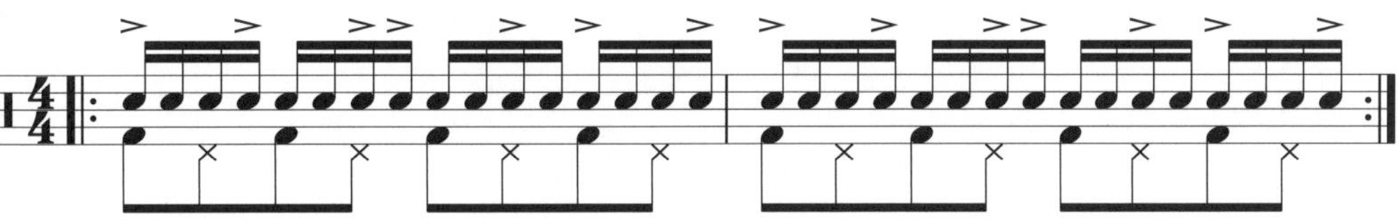

Mbaqanga is a style from South Africa and was brought to worldwide attention by various pop artists. Miriam Makeba and Mahlathini & the Mahotella Queens are two of the most well-known mbaqanga artists. Notice the syncopated backbeat on the "and" of beat 1 in each bar.

10.

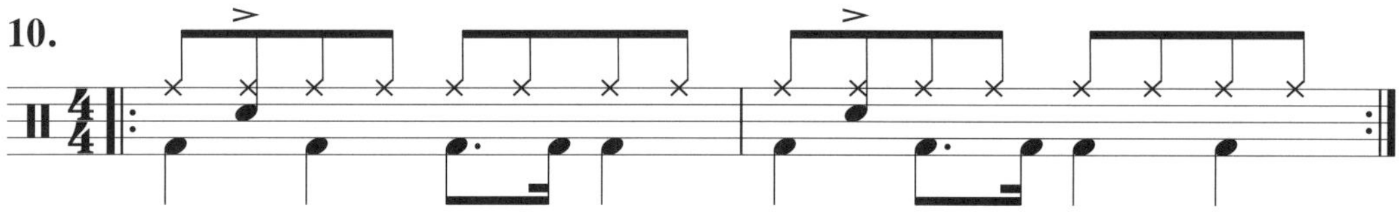

King Sunny Adé is one of the most well-known juju artists. *Juju* is a broad style that encompasses a number of different rhythms, but this is a commonly played groove.

11.

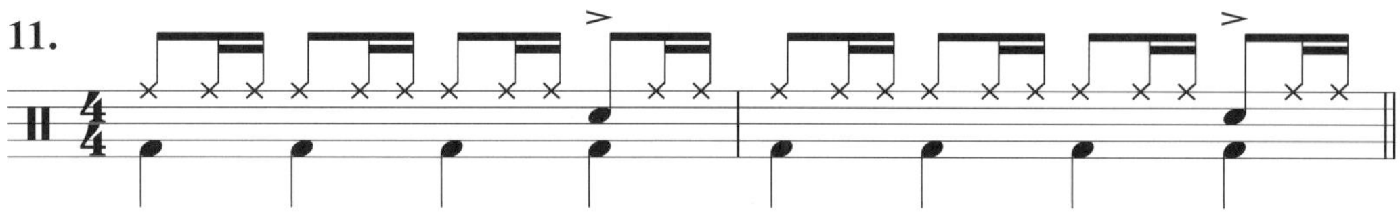

CHAPTER 4
MAMBO

Mambo is a term that loosely describes the style we are referring to in this section. In Cuban music, the tempo can sometimes distinguish one particular style from another, and the Mambo style is generally played at fast tempos.

Although the drumset has never traditionally been part of the Mambo style, contemporary drummers have adapted the rhythms played on traditional percussion instruments in this popular style. The traditional ensemble generally utilizes congas, timbales, guiro, claves, bongos/bell, bass, piano, horns and vocals.

The following page contains basic Mambo patterns with 3+2 and 2+3 clave patterns, played by a cross-stick on the snare drum, along with the tumbao figure that is played on the bass drum in the Mambo style and variations for the left-foot hi-hat. The cymbal pattern is the standard "cascara" pattern — a two-bar phrase that can be played in 2+3 or 3+2 son or rumba clave. The literal translation for the word "cascara" is "shell." This is the pattern traditionally performed by the timbale player on the side or shell of the timbale or on a mambo bell. Drumset players can play it on ride cymbal, cowbell (mambo bell), closed hi-hat, or on the side (shell) of the floor tom. When using a mambo bell, play the accents on the open end and the other notes on the body of the cowbell.

Following the page with the basic Mambo/cascara patterns are several pages showing ride-cymbal (or mambo bell) variations in the four different clave feels. These can all be played with the different bass drum/hi-hat patterns from the patterns on pages 3–4. Typically, a Latin-jazz drummer will play the standard two-bar cascara pattern on hi-hat or the shell of the floor tom during the A section of a standard AABA-style tune, and play a two-bar variation on ride cymbal or cowbell during the B section or "bridge." Variations are also frequently used during solo sections. This corresponds to what the timbale player would do in a traditional Afro-Cuban song.

Begin by playing a pattern from page 3 or 4 and then play a two-bar variation in the same clave, alternating between the two patterns. Before attempting to play each exercise on the drumset, you may find it very helpful to sing the cascara pattern and each ride cymbal (or mambo bell) variation while clapping the clave rhythm. This will help you internalize the clave and play each variation with a better feel. Choose two different syllables to sing: one for the accented notes and one for the unaccented notes. Sing both syllables with a short sound. Clap the clave rhythm and repeat the cascara pattern and each variation as needed before combining the two phrases. Do the same with each summary.

3+2 Son Clave

1.

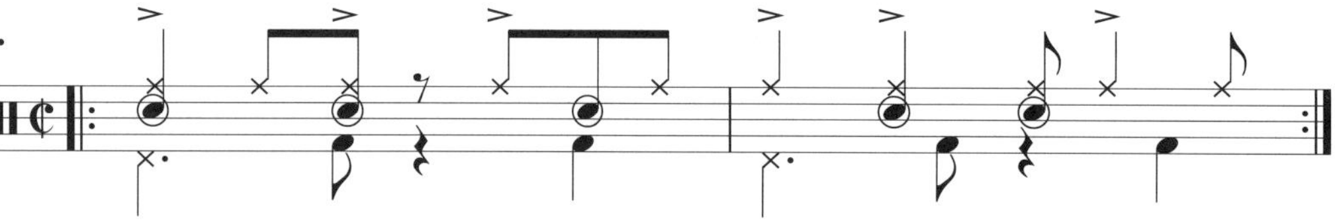

2.

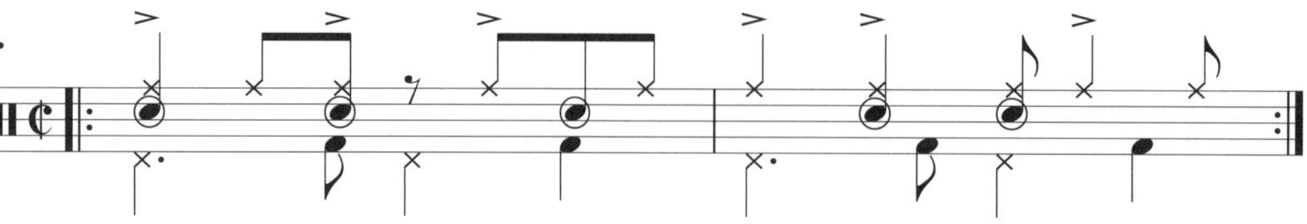

3.

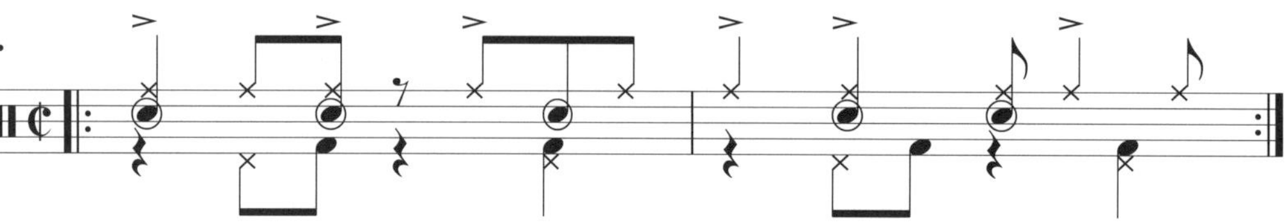

2+3 Son Clave

4.

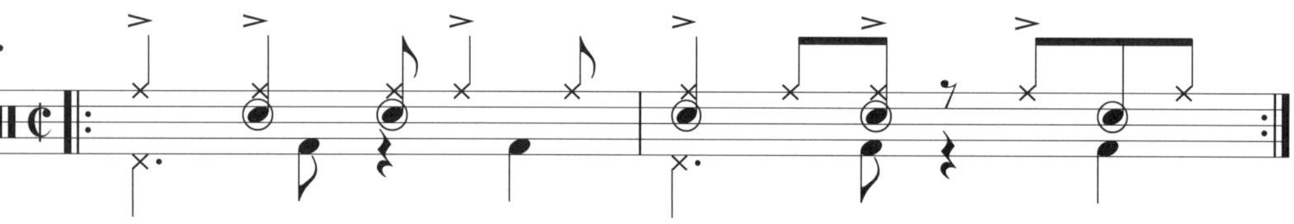

5.

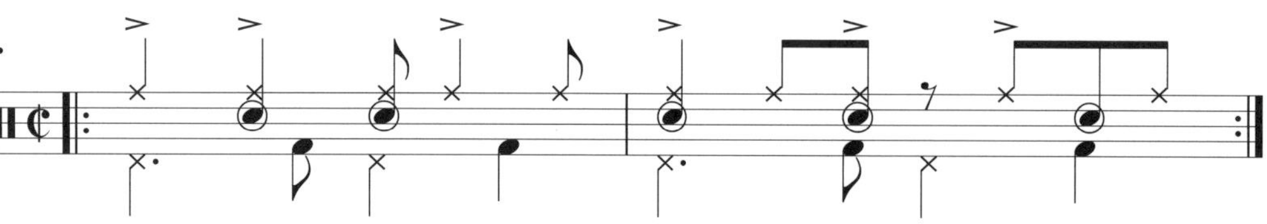

6.

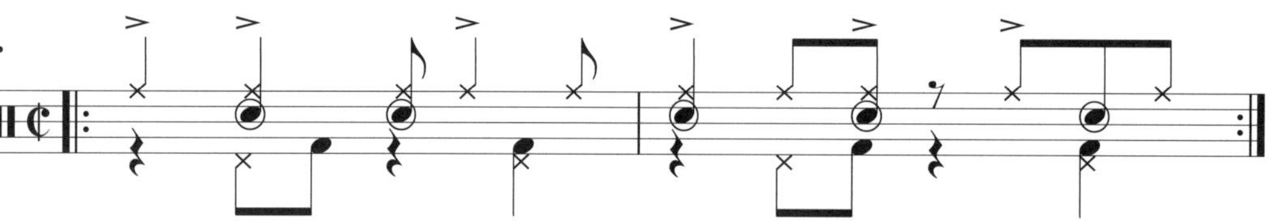

3+2 Rumba Clave

7.

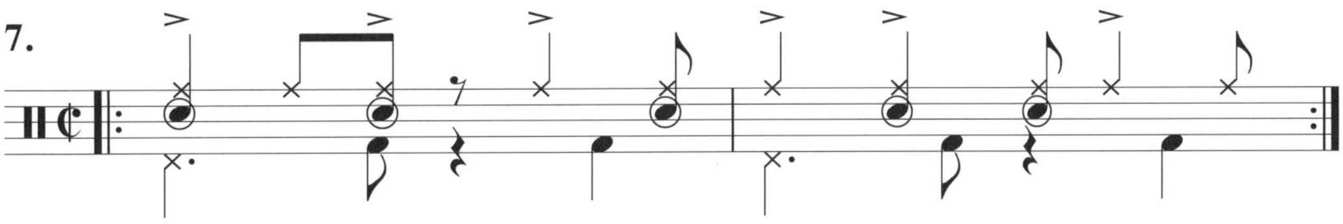

8.

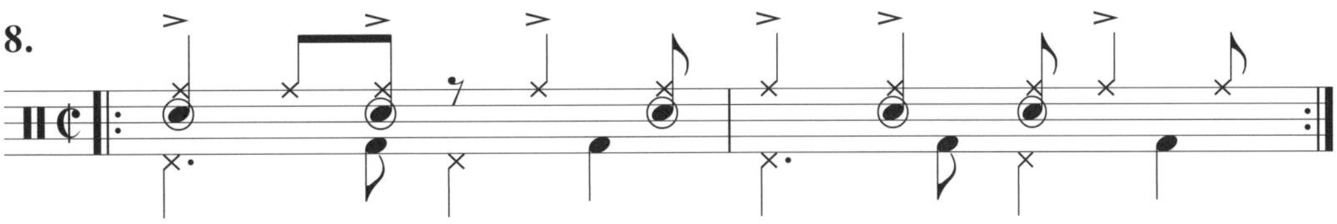

9.

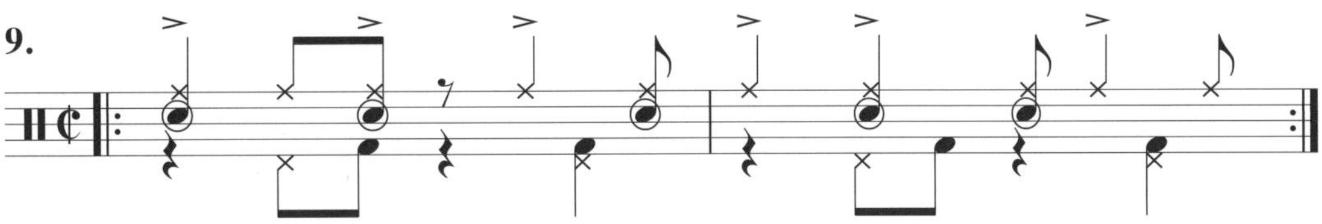

2+3 Rumba Clave

10.

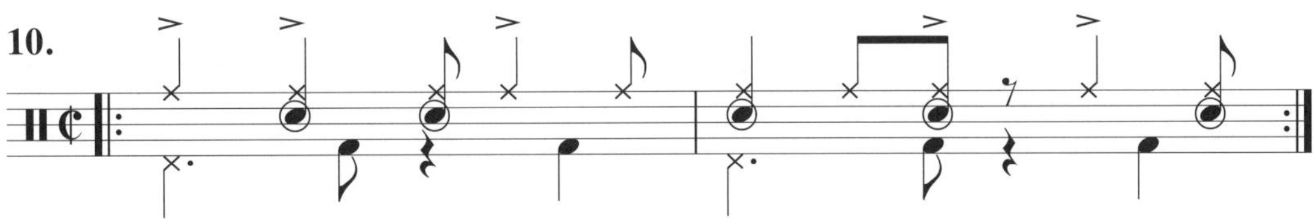

11.

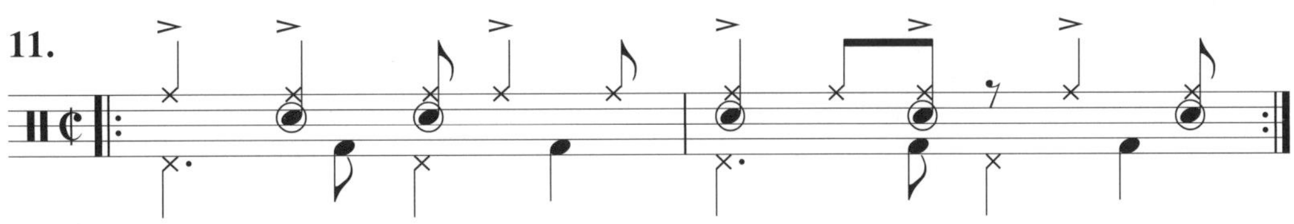

12.

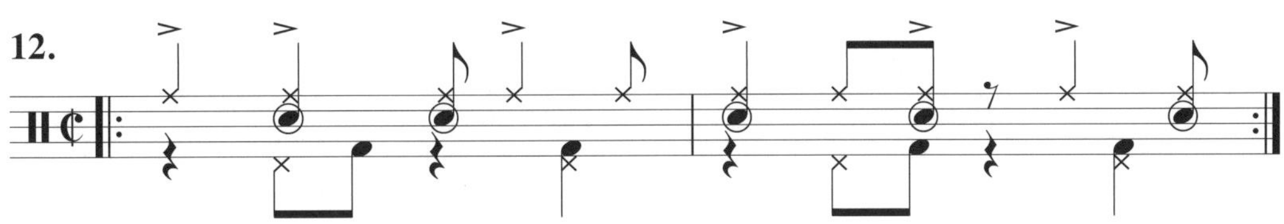

RIDE CYMBAL VARIATIONS

3+2 SON CLAVE

1.

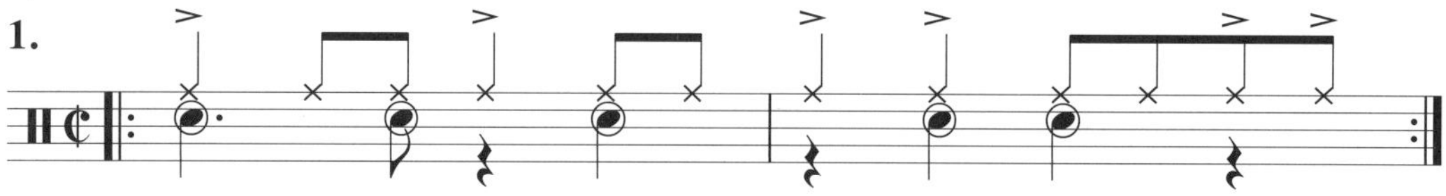

2.

3.

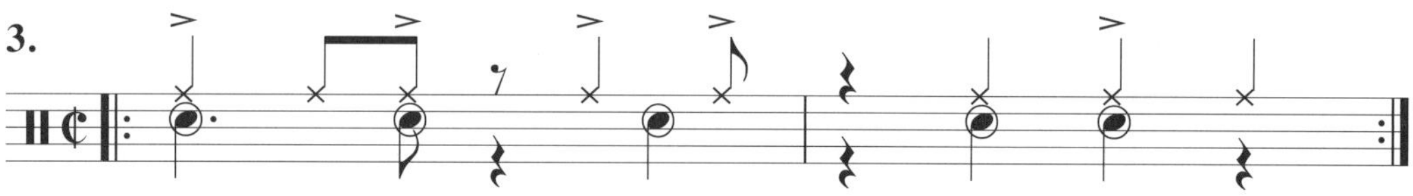

4.

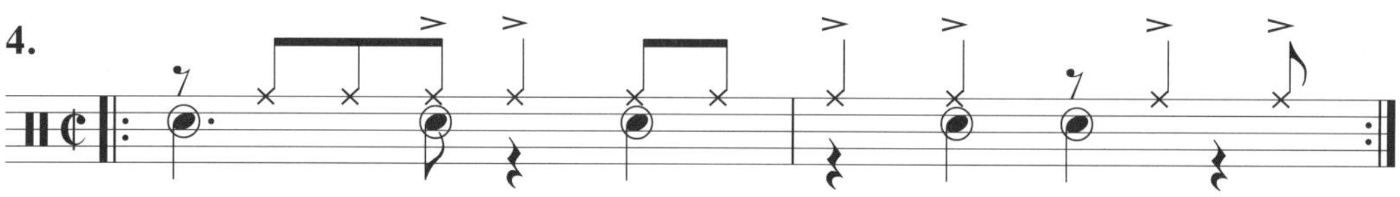

5.

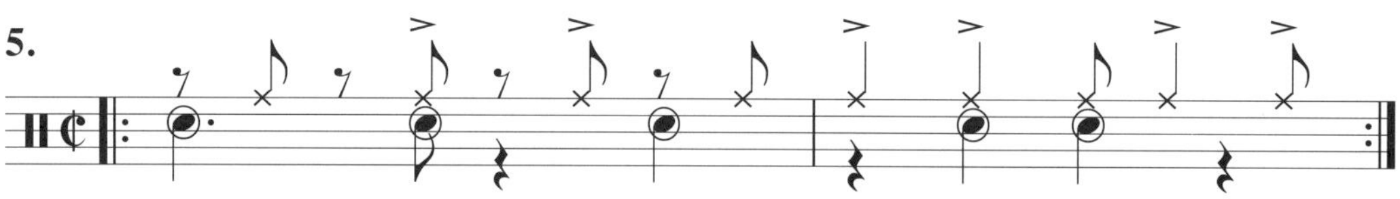

3+2 SON CLAVE, continued

6.

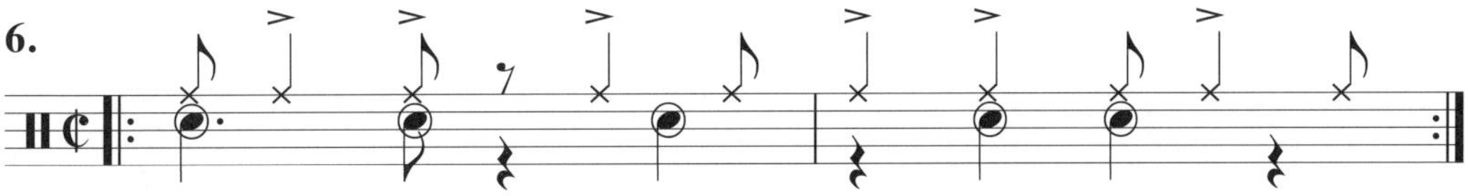

7.

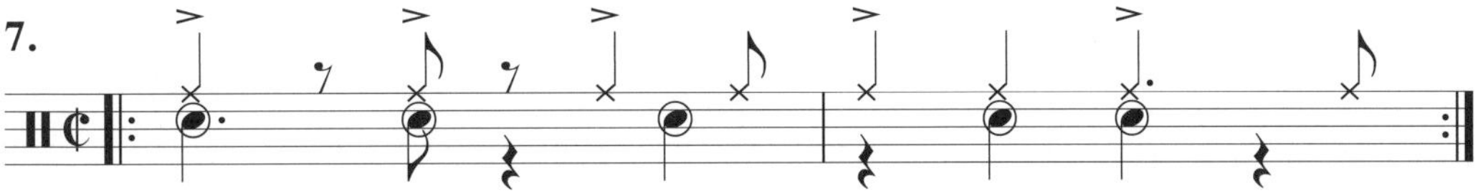

8.

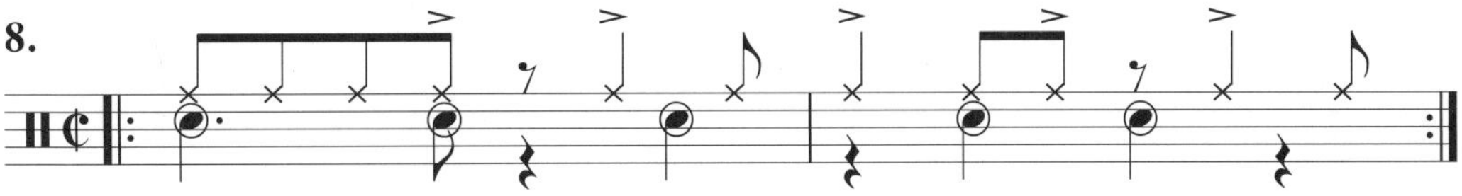

9.

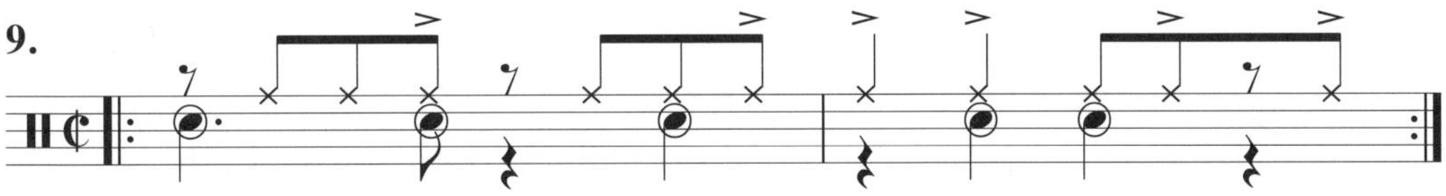

10.

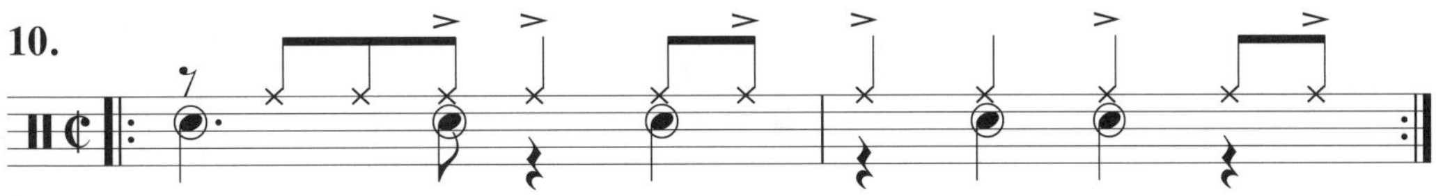

3+2 SON CLAVE, continued

11.

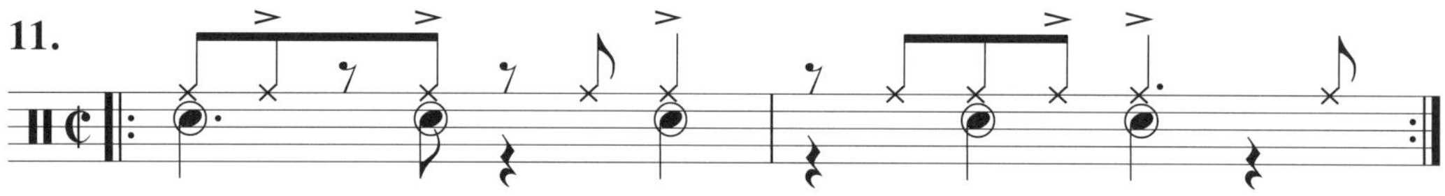

12.

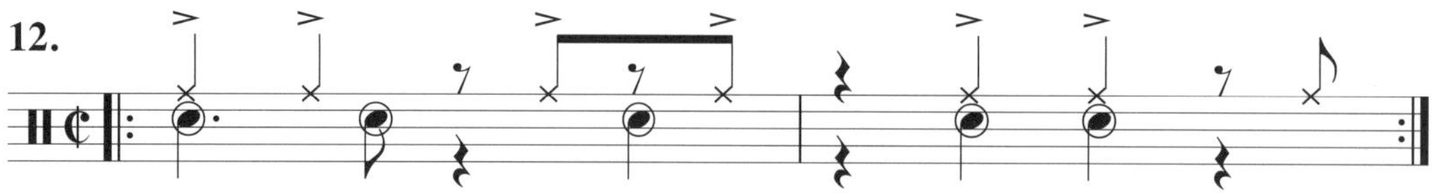

13.

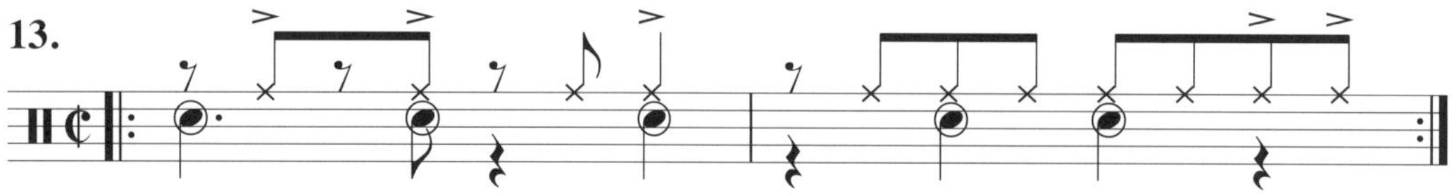

14.

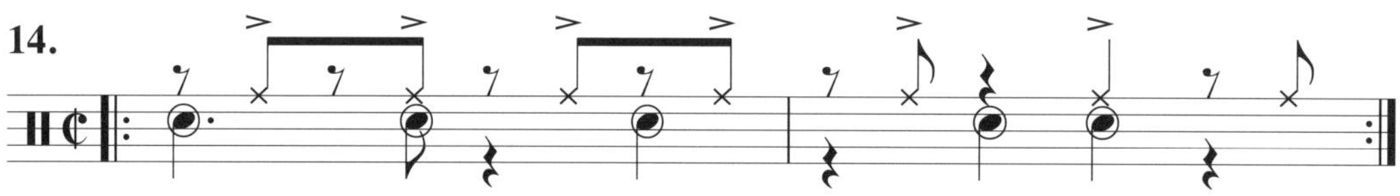

15.

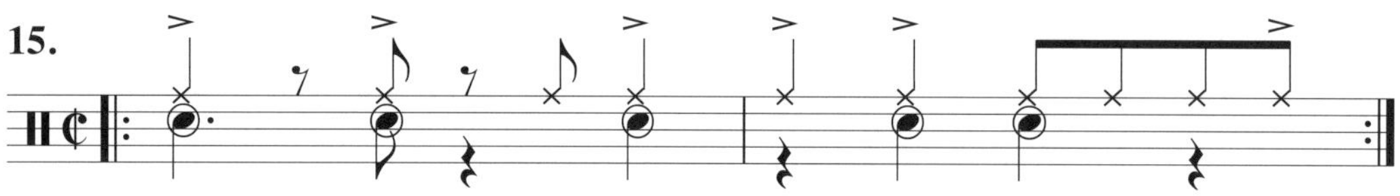

3+2 SON CLAVE, continued

16.

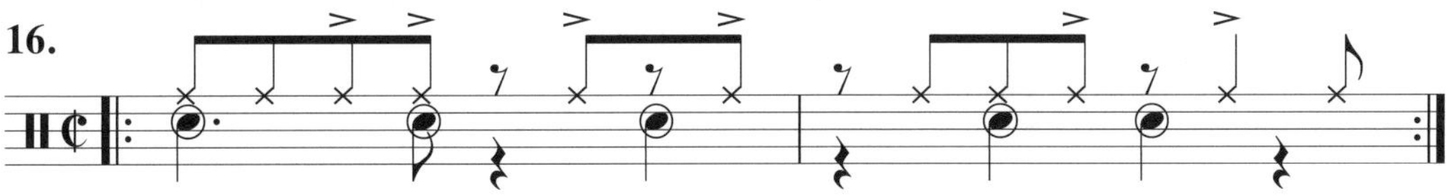

17.

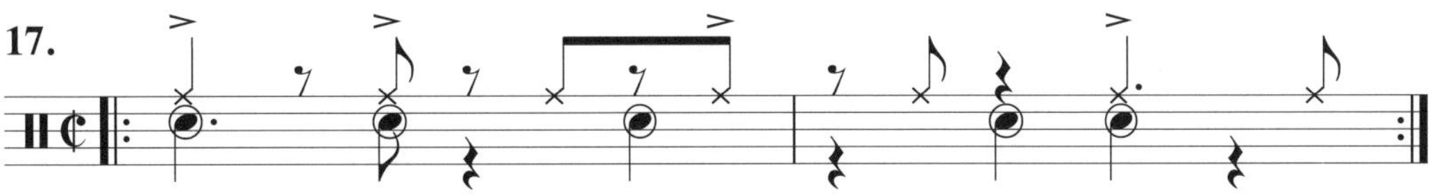

18.

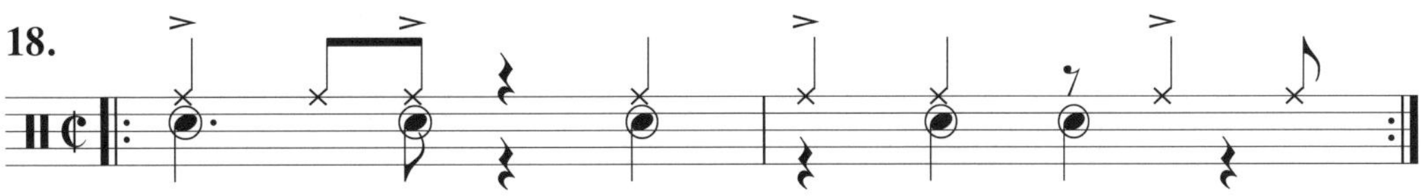

19.

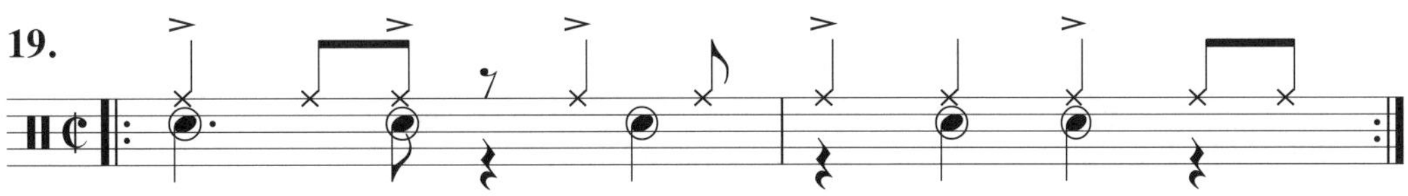

20.

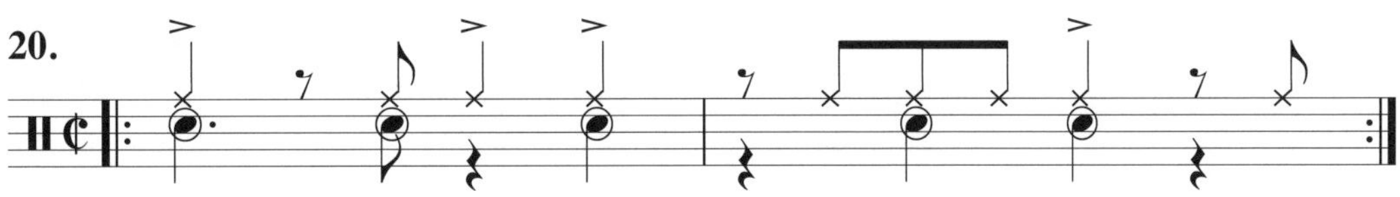

2+3 SON CLAVE

1.

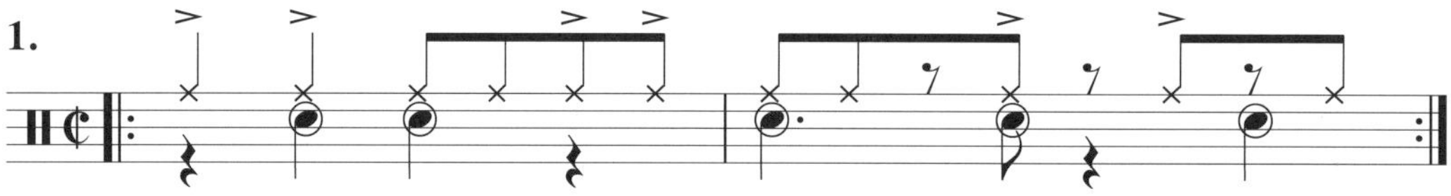

2.

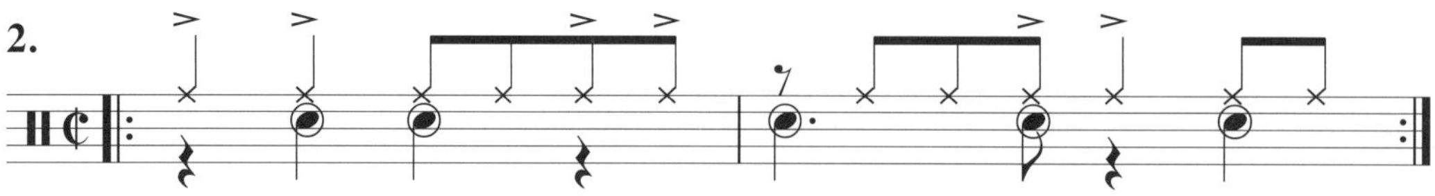

3.

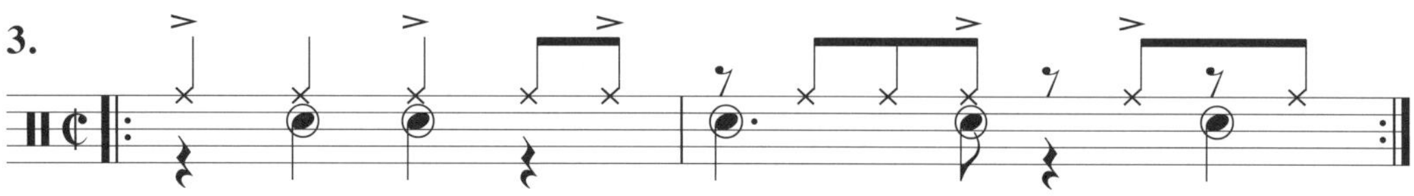

4.

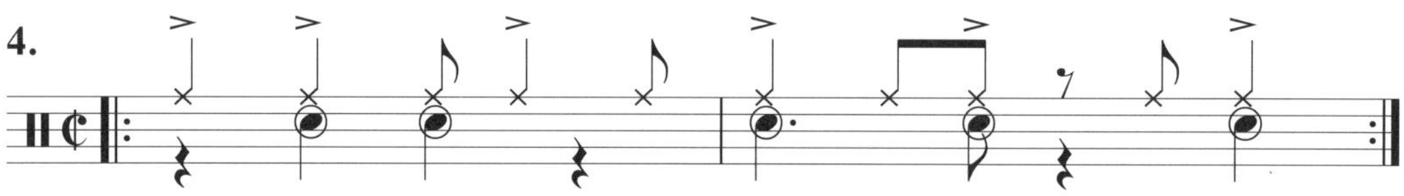

5.

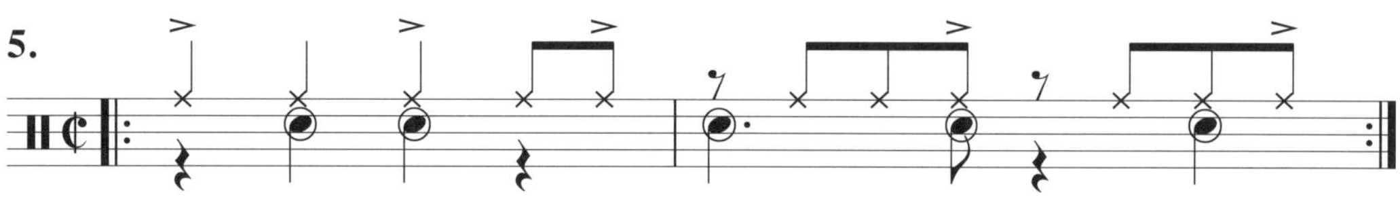

2+3 SON CLAVE, continued

6.

7.

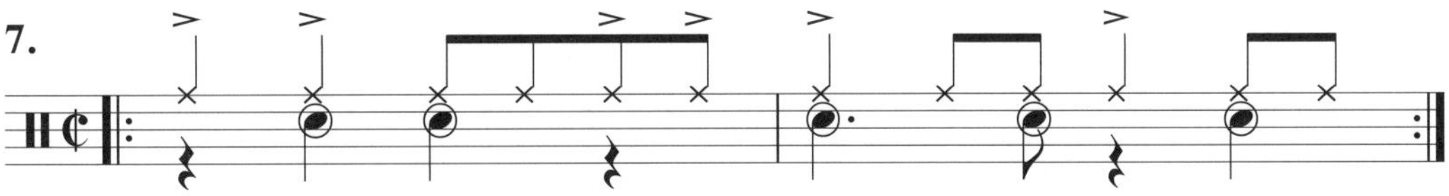

8.

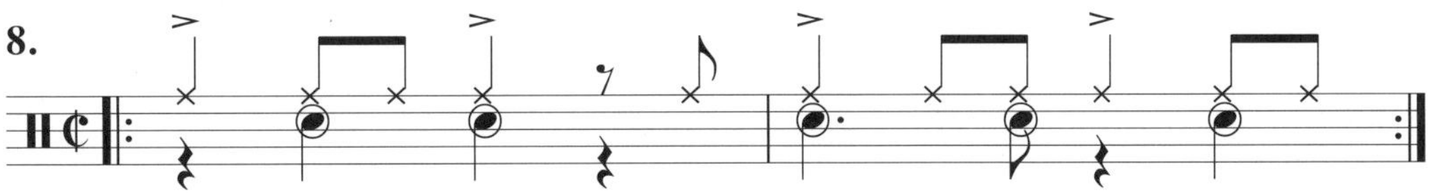

9.

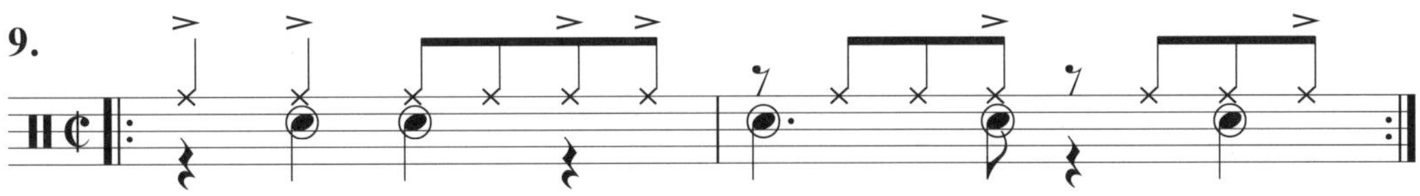

10.

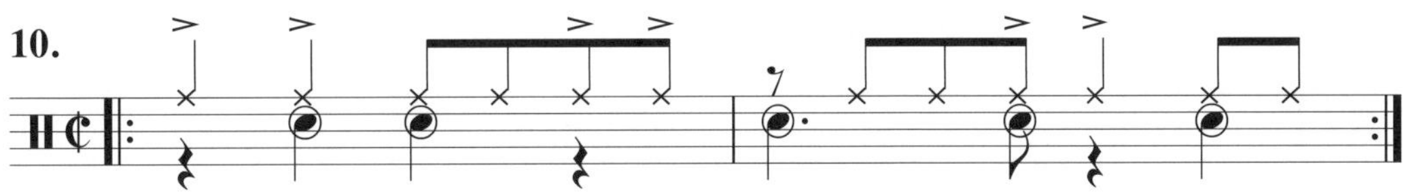

2+3 SON CLAVE, continued

11.

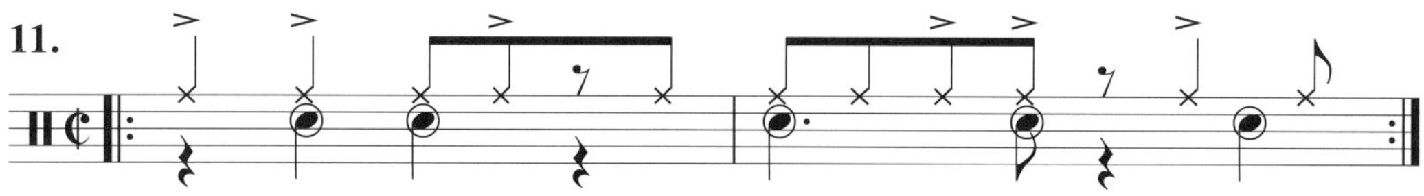

12.

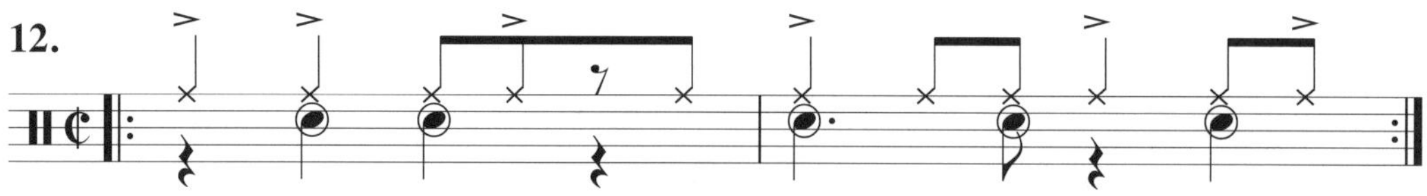

13.

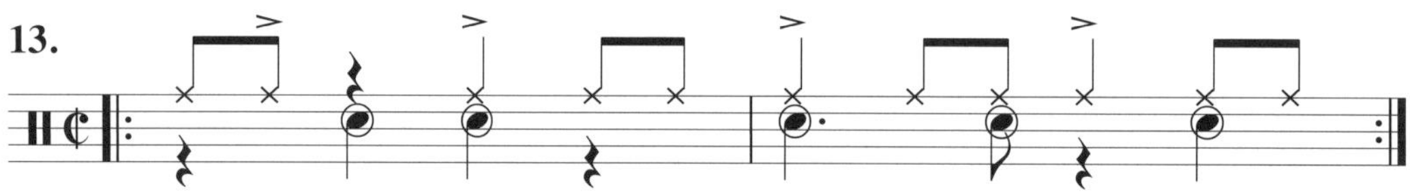

14.

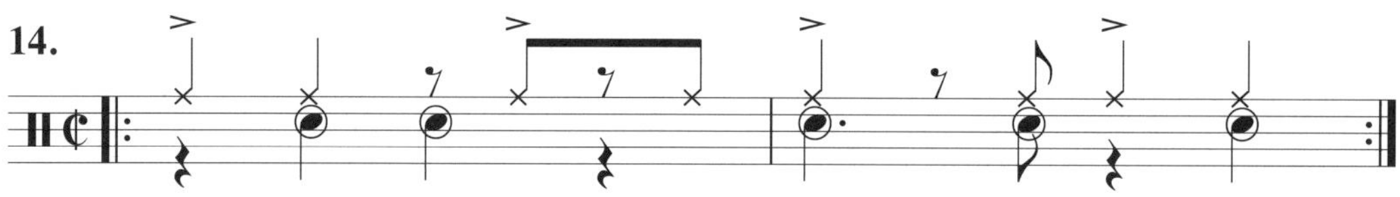

15.

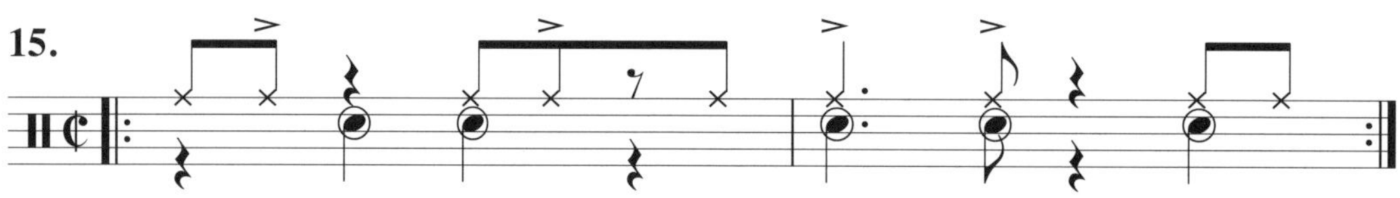

2+3 SON CLAVE, continued

16.

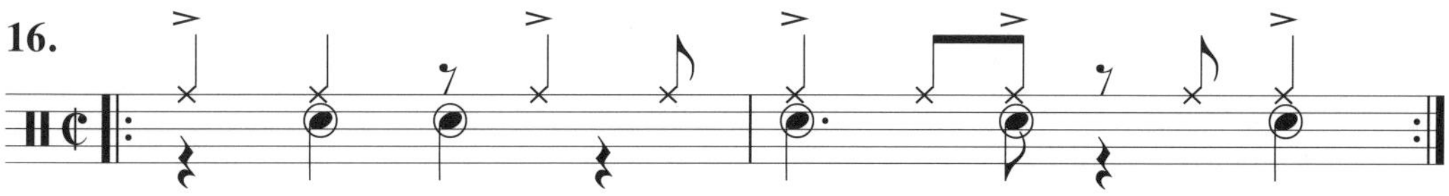

17.

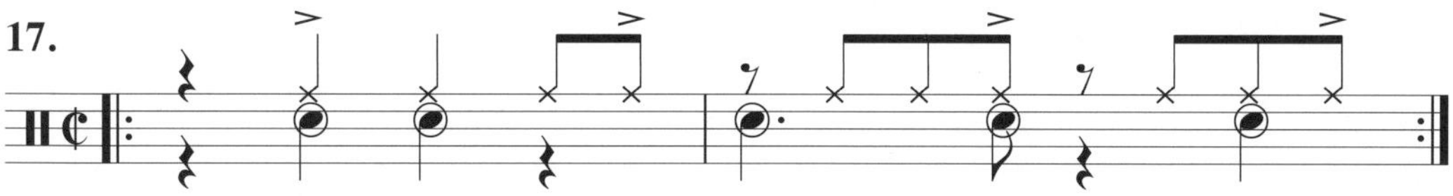

18.

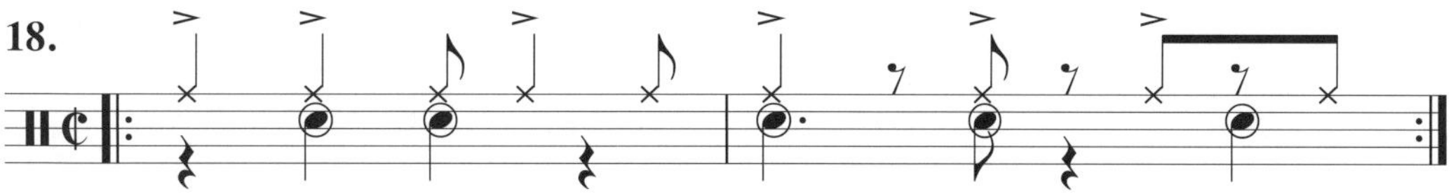

19.

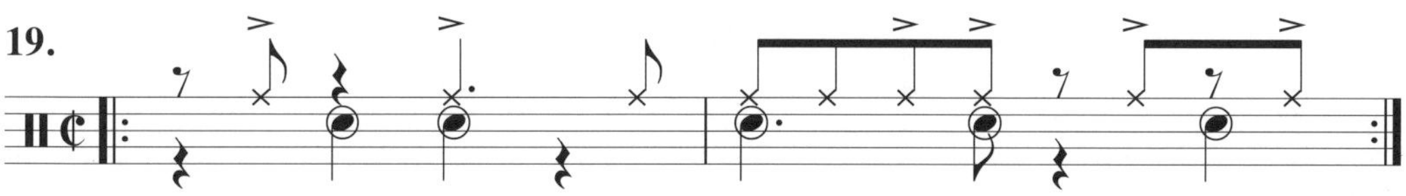

20.

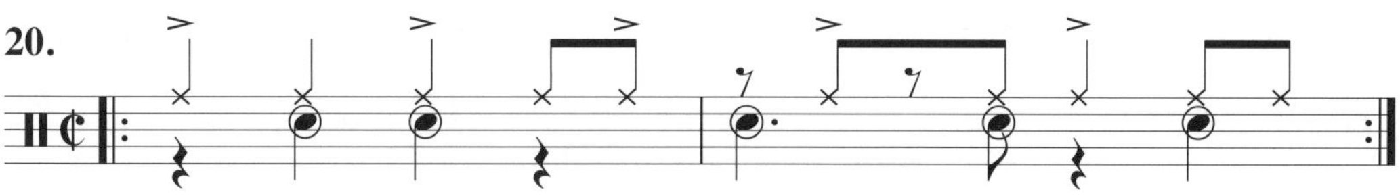

3+2 RUMBA CLAVE

1.

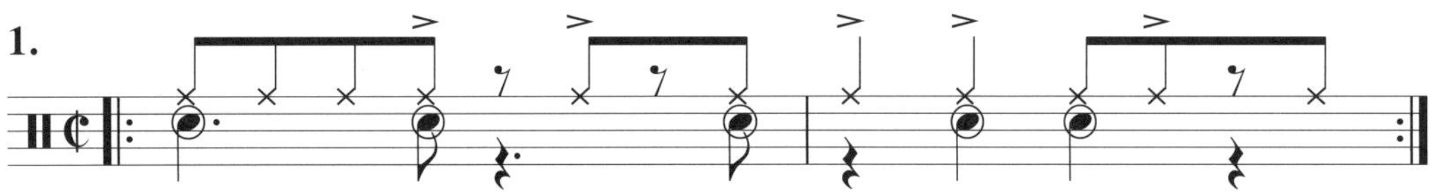

2.

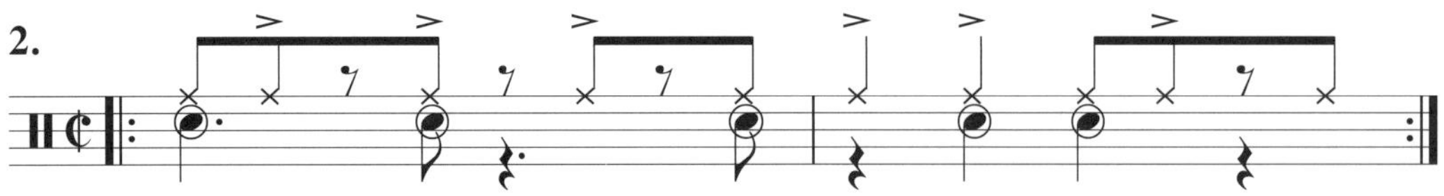

3.

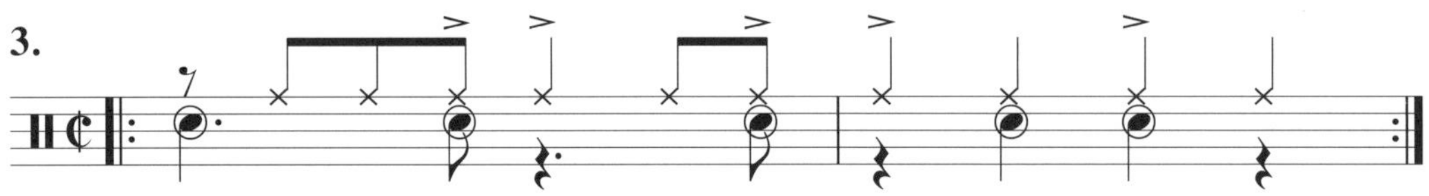

4.

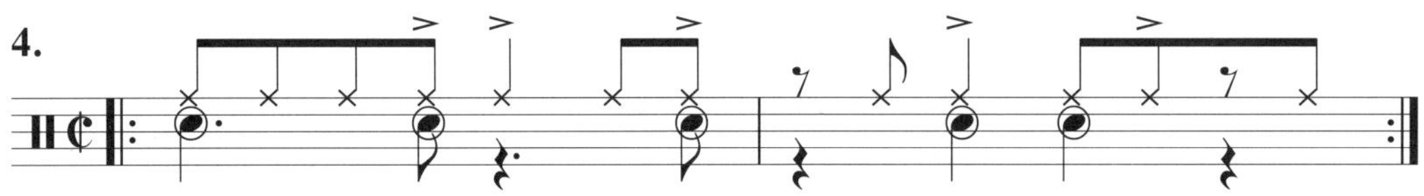

5.

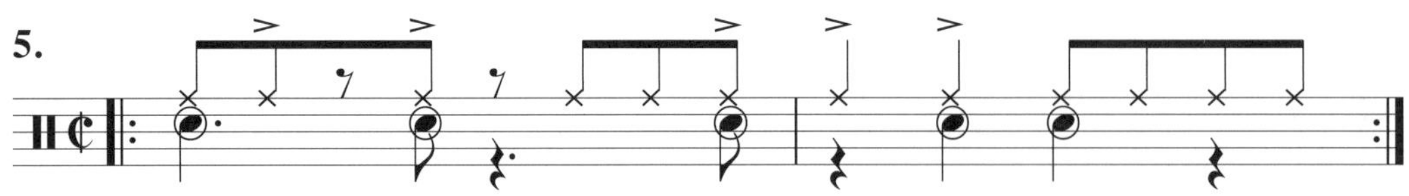

6.

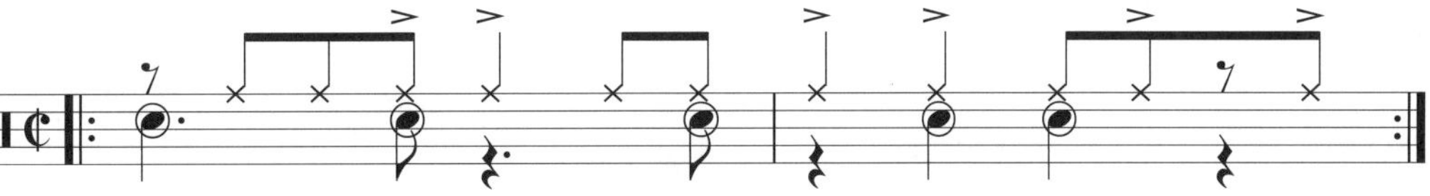

7.

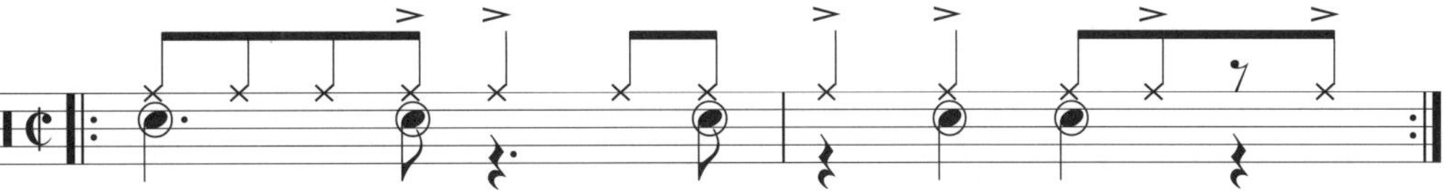

8.

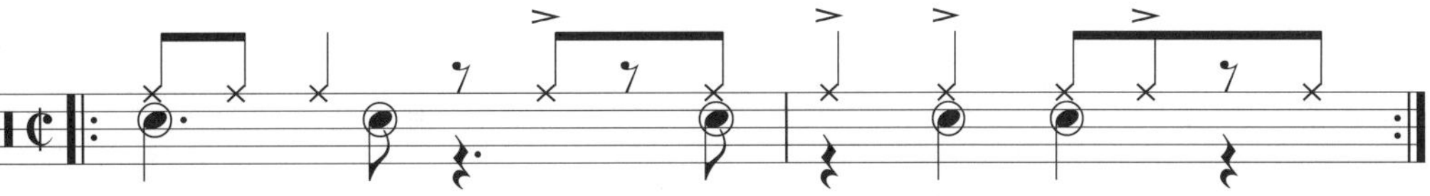

9.

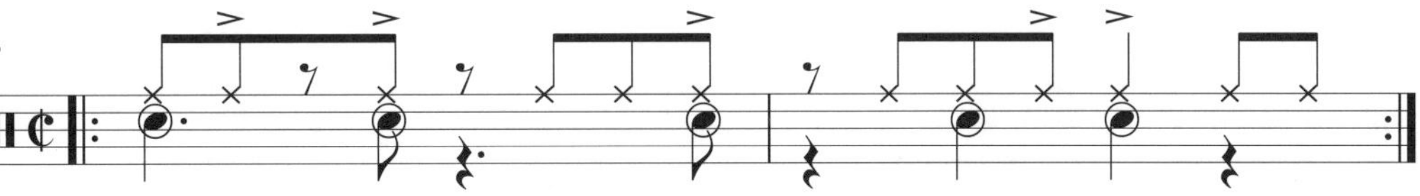

10.

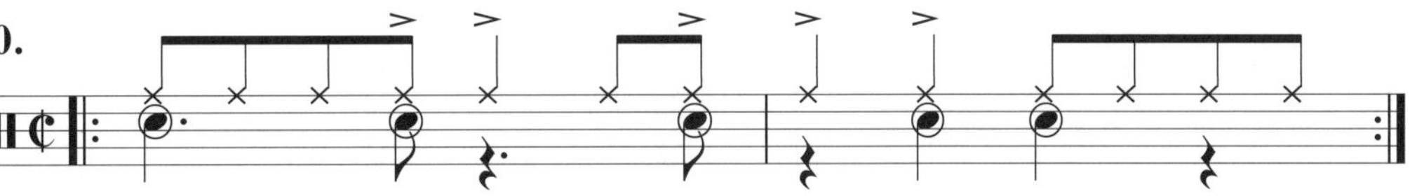

11.

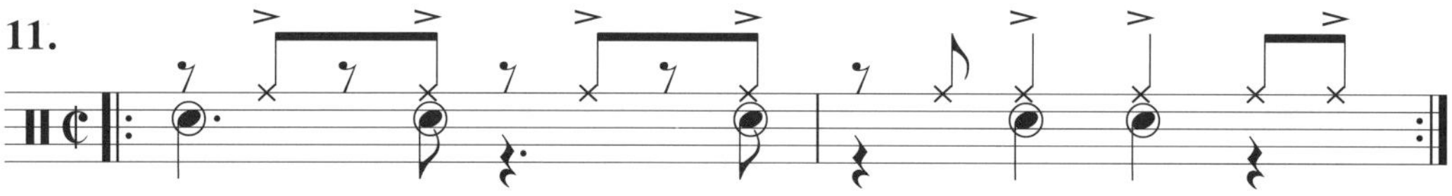

12.

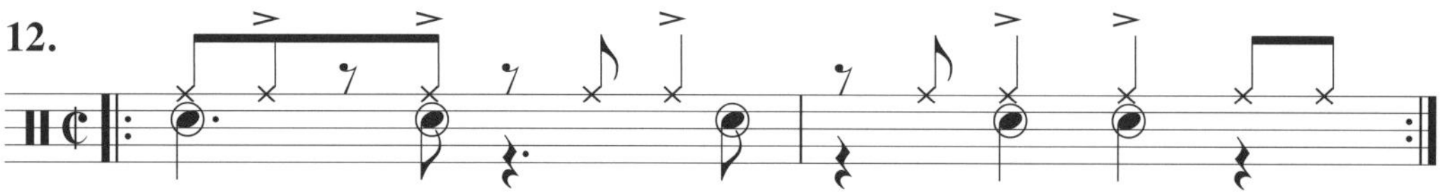

13.

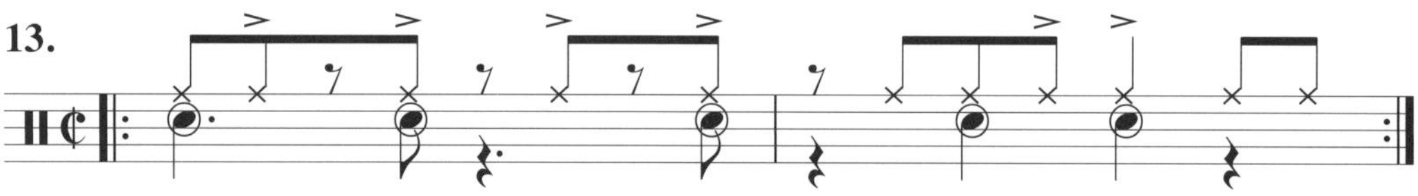

14.

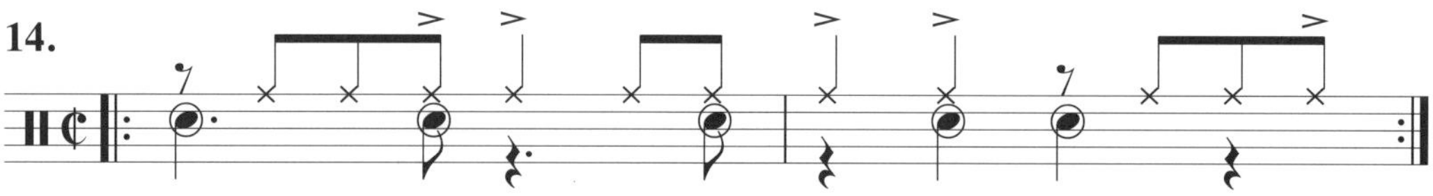

15.

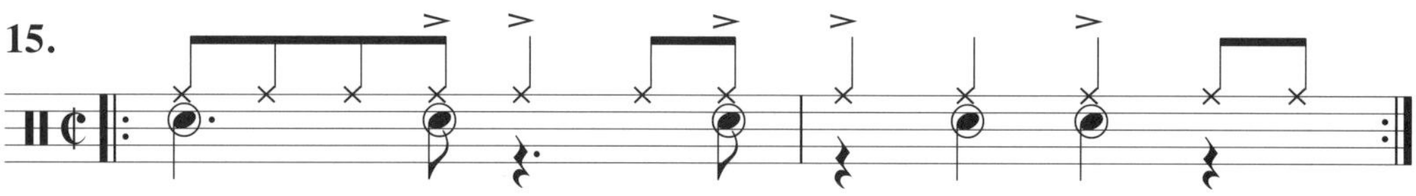

16.

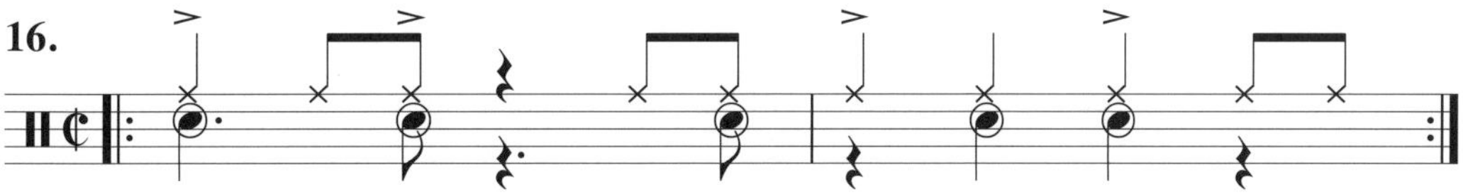

17.

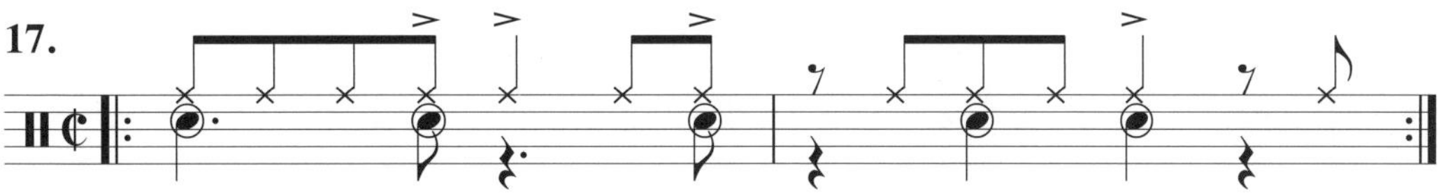

18.

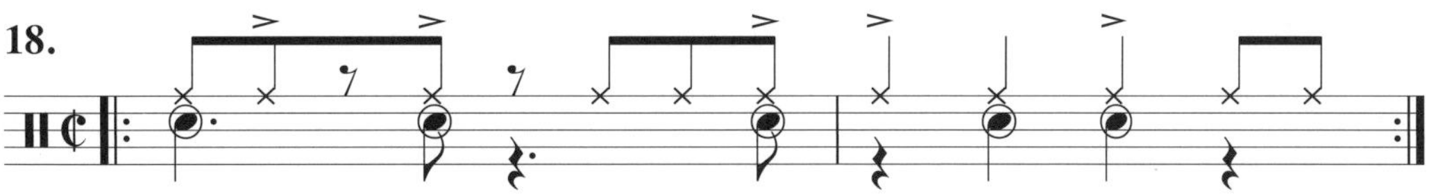

19.

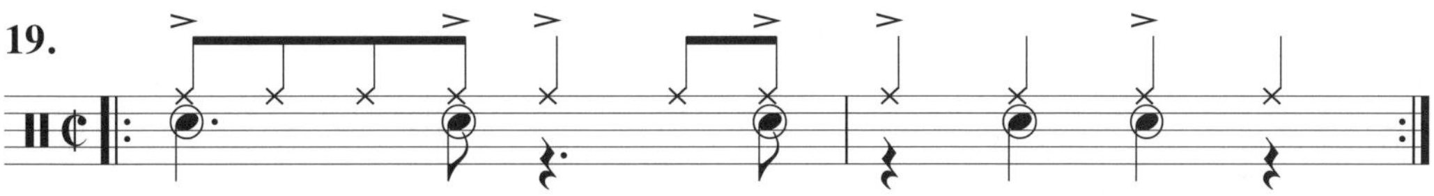

20.

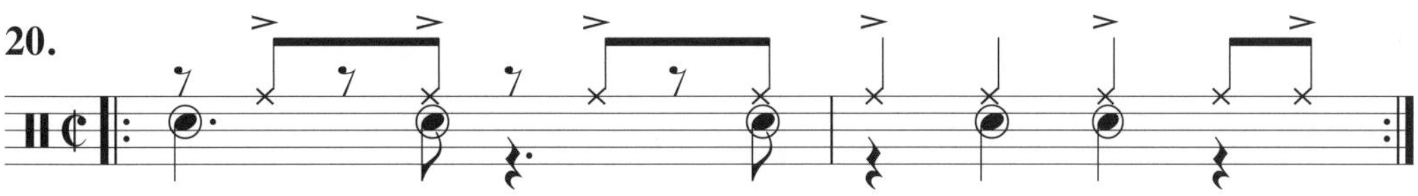

2+3 RUMBA CLAVE

1.

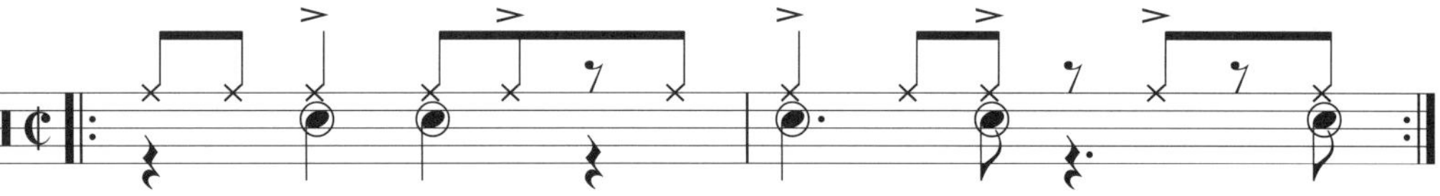

2.

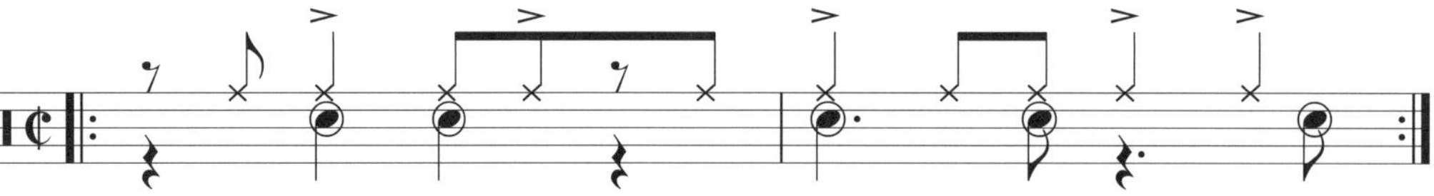

3.

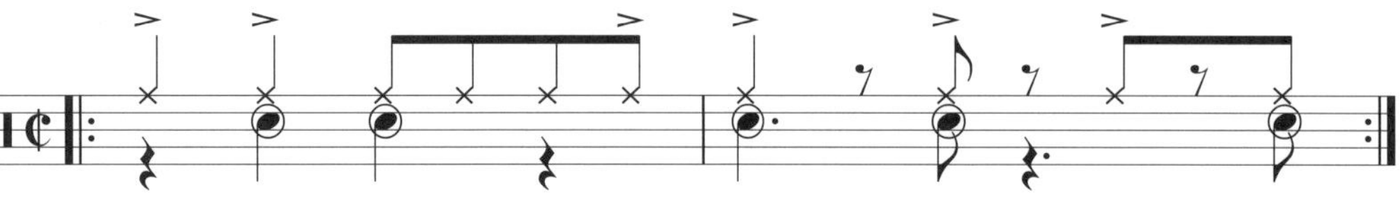

4.

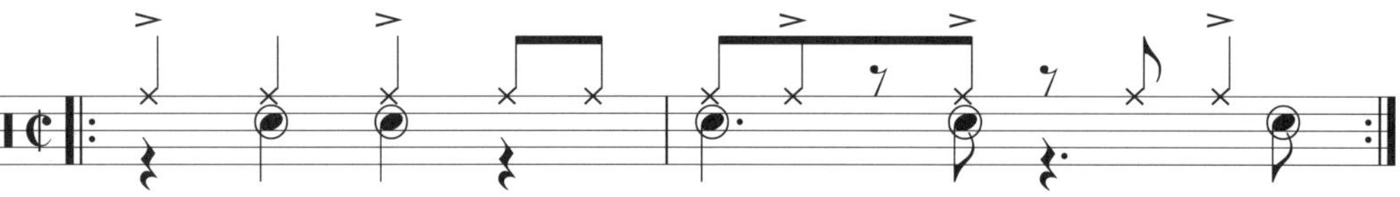

5.

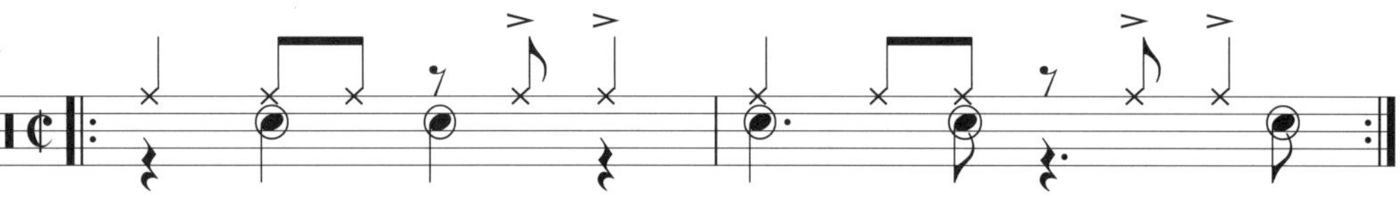

6.

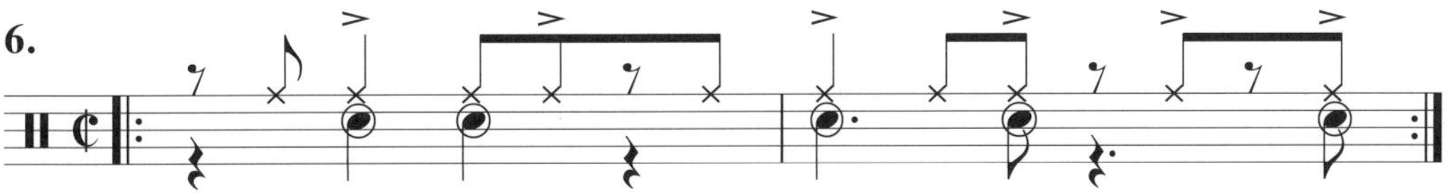

7.

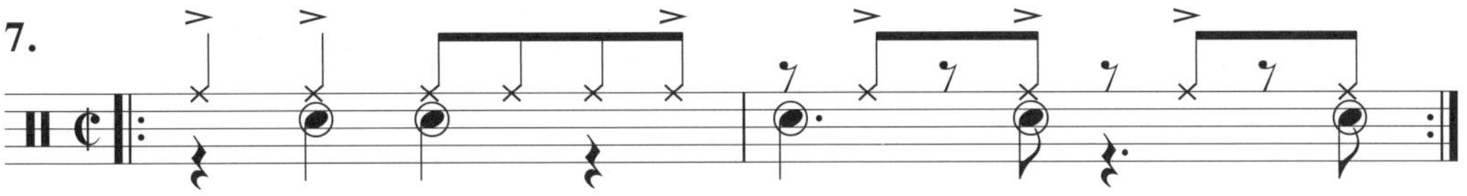

8.

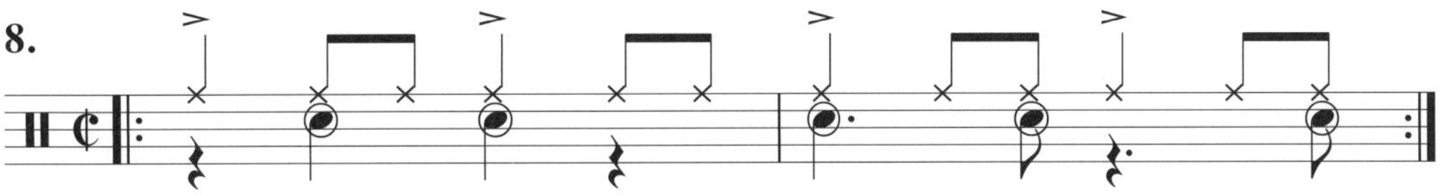

9.

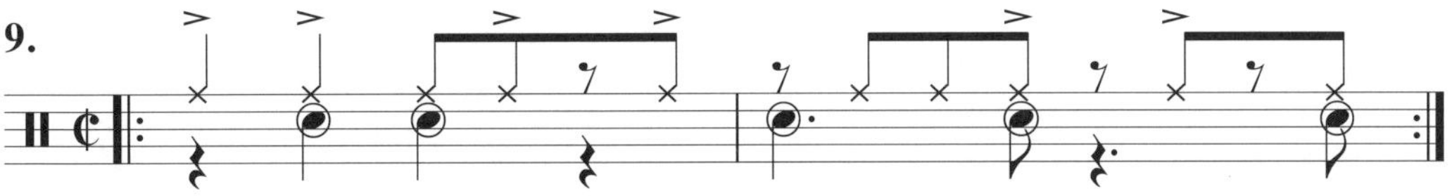

10.

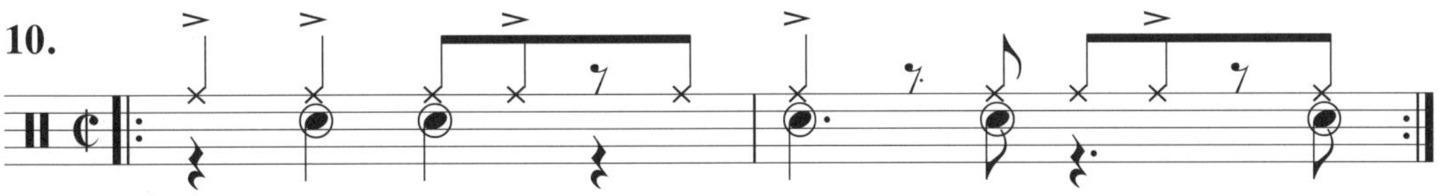

2+3 RUMBA CLAVE, continued

11.

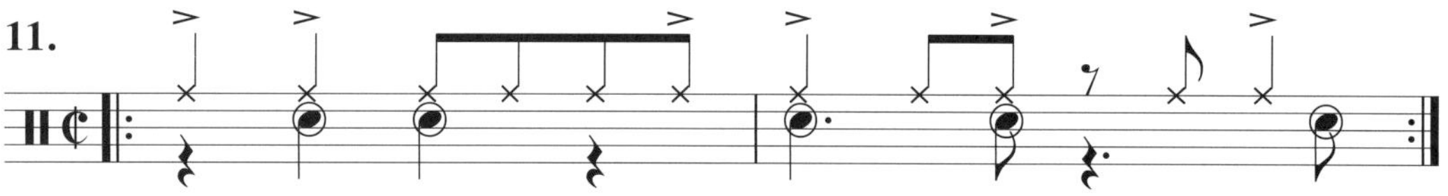

12.

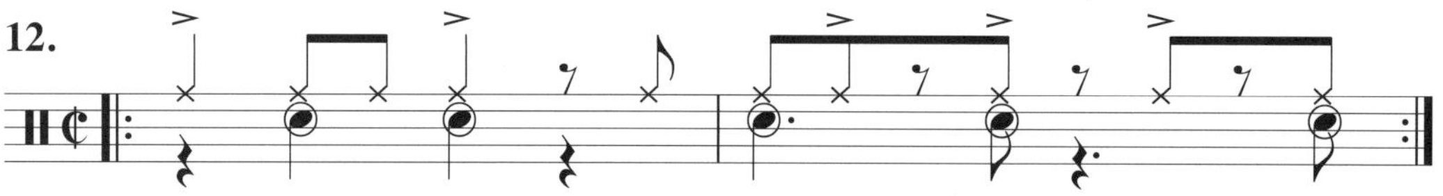

13.

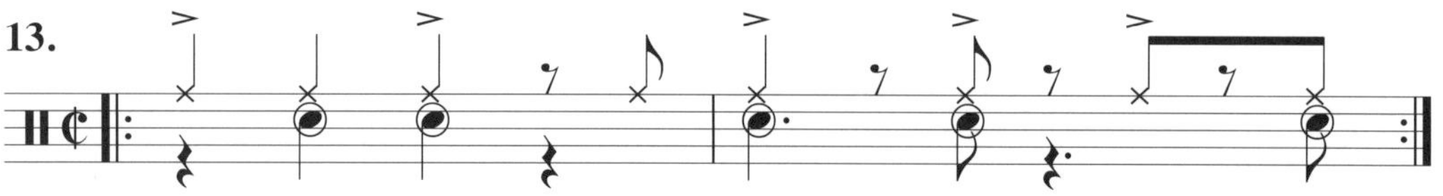

14.

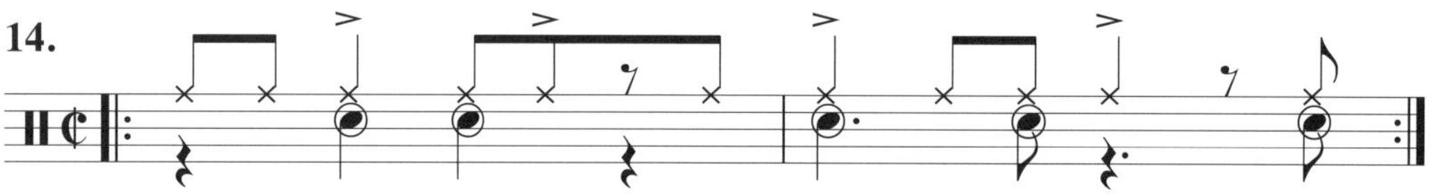

15.

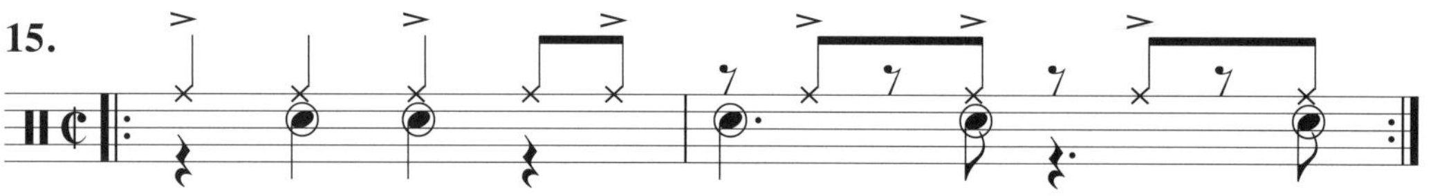

16.

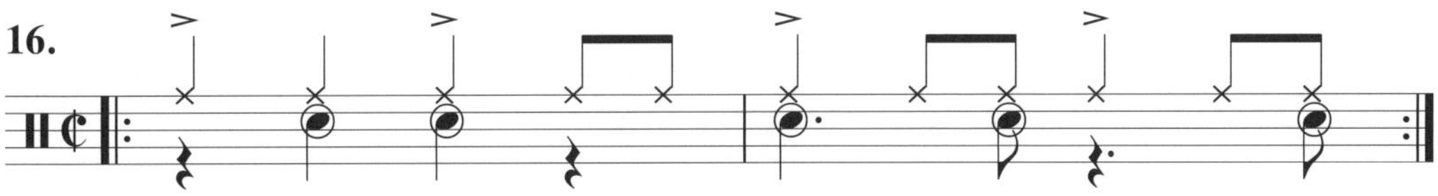

17.

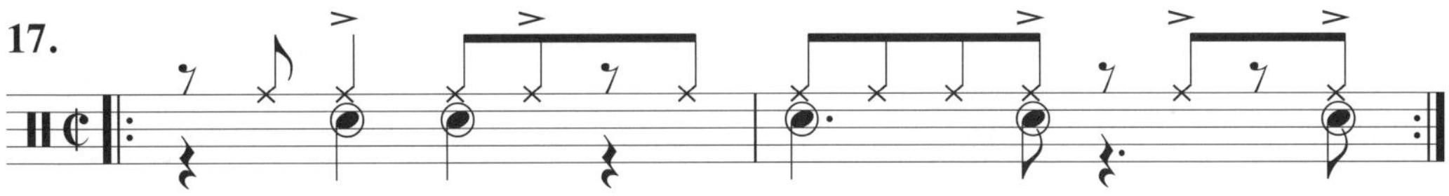

18.

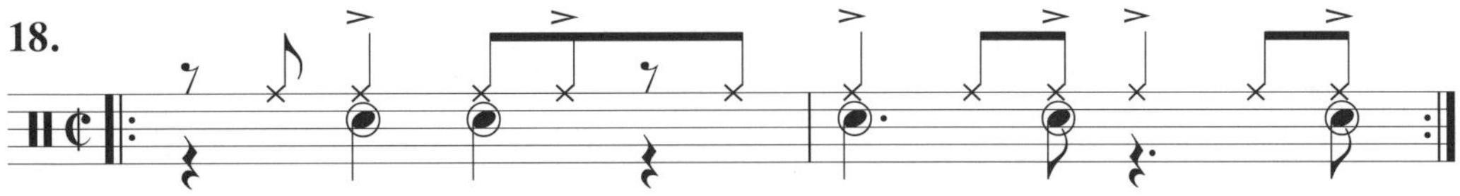

19.

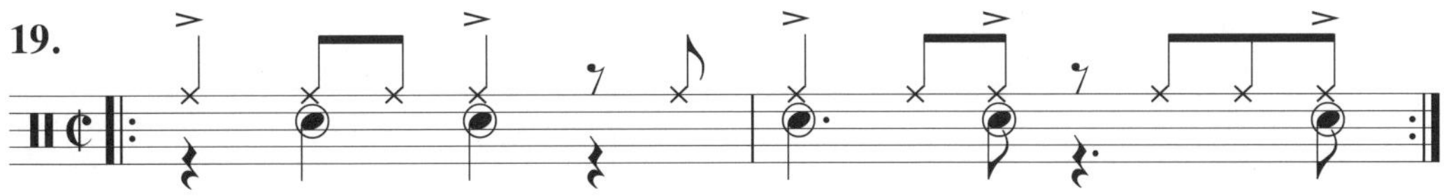

20.

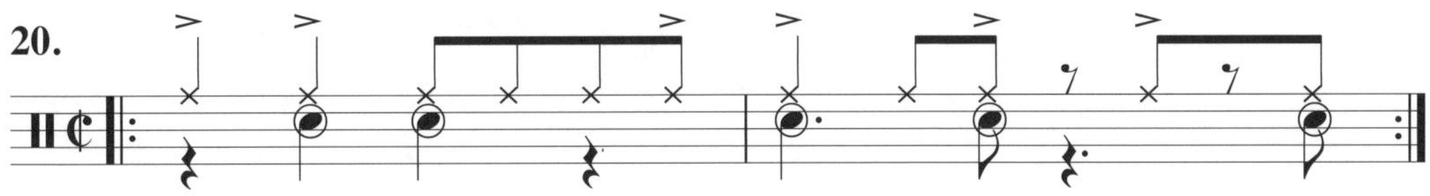

SUMMARY, 3+2 SON CLAVE

1.

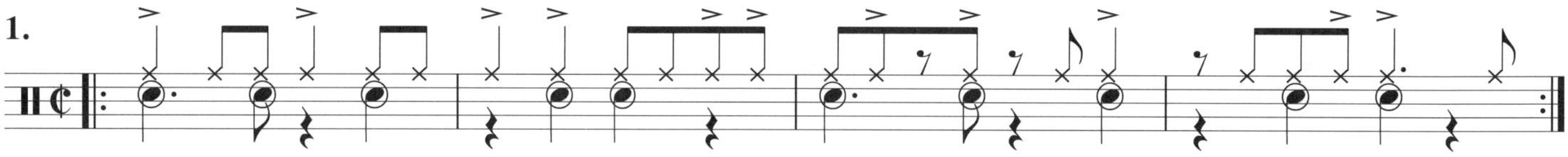

2.

3.

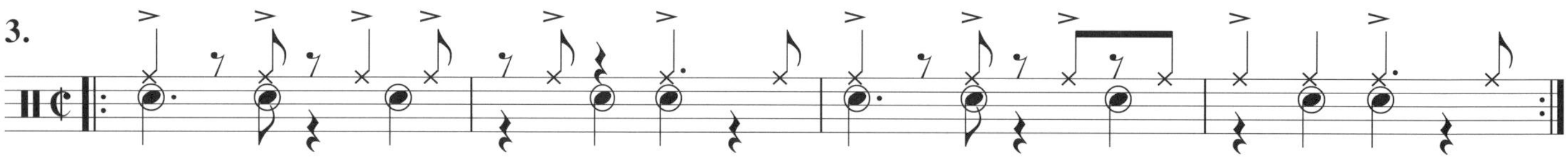

4.

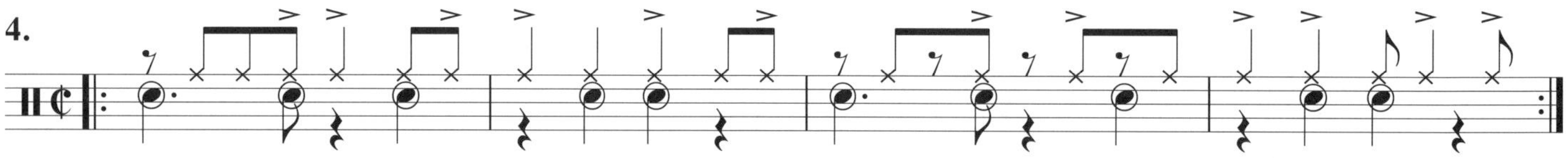

SUMMARY, 3+2 SON CLAVE, continued

5.

6.

7.

8.

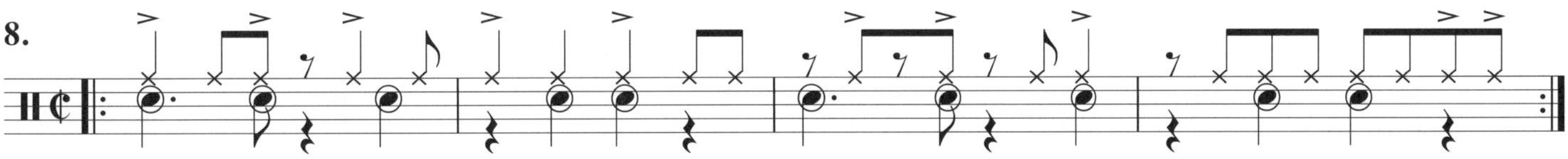

SUMMARY, 2+3 SON CLAVE

1.

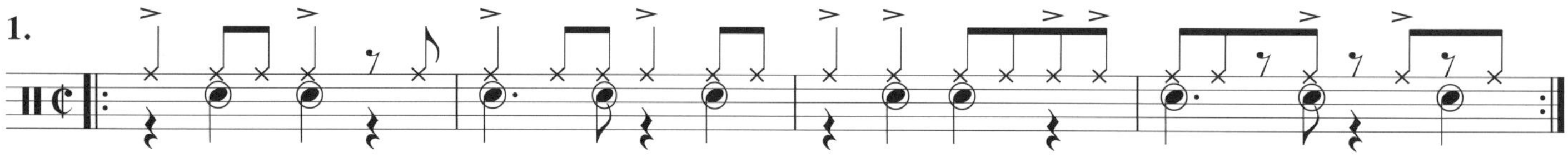

2.

3.

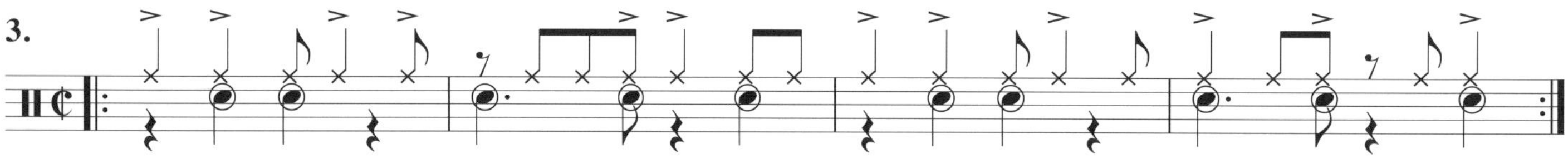

4.

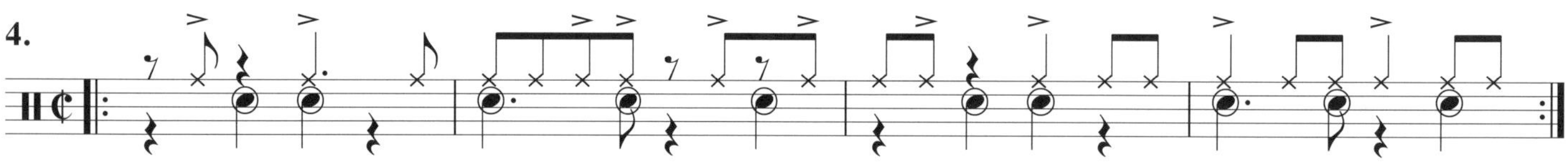

SUMMARY, 2+3 SON CLAVE, continued

5.

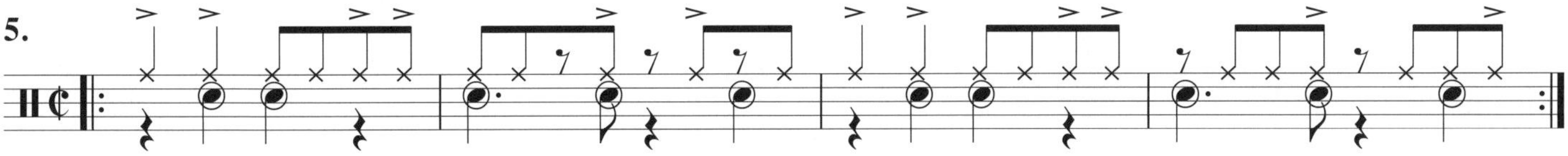

6.

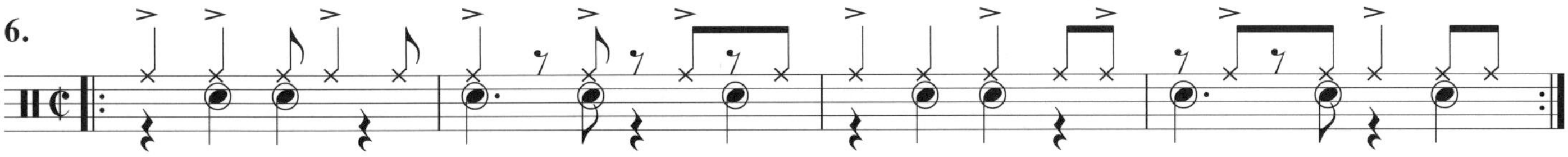

7.

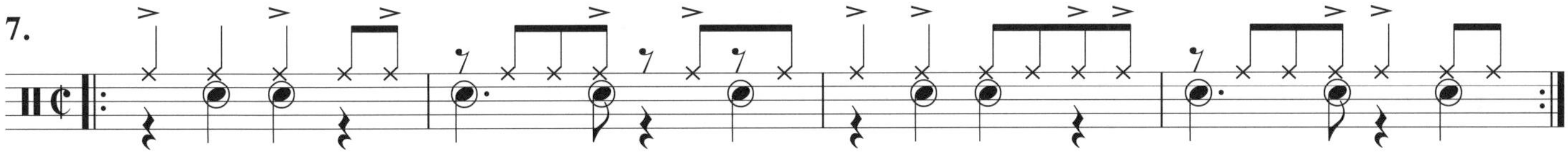

8.

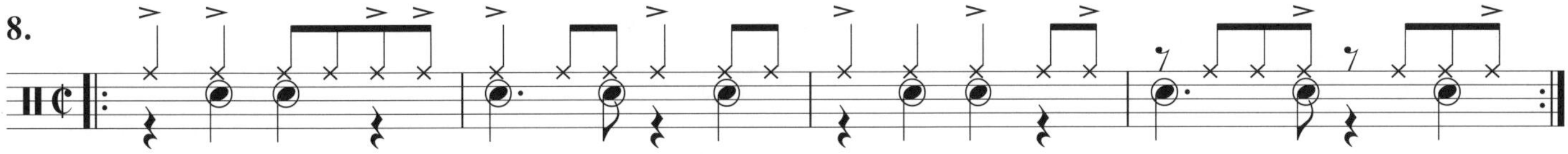

SUMMARY, 3+2 RUMBA CLAVE

1.

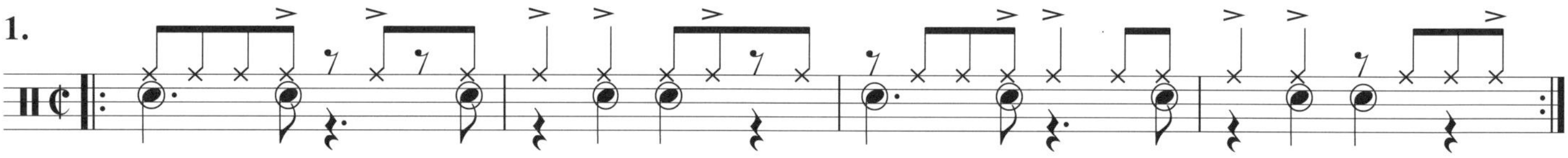

2.

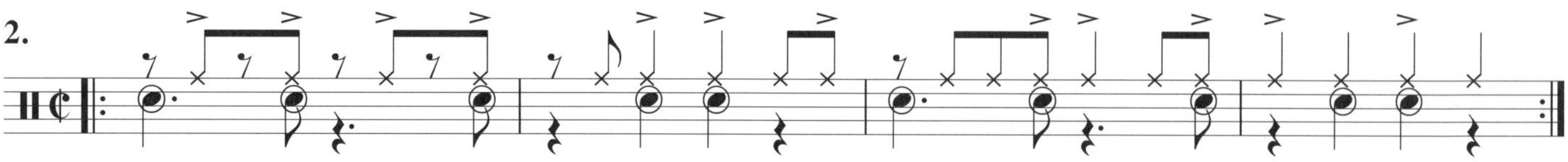

3.

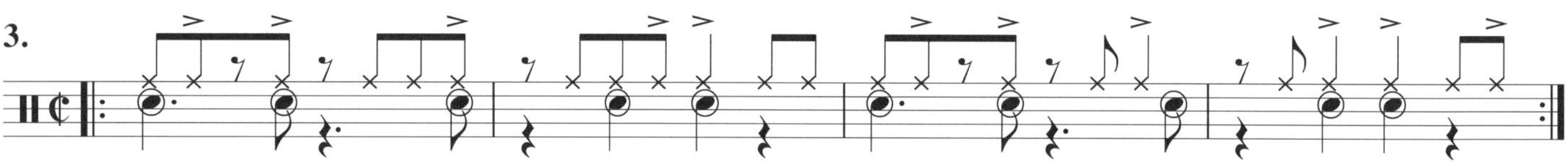

4.

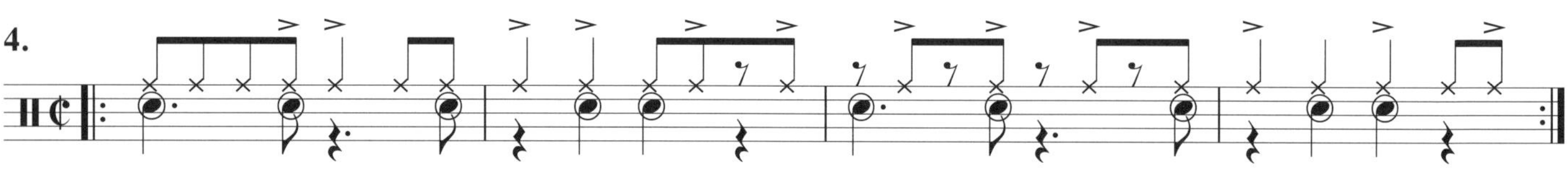

SUMMARY, 3+2 RUMBA CLAVE, continued

5.

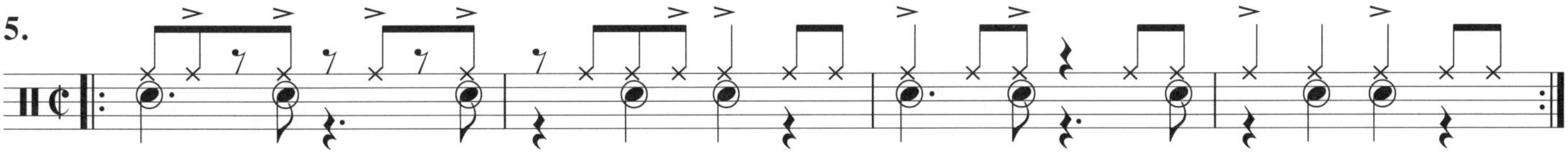

6.

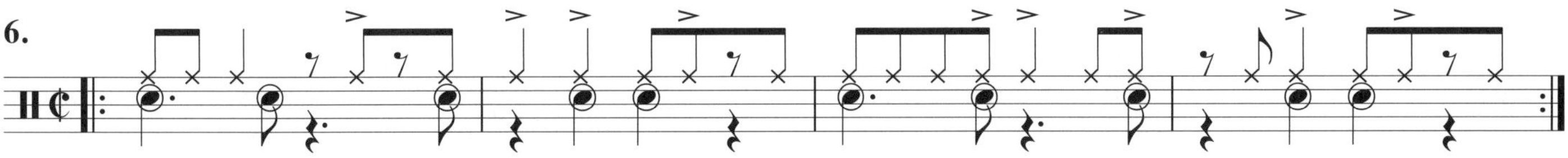

7.

8.

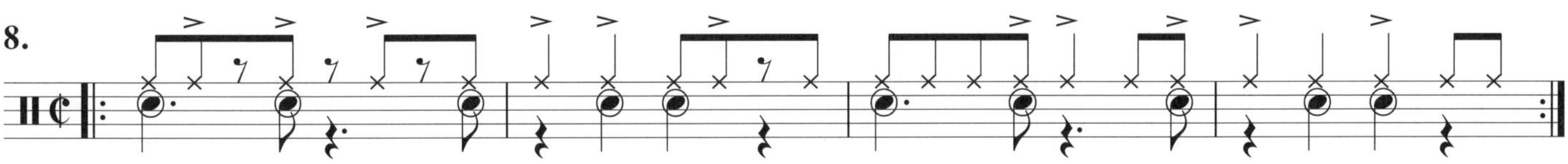

SUMMARY, 2+3 RUMBA CLAVE

1.

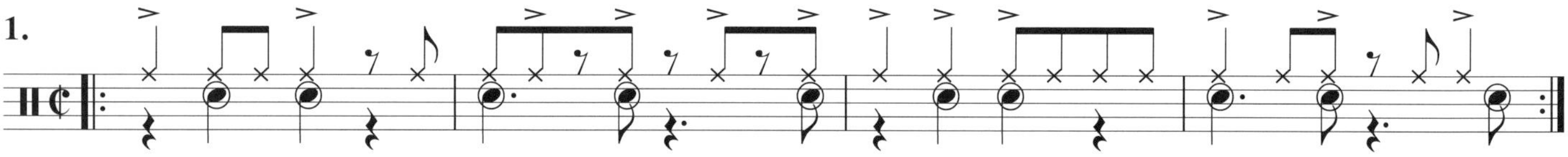

2.

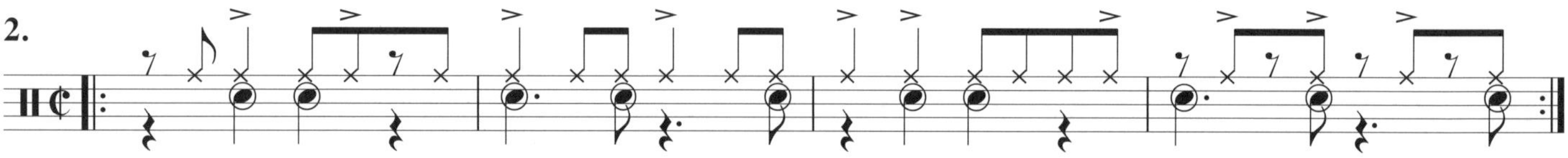

3.

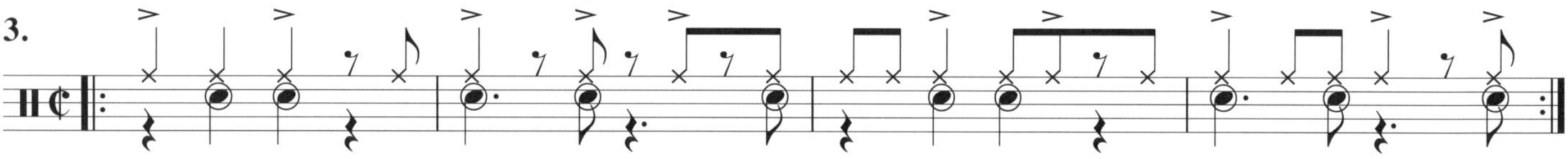

4.

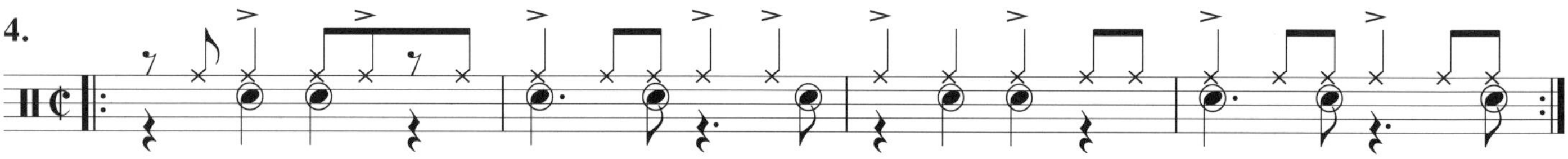

SUMMARY, 2+3 RUMBA CLAVE, continued

5.

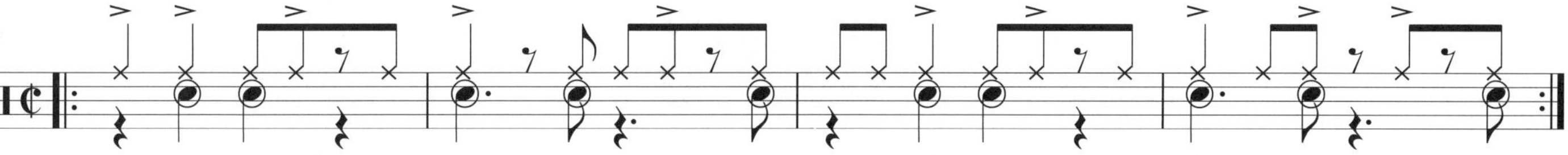

6.

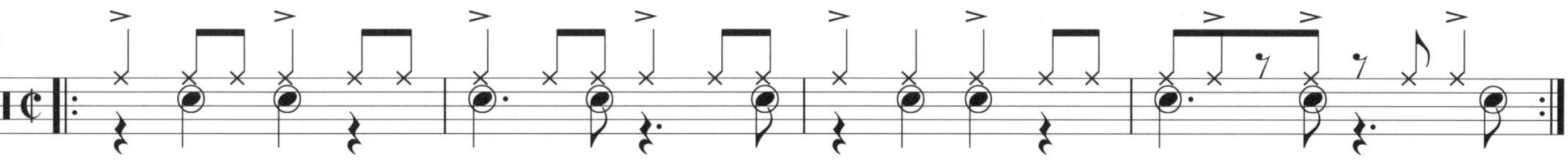

7.

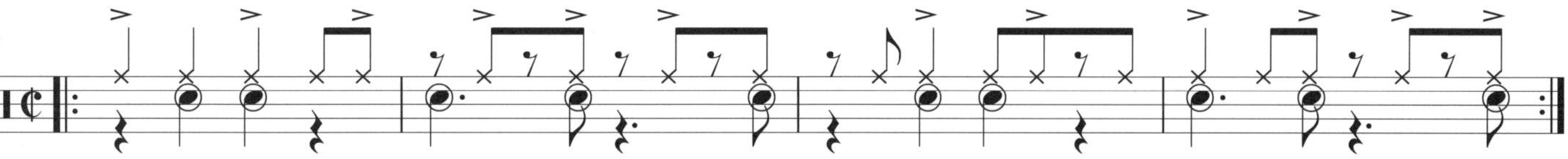

8.

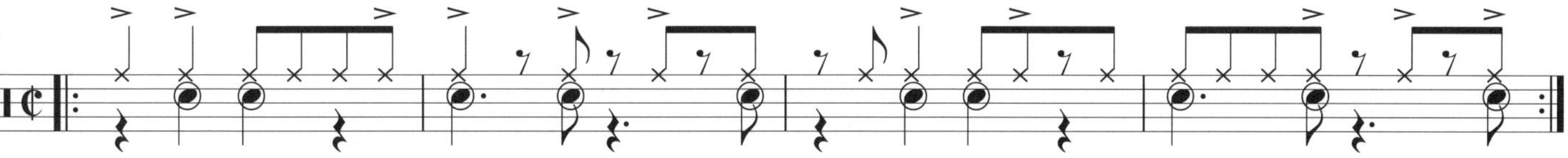

CHAPTER 5
SONGO

The Songo style of drumming is more of a concept than one particular "beat." Songo is a blend of folkloric and contemporary Cuban styles with elements of funk and jazz. In many ways, Songo is the "jazz" of Cuban drumming. Although there are many different ways to play Songo, the rhythmic style originated from approximately six to eight different grooves invented by Jose Luis Quintana, better known as "Changuito."

The following Songo ostinatos are very popular grooves often played and heard in the "Latin-jazz" style of music. Examples 6–10 feature Songo ostinatos with left-foot clave patterns. Pages 82–85 contain bass drum variations that can be played with the Songo ostinatos in order to develop the freedom and coordination to improvise bass drum patterns of your own.

Although the clave rhythm is not always played on the drumset, it plays an important role and it is important to always be aware of the clave while playing the Songo style. Although patterns 1–6 are only shown in 3+2 clave, they should all be practiced in 2+3 clave as well by starting on the second bar.

3+2 Rumba or Son Clave

1.

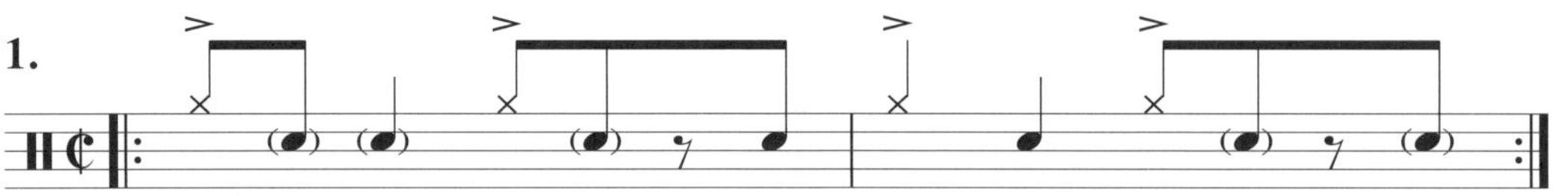

3+2 Rumba or Son Clave

2.

3+2 Rumba or Son Clave

3.

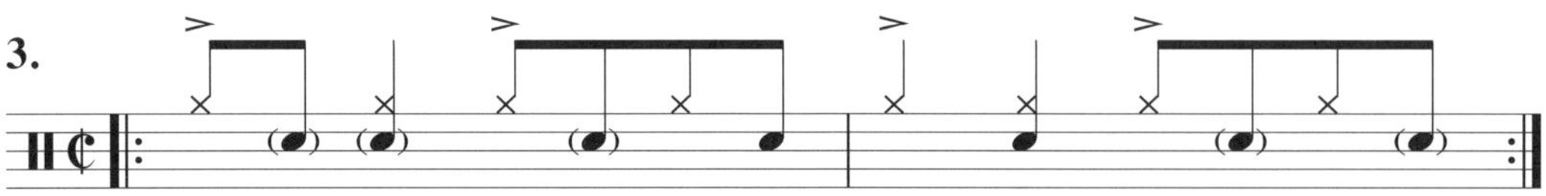

3+2 Rumba or Son Clave

4.

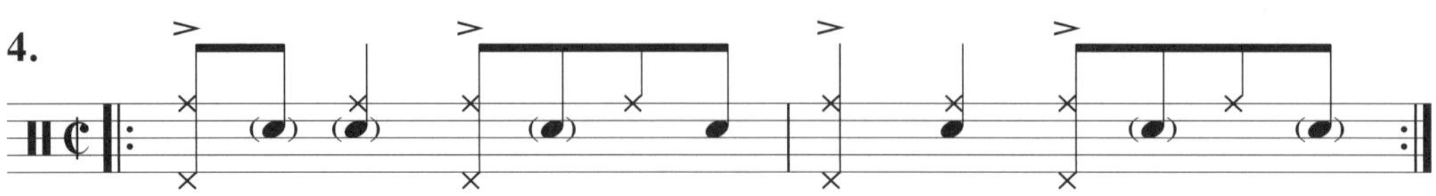

3+2 Rumba or Son Clave

5.

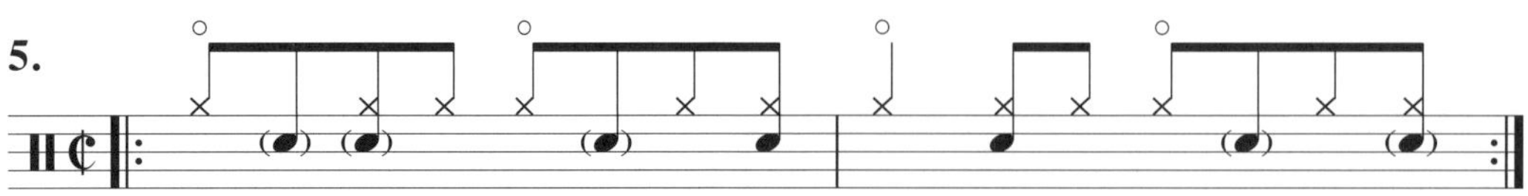

3+2 Rumba or Son Clave

6.

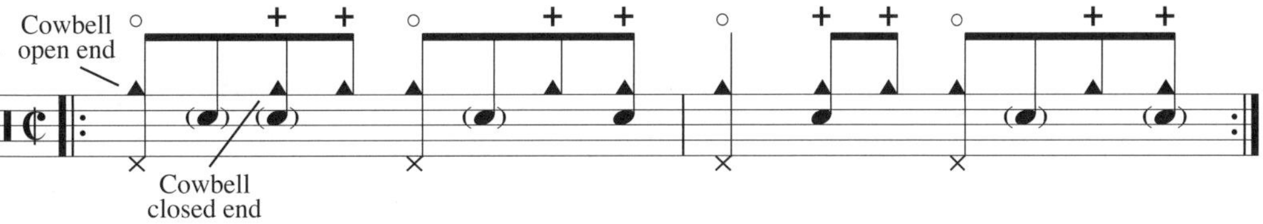

3+2 Rumba or Son Clave

7.

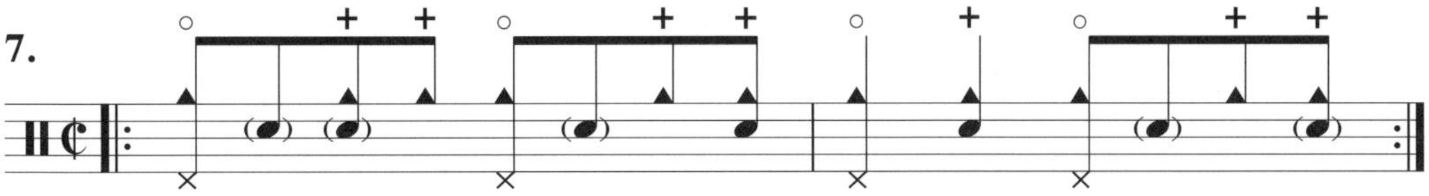

2+3 Rumba or Son Clave

8.

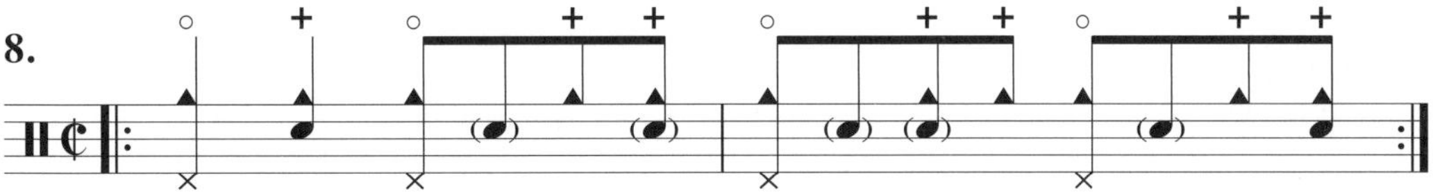

3+2 Rumba or Son Clave

9.

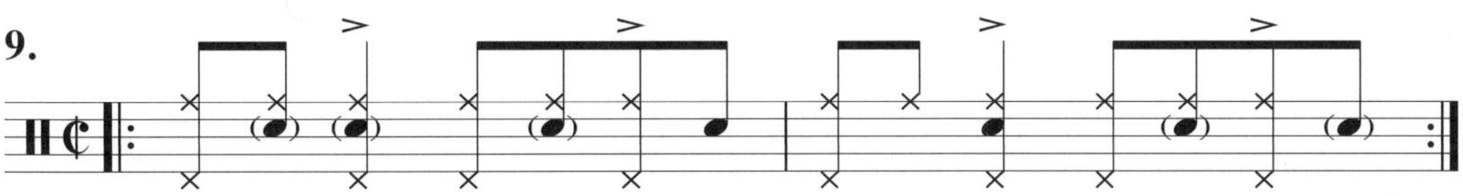

2+3 Rumba or Son Clave

10.

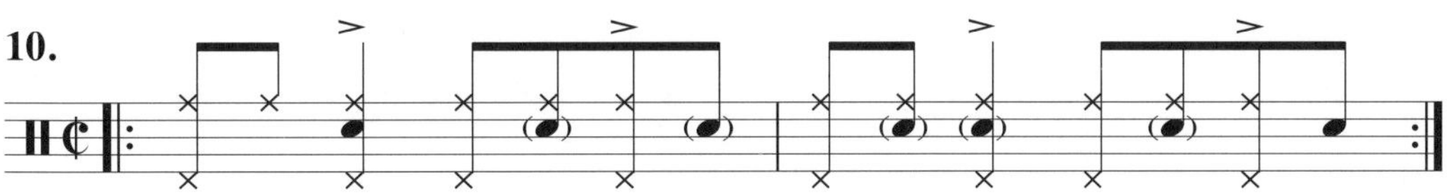

SONGO BASS DRUM VARIATIONS

1.

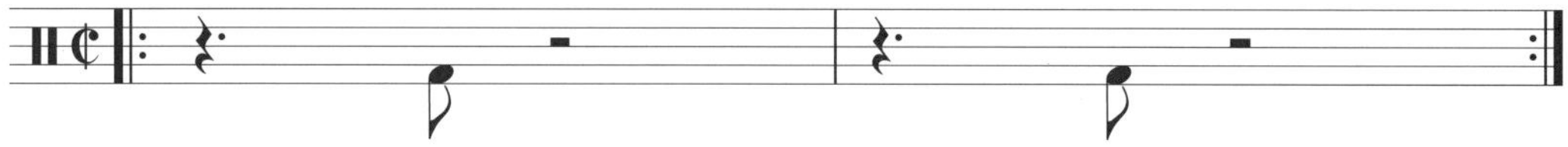

2.

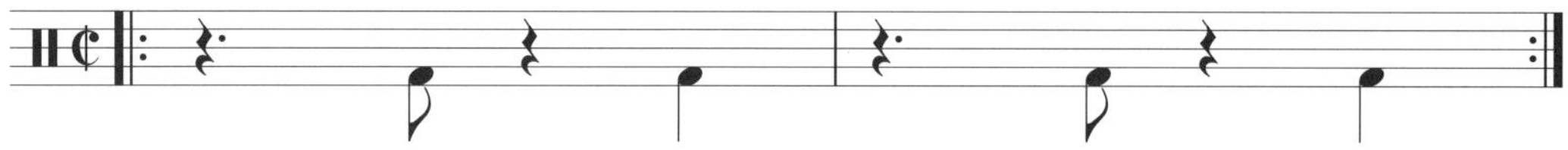

3.

4.

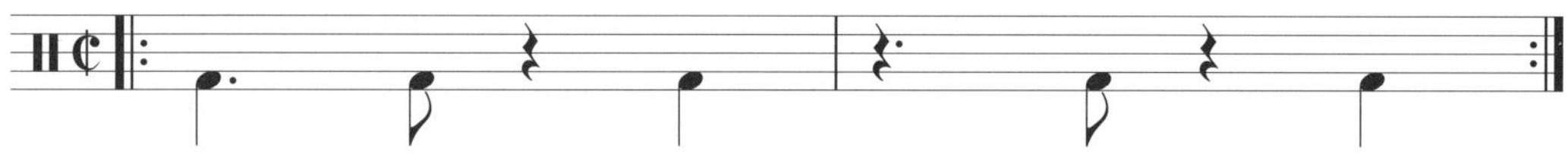

5.

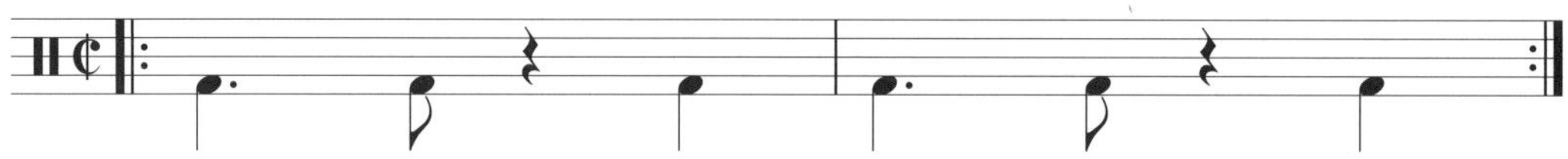

SONGO BASS DRUM VARIATIONS, continued

6.

7.

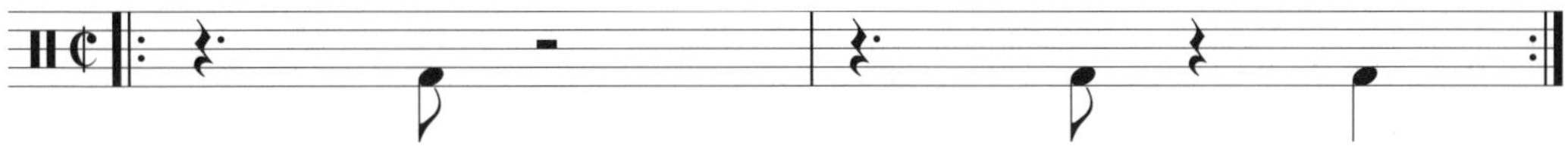

8.

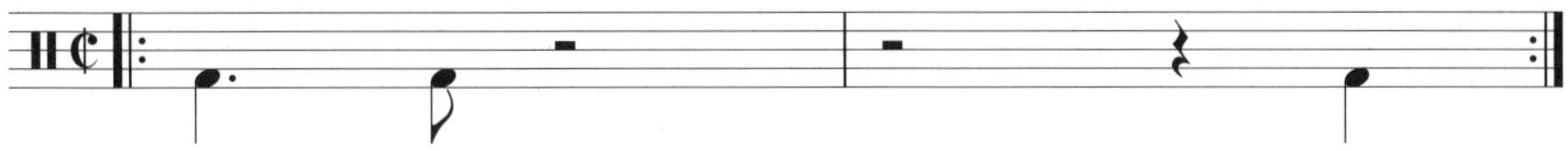

9.

10.

11.

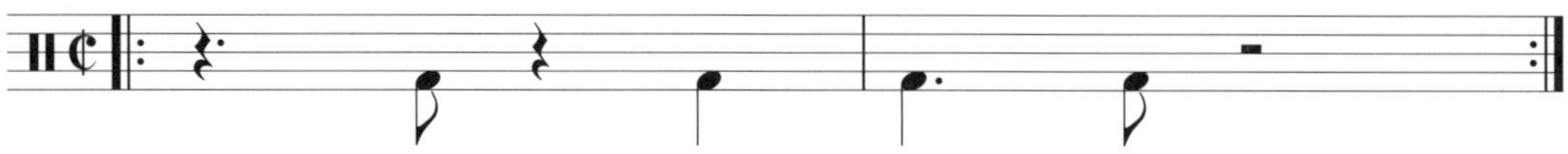

12.

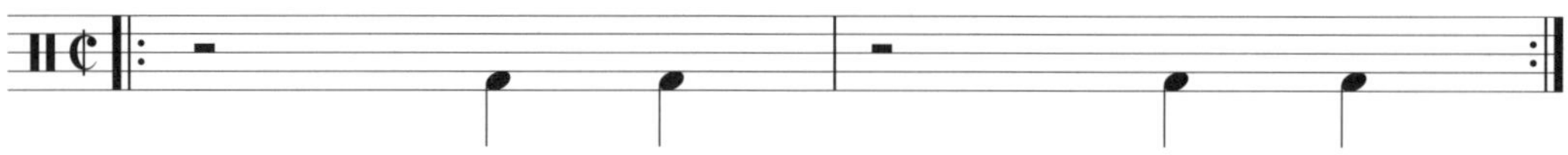

13.

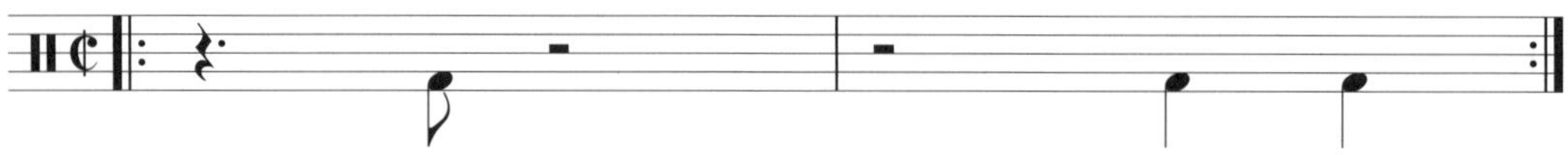

14.

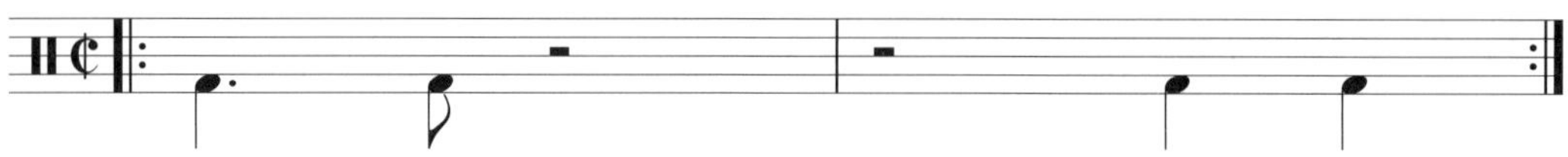

15.

SONGO BASS DRUM VARIATIONS, continued

16.

17.

18.

19.

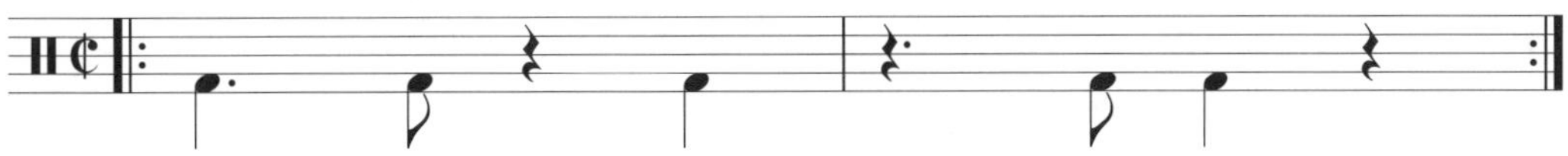

20.

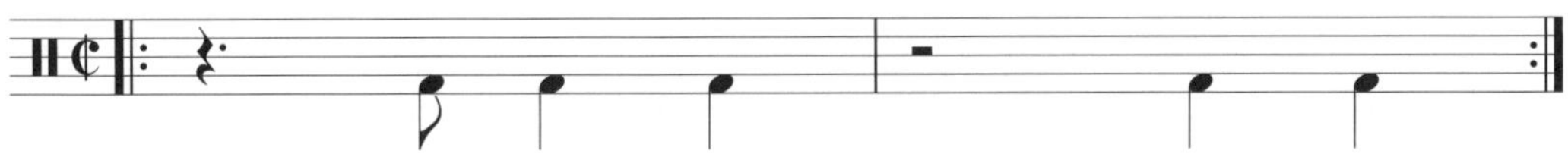

MOZAMBIQUE

The Mozambique rhythm is traditionally a form of Carnival music from Cuba and was created in the 1960s by Pello Izquierdo, better known as Pello "El Afrokan." The traditional instrumentation consists of two cowbells (which are the signature sound of the Mozambique rhythm), two bass drums (high and low), three congas, horns (trombone), chorus and lead vocals. Later, timbales, percussion, electric guitar, and bass were added to the ensemble.

Although the drumset has never traditionally been part of the Mozambique style, the adaptations by many contemporary drummers has made the Mozambique popular, particularly with "Latin-jazz" bands. The grooves written on the next page are more of a traditional approach for the drumset, and are written in 3/2 rumba clave (which is played with the cross-stick). Patterns 1 and 2 have the traditional high and low bass drum parts being played by the bass drum and with muted and open strokes on the floor tom. Patterns 3 and 4 include the cowbell parts that create the traditional sound of the Mozambique. These four patterns are all written in 3+2 Rumba clave, but they can also be played in 2+3 by starting on the second bar.

1.

2.

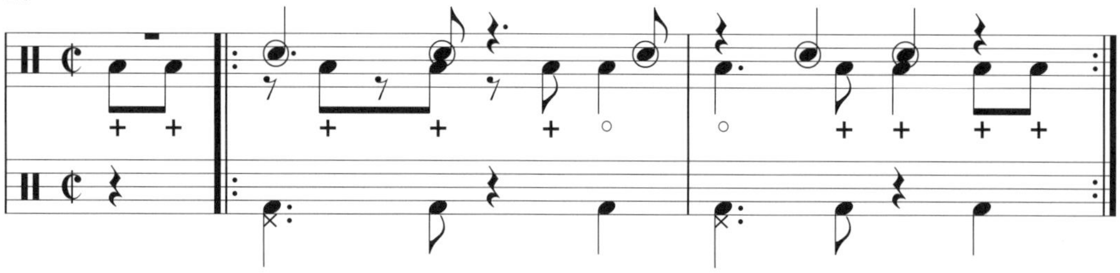

3.

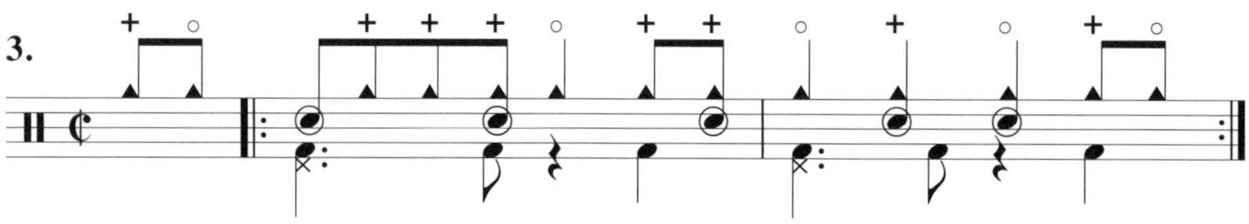

4.

NEW YORK MOZAMBIQUE, 2-BAR PHRASES

Contemporary Mozambique is sometimes referred to as "New York Mozambique" and is a hybrid of the traditional approach combined with elements of funk. The following pages contain a variety of bass drum variations that can be played with the New York Mozambique ostinato of ride cymbal (which plays the typical New York Mozambique cowbell part), snare drum, high tom, floor tom, and hi-hat with foot. Individual lines of the summaries can be played as 4-bar phrases. The New York patterns are all written in 2/3 clave, which is most common in contemporary Mozambique music.

1.

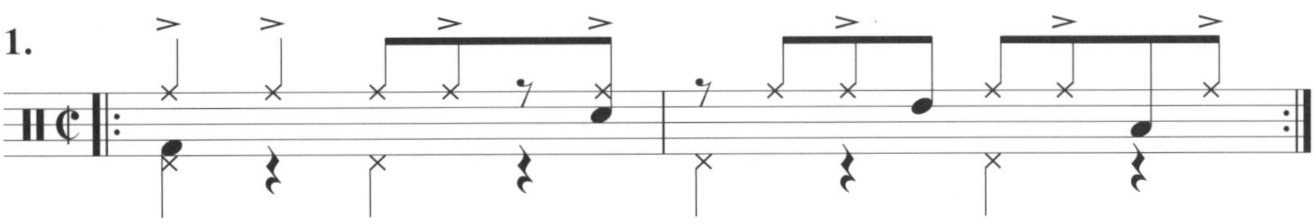

2.

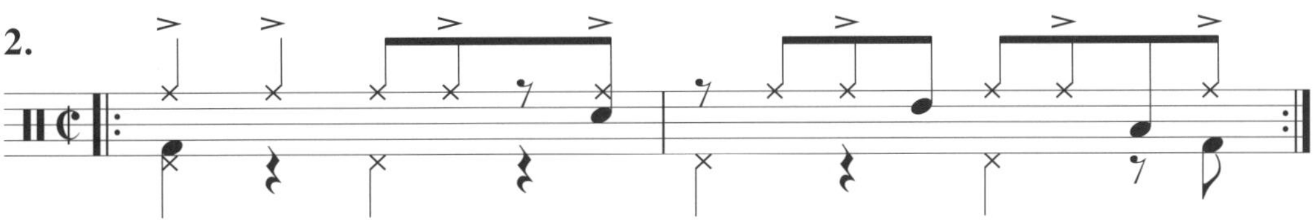

3.

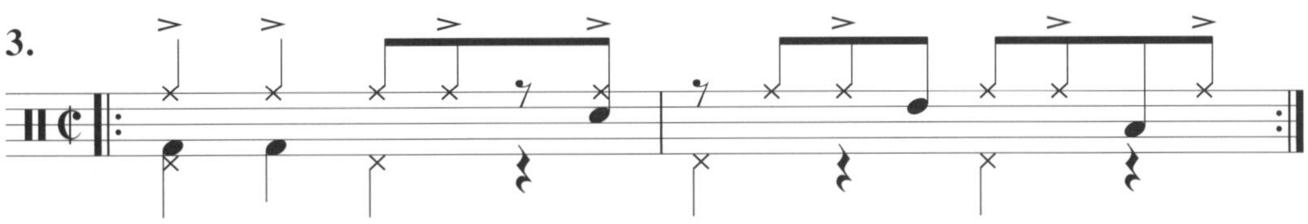

4.

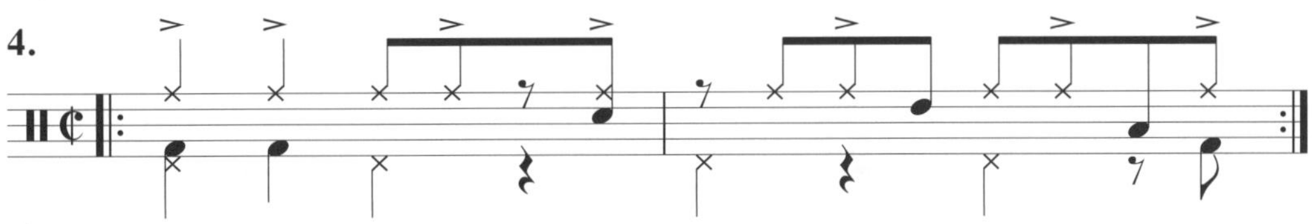

NEW YORK MOZAMBIQUE, 2-BAR PHRASES, continued

5.

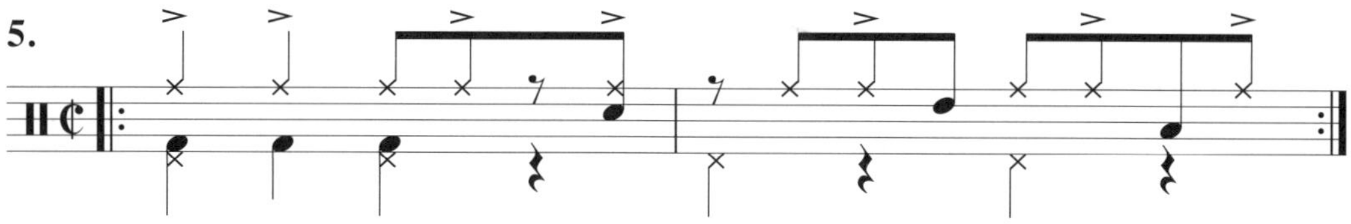

6.

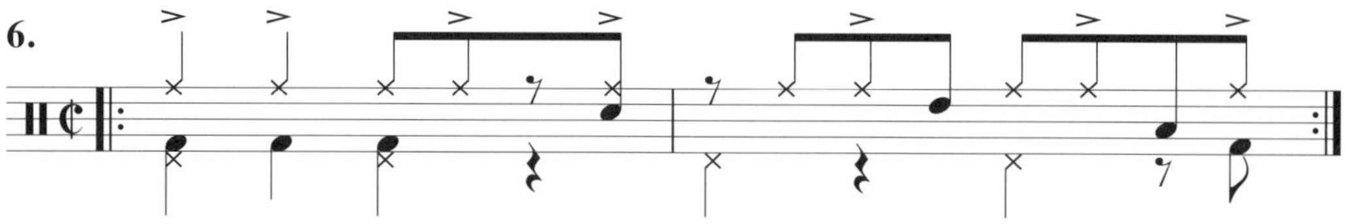

7.

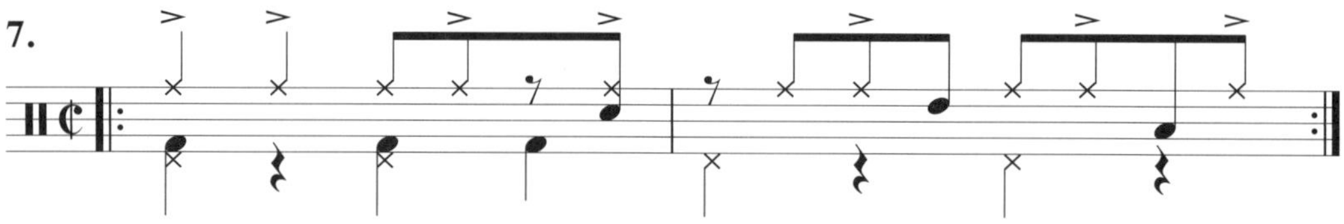

8.

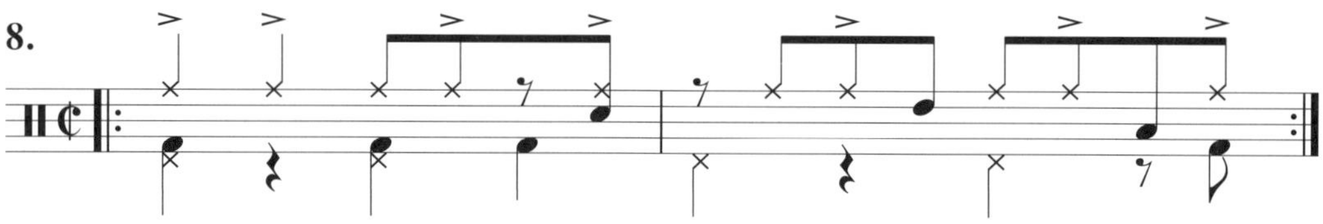

9.

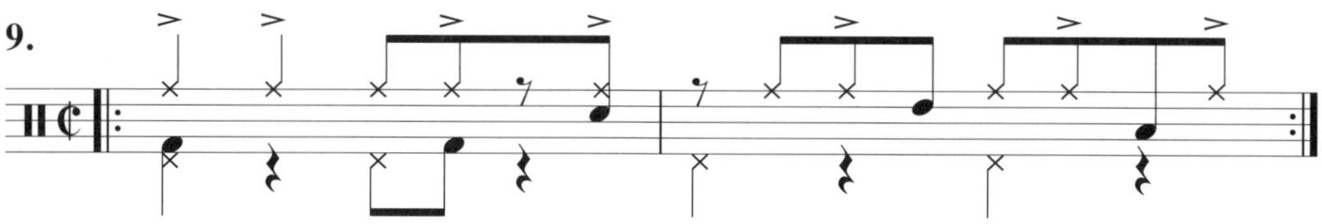

NEW YORK MOZAMBIQUE, 2-BAR PHRASES, continued

10.

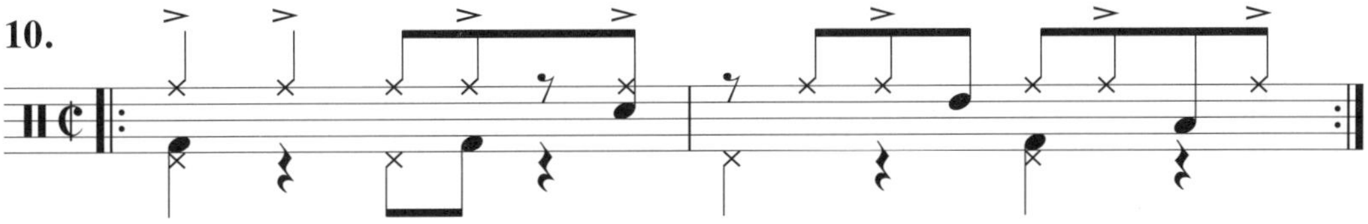

11.

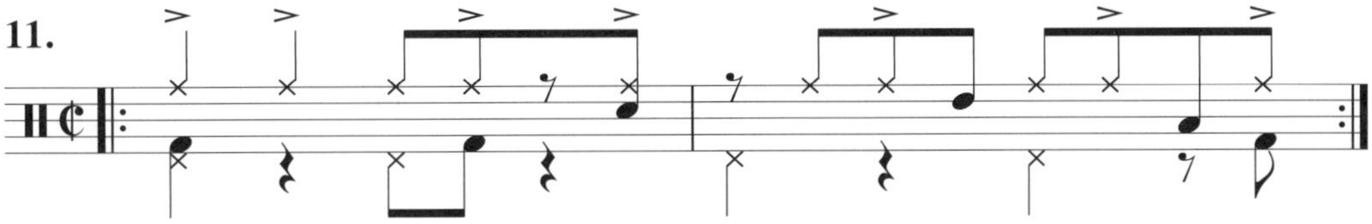

12.

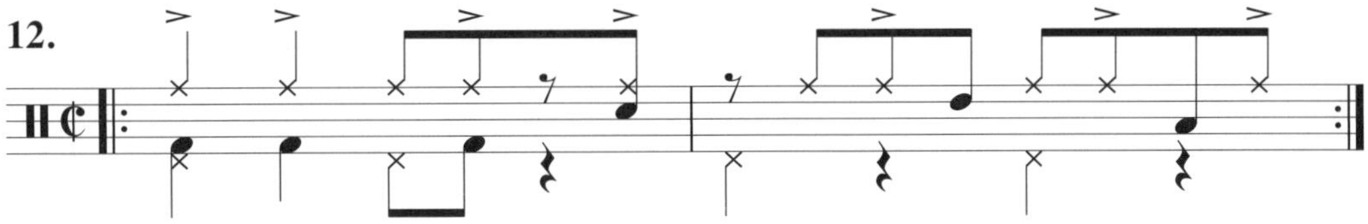

13.

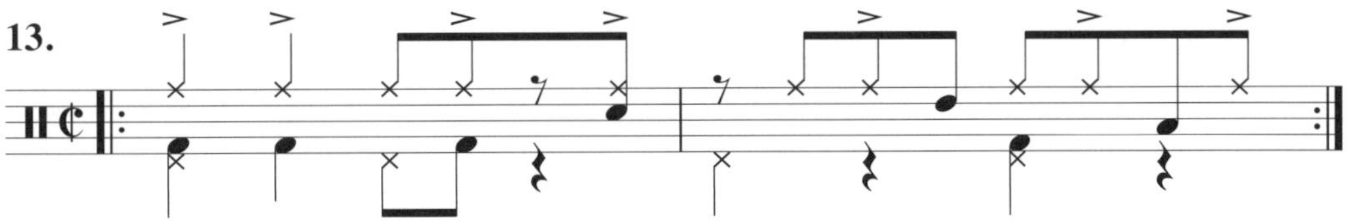

14.

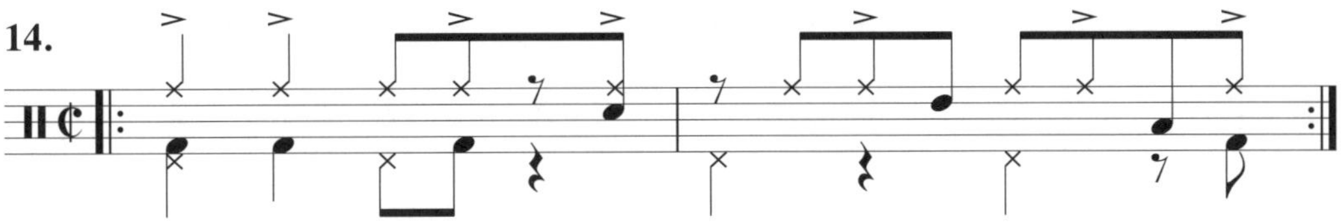

NEW YORK MOZAMBIQUE, 2-BAR PHRASES, continued

15.

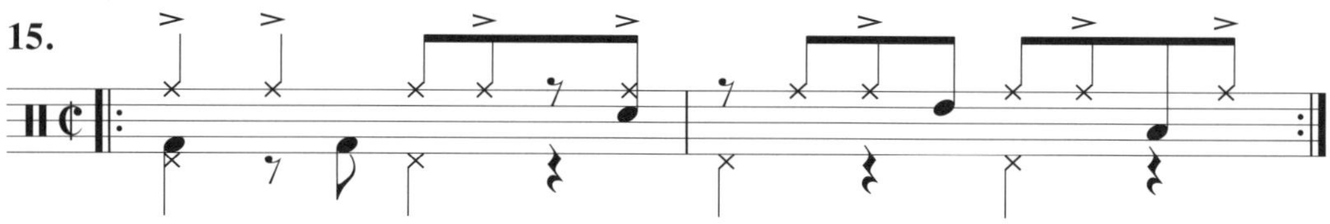

16.

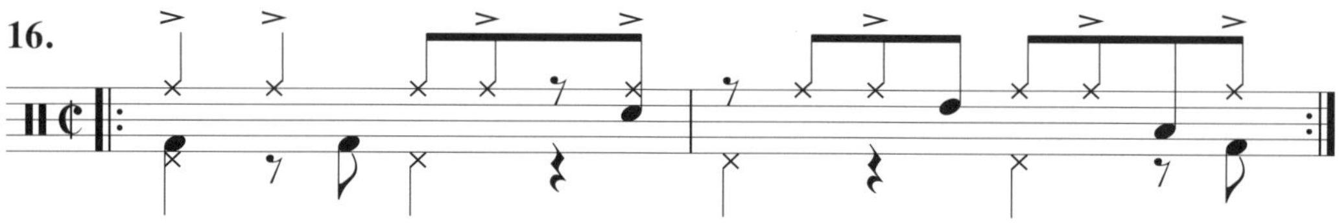

17.

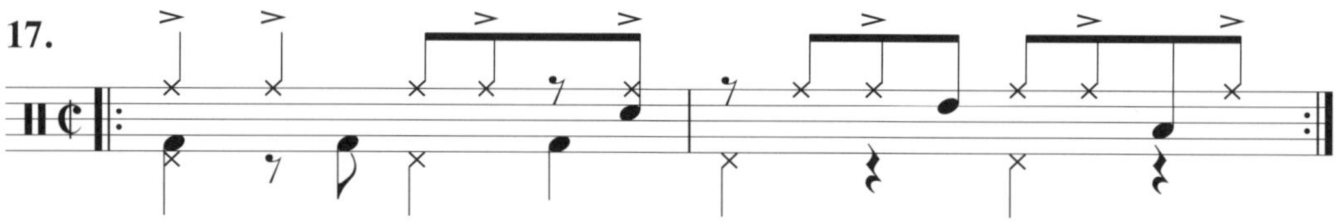

18.

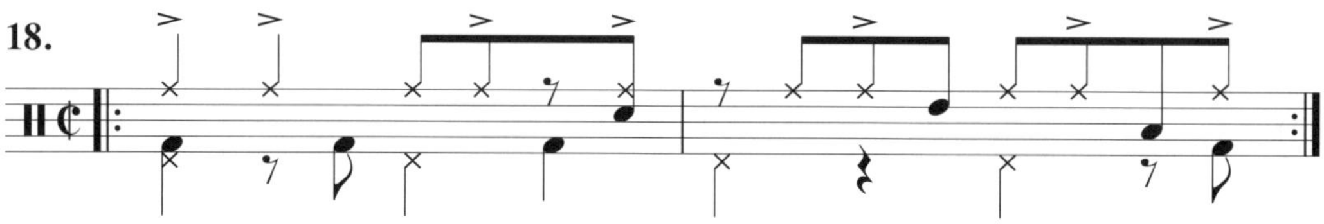

NEW YORK MOZAMBIQUE, 2-BAR PHRASES, continued

19.

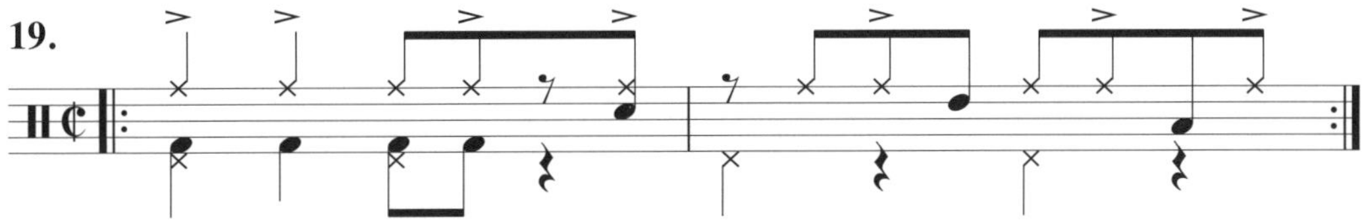

20.

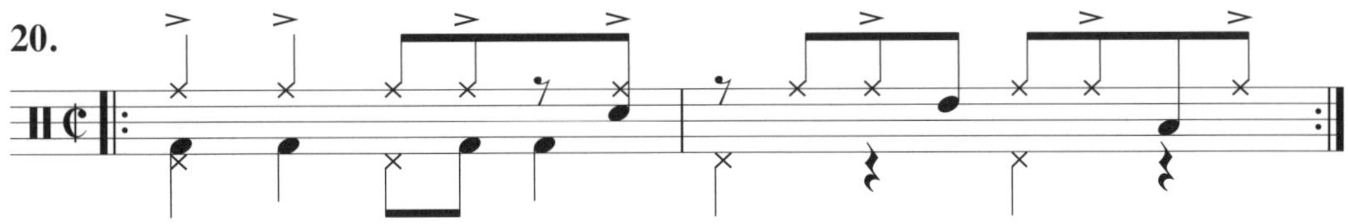

21.

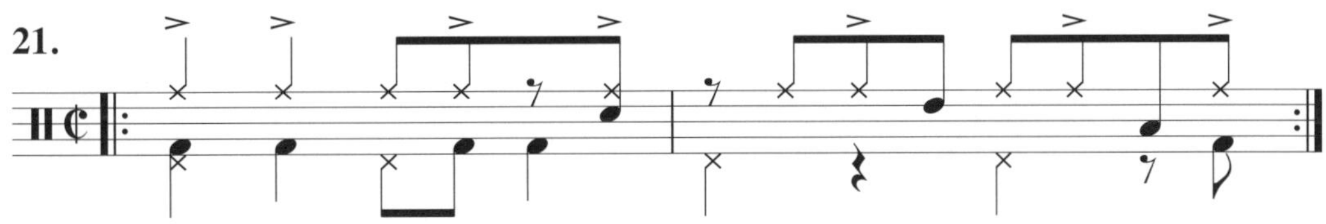

22.

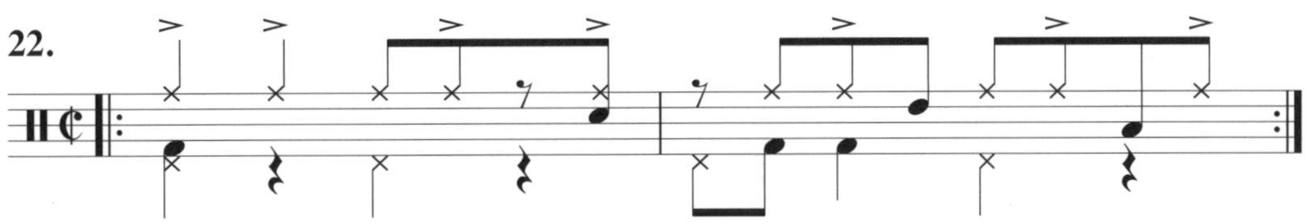

23.

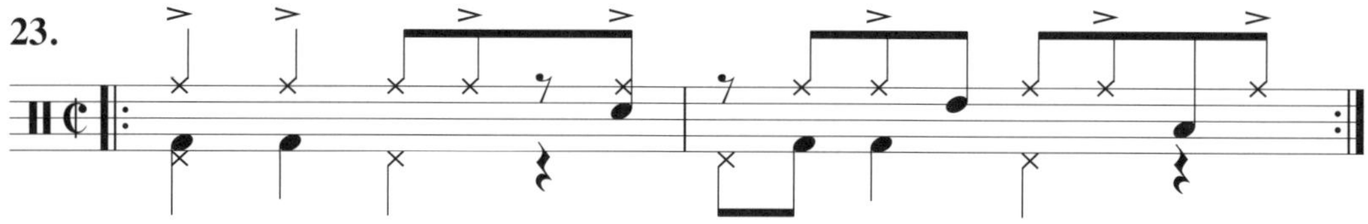

24.

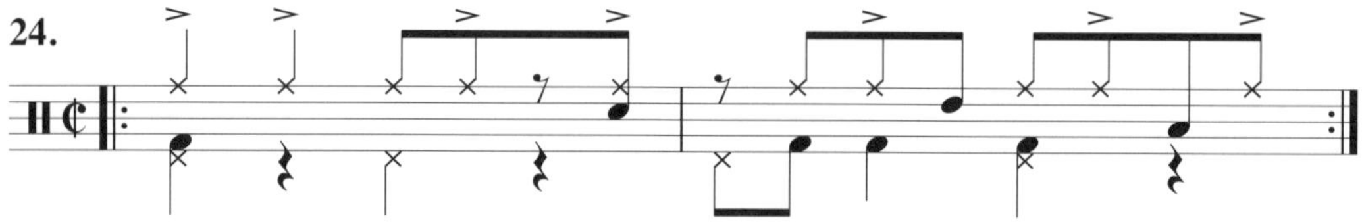

25.

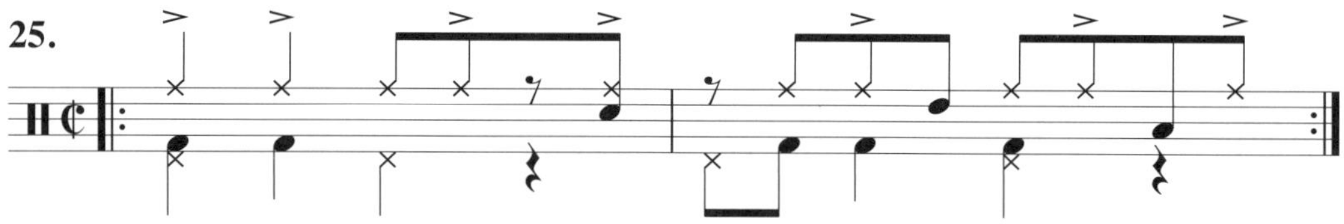

26.

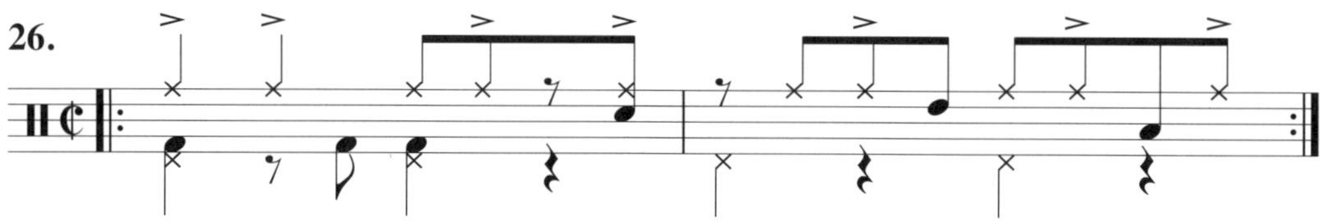

NEW YORK MOZAMBIQUE, 2-BAR PHRASES, continued

27.

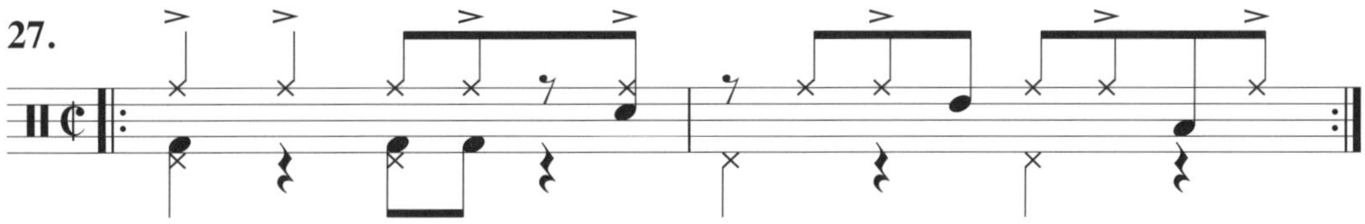

28.

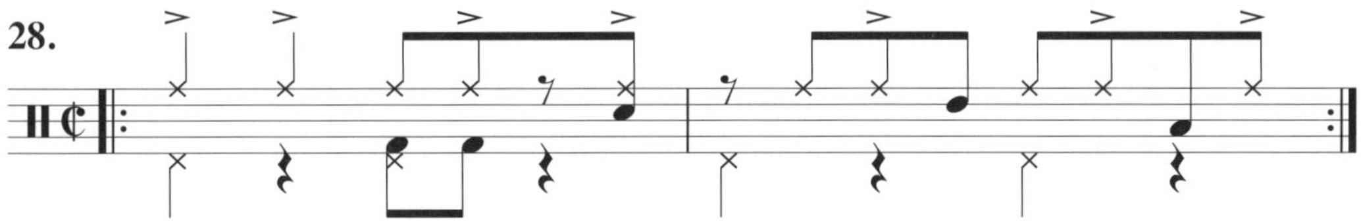

29.

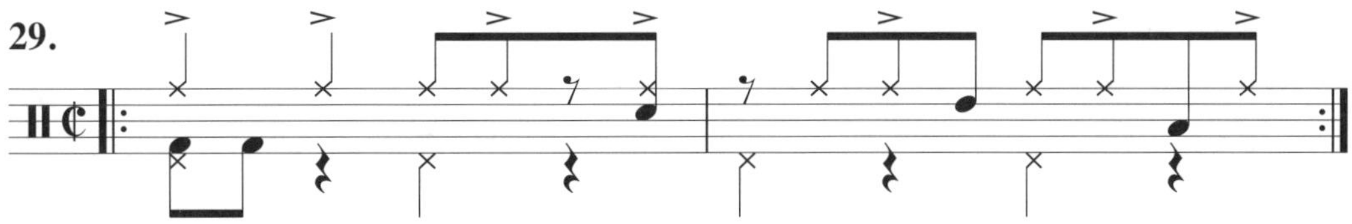

30.

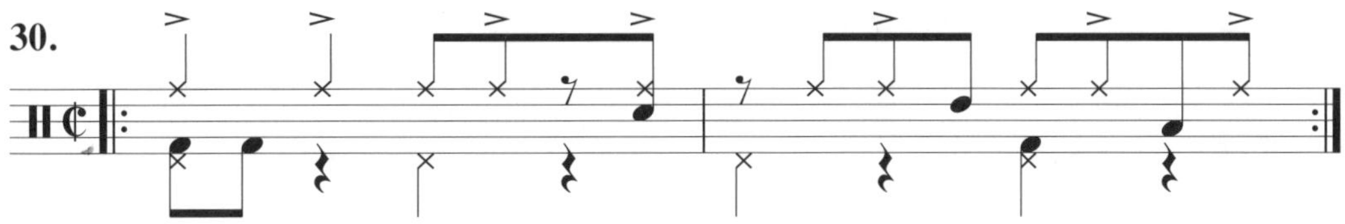

NEW YORK MOZAMBIQUE SUMMARY 1

1.

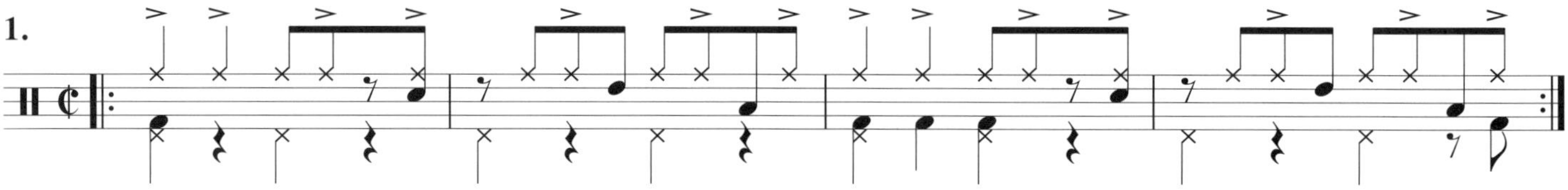

2.

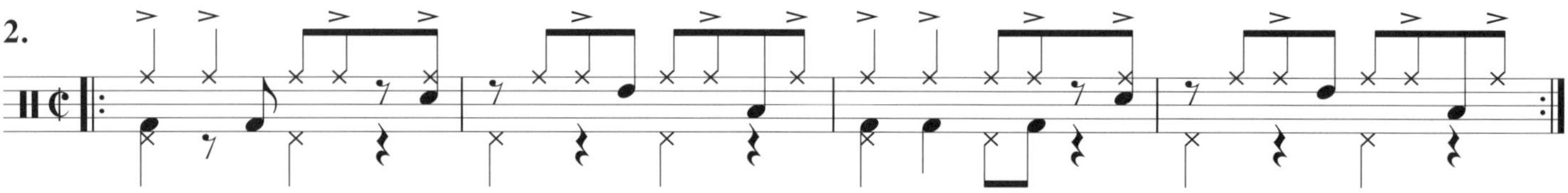

3.

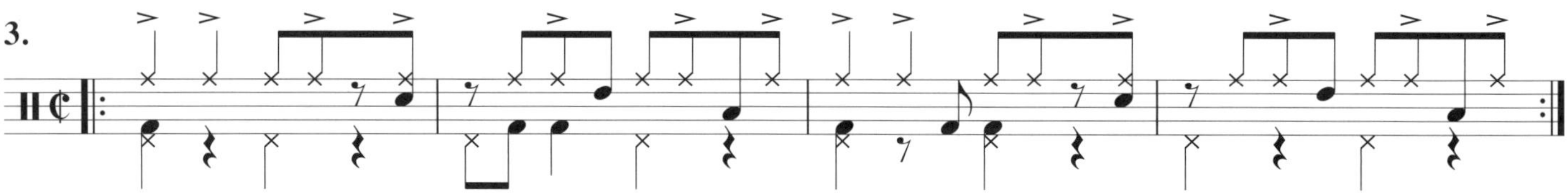

4.

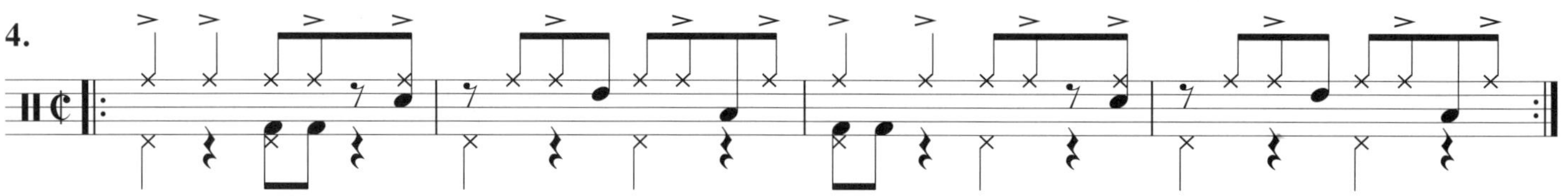

5.

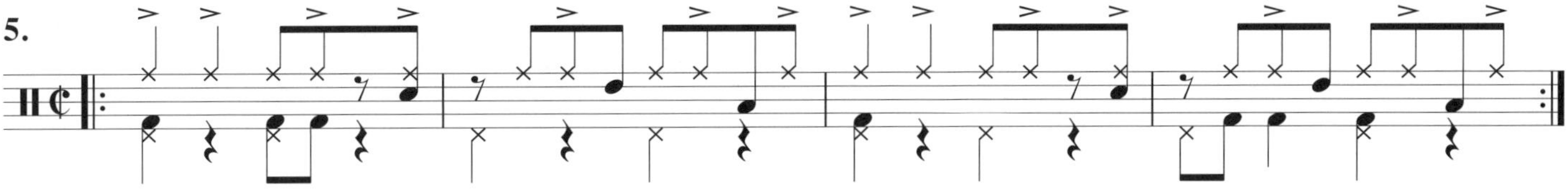

6.

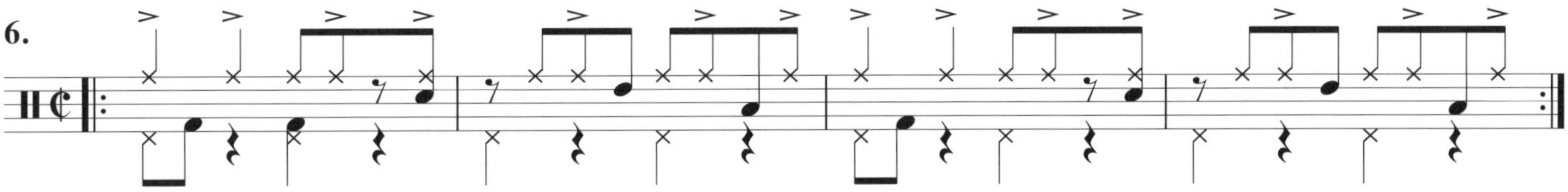

7.

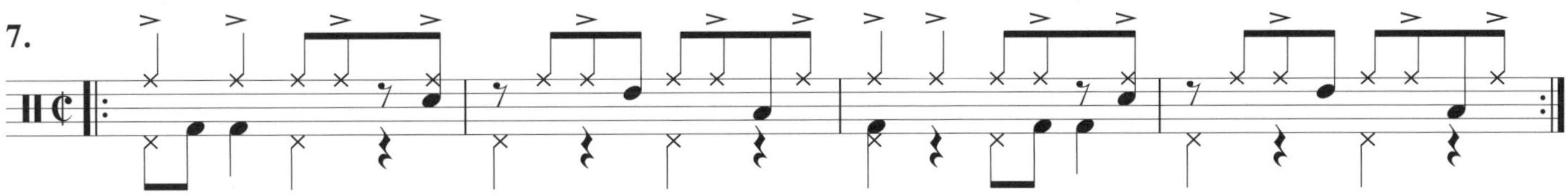

8.

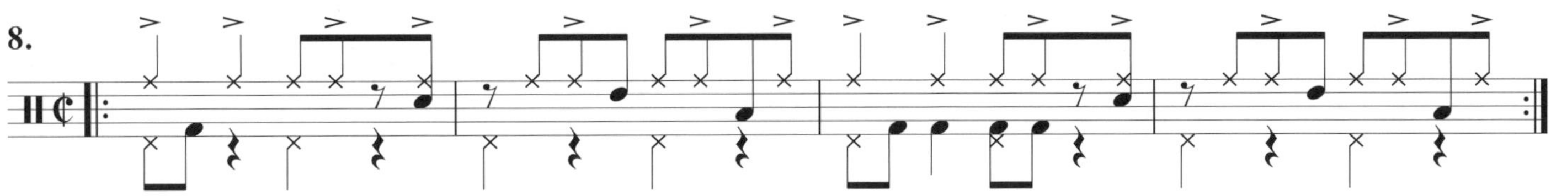